An Altitude
SuperGuide

W9-CYN-064

Classic Hikes
OF SOUTHWESTERN
British Columbia

An Altitude SuperGuide

Classic Hikes

OF SOUTHWESTERN

British Columbia

Anita Cancian

Altitude Publishing Canada Ltd.
Canadian Rockies/Vancouver

Publication Information

Altitude Publishing Canada Ltd.
The Canadian Rockies

1500 Railway Avenue
Canmore, Alberta T1W 1P6

www.altitudepublishing.com

Canadian Cataloguing in Publication Data

Cancian, Anita, 1961–
Classic Hikes of the Lower Left-hand Corner of British Columbia
(SuperGuide)
Includes index.
ISBN 1-55153-705-2 (pbk.)
1. Hiking-B.C.-Lower Mainland-Guidebooks
2. Hiking-B.C.-Vancouver Island-Guidebooks
3. Trails-B.C.-Lower Mainland-Guidebooks
4. Trails-B.C.-Vancouver Island-Guidebooks
5. Lower Mainland (B.C.)-Guidebooks
6. Vancouver Island (B.C.)-Guidebooks
I. Title.
GV199.44.C22L68 1998 917.11'3044 C97-910153-0

Altitude GreenTree Program

Altitude Publishing will plant in Canada twice as many trees as were used in the manufacturing of this product.

Front cover: West Coast Trail, photo: Al Harvey
Back cover: Hiking the Coast Mountains, photo: Al Harvey

Project Development

Design	Stephen Hutchings
Layout	Sabrina Grobler, Kelly Stauffer
Maps	Mark Higenbottam
Editor	Sabrina Grobler
Index	Noeline Bridge

Made in Western Canada

Printed and bound in Canada
by Friesen Printers, Altona, Manitoba

We acknowledge the financial support of the Government of Canada through the Book Publishing Industry Development Program (BPIDP) for our publishing activities.

A Note from the Publisher

The world described in *Altitude SuperGuides* is a unique and fascinating place. It is a world filled with surprise and discovery, beauty and enjoyment, questions and answers. It is a world of people, cities, landscapes, animals and wilderness as seen through the eyes of those who live in, work with, and care for this world. The process of describing this world is also a means of defining ourselves.

It is also a world of relationship, where people derive their meaning from a deep and abiding contact with the land—as well as from each other. And it is this sense of relationship that guides all of us at Altitude to ensure that these places continue to survive and evolve in the decades ahead.

Altitude SuperGuides are books intended to be used, as much as read. Like the world they describe, *Altitude SuperGuides* are evolving, adapting and growing. Please write to us with your comments and observations, and we will do our best to incorporate your ideas into future editions of these books.

Stephen Hutchings
Publisher

Contents

The *Classic Hikes* of Southwest B.C. are organized according to this colour scheme:

Vancouver Island

North Shore

Squamish

Pemberton

Golden Ears

Fraser Valley

Manning Park

Information/Reference

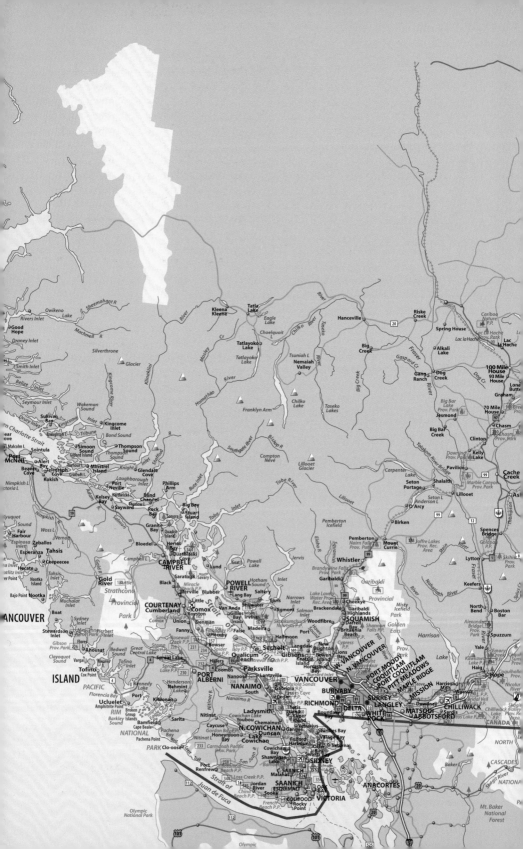

Foreword

As you leaf through the pages of this book, you will open up a world of hiking adventure that will take you through a remarkable environment of great beauty and variety. What makes hiking in southwestern B.C. so special are the vast stretches of isolated wilderness that make up much of the landscape. Development in this area is restricted by rugged mountains, glaciers, fjords and ocean, leaving the wilderness for hikers to explore. The mild climate produces lush rainforests and makes it possible to hike all year round at lower elevations along the coastal areas.

Often when you hike in southwestern B.C., you retrace a path that was established hundreds of years ago. The sport of hiking and the trails themselves have a long history. Native people were the first to hike in this area, and they established many of the trails, such as the Skyline Trail in Manning Park, that are still in use today. Many trails were originally used as transportation routes that linked communities and people to one another. Historical records show that people were keen to go out trekking in the backcountry as soon as they settled in this region. Mountain climbers and clubs like the British Columbia Mountaineering Club were responsible for pushing into uncharted terrain. They created trails, introduced people to the backcountry through organized trips and instigated the preservation of many of the parks that exist today.

Today, hiking is an enormously popular recreational activity. People are still compelled to explore this great, beautiful landscape. However, with this popularity comes the risk of loving the wilderness out of existence. We must be diligent in keeping our environment pristine, protected and wild. Treat it with respect and care, for it is all that we have. If we lose it, it is gone forever.

This book is a guide to the best hiking trails to be found in southwestern B.C. It contains all of the trails to which people return year after year. The book has been divided by region, as each region has its own unique character and geography. The trails range from short day hikes to multi-day trips for all levels of ability. The terrain covered varies widely, ranging from ocean beaches to rocky mountain peaks. Indeed, there should be a hike to suit everyone in this book. Enjoy it, and let your adventure begin.

Hiking in Southwestern B.C.

There are some things you should keep in mind when you hike in southwestern B.C. The trails in this book take you through a wide variety of areas and often through isolated wilderness. Since most of the hikes are located less than three hours from Vancouver, it is easy to forget how rugged these areas are. It may take a long time for help to reach you if something goes wrong. This means that you must be self-reliant and properly equipped. Always carry the ten essentials and notify someone of your plans or use the volunteer registration provided at some trailheads.

The weather in this area can change very quickly, making it easy to lose your way. It may change from clear sky to a foggy whiteout in a matter of minutes. It is recommended that you always carry a map and compass when you hike.

The thick, jungle-like coastal forest may grow over parts of trails in the course of a single season. However, the more commonly used trails are often well maintained. Southwestern B.C. is often subject to heavy rainfall and flash flooding, especially in the winter months. Some sections of the trails and some bridges may be washed out.

Park use permits are sometimes required for backcountry camping and hiking. There are no quotas on any of the *Classic* hikes except on the West Coast Trail and the Juan de Fuca Trail. It is legal to camp on Crown land in B.C.

Hikers will invariably encounter

left: map of the lower left-hand corner of British Columbia

wildlife. Most wildlife is harmless, although there are a few incidents involving humans and wild animals each year. Use common sense and caution when hiking in wildlife habitat.

Black bears and grizzlies occasionally clash with humans. They are usually attracted to food. Cougars are rarely seen and are more timid than bears, however cougars sometimes see small children or dogs as easy prey. Keep children and dogs near you when hiking. Remember to make noise so that these animals know that you are in the area. As a general rule, both bears and cougars prefer to avoid humans. Small rodents can eat through your pack or tent in search of food, so always hang up your food in a bag away from your tent.

Prairie rattlesnakes are the only venomous snakes in southwestern B.C. Bees, hornets and wasps usually sting in self-defense. Horseflies can be a nuisance and their bite is painful. Be wary of ticks, as they can carry serious diseases such as Rocky Mountain spotted fever and Lyme disease.

Firearms are not allowed in national or provincial parks. It is illegal to collect or remove natural objects in national parks, including marine life, plants and fossils.

Shellfish collectors should be on guard for paralytic shellfish poisoning, sometimes known as "red tide." This is caused by microscopic algae that are ingested by filter-feeding shellfish. Contaminated shellfish produces a poison that causes muscle paralysis and possible death. If you eat contaminated shellfish, induce vomiting and contact a physician immediately. Warning signs are posted in most contaminated areas, but be aware that isolated areas may not be signed. The Canadian Parks Service recommends that hikers not eat shellfish on the West Coast Trail.

Assumption of Risk

An element of risk is involved any time you go out on a hike. In fact, you may encounter an endless range of possible risks. In southwestern B.C., these risks include large ocean waves and swells, surge channels, high tides, aggressive wildlife, rough trails, slippery boardwalks, logs, tree roots and bridges, inclement weather, contaminated drinking water, loose rock, swollen streams, poisonous shellfish and insect bites. More often than not, however, these risks are manageable.

Great care has been taken to make this book as accurate as possible. However, trail conditions often change and are subject to dynamic elements such as weather and erosion. Therefore, the inclusion or exclusion of any information does not mean that you will find conditions as they are described in this book. In particular, trails and bridges may or may not be present, trail signs and markers may be missing, cable cars and ladders may be broken and ponds, stream crossings and snow patches may change from year to year.

Classic Hikes of the Lower Left-hand Corner of British Columbia contains much information to help you prepare yourself for a safe backcountry hiking experience. However, you are solely responsible for your safety in the backcountry. Neither the author nor the publisher can be held responsible for any difficulties, injuries, misfortune or loss of property that may arise from using the information presented.

In this book, "backpacking" means to hike and camp self-sufficiently in the backcountry. It in no way implies that any services associated with low-budget travel (also called "backpacking" in Europe and Australasia) will be present.

How To Use This Book

Hike Descriptions

This book covers the best hikes in southwestern B.C. The hikes were chosen after careful consideration and consultation with other experienced hikers who know the area well. Criteria used for choosing the best hikes in this area include accessibility, outstanding physical features and the trail's reputation for being enjoyable to hike.

Each hike features boxed introductory information that identifies the route and the trailhead. Information about distance, difficulty rating, mountain biking, dogs, camping and topographical maps is also included.

The distances and elevations provided cover the area between the trailhead and the destination. Distances and elevations between landmarks such as campgrounds, lakes, mountain passes and junctions are also given. To get an overall impression of a hike, compare the elevation losses or gains over the different sections of the hike.

Many day hikes can be extended into overnight trips and some overnight hikes may be done as very long day hikes. Some hikes, like the Howe Sound Crest Trail or Long Beach, can be hiked in sections or in their entirety. The choice is yours, and can be based on factors such as your experience, fitness level, time limitations, individual goals and the weather. Consult park information centres for closures, current conditions, weather and additional information.

Trails

In the text, "trail" refers to a marked route that is maintained. Some trails are marked and maintained better than others. In general, the more popular the trail is, the better it is marked and maintained. However, some trails are by nature very rough, and you will need sturdy boots to hike them. The term "trail" is also used to refer to beach routes.

Some creeks or streams must be waded, and this is stated in the trail description. Note that many trails are shared by mountain bikers, hikers and dogs. An ice axe is recommended on a few of the trails. These trails are appropriate for those who are familiar with snow travel and skilled in ice-axe self-arrest.

Maps

Maps accompanying the hikes have been created especially for this book. They show all trails as accurately as possible. The topographical map for each hike is also listed at the bottom of the route information box.

Topographical maps are essential for back-country travel. Some *Classic* trails are shown in the 1:50 000 series maps produced by the Department of Energy, Mines and Resources (National Topographic Series). With a few exceptions, the trails shown on these maps are accurate.

Distances and Hiking Time

A distance and hiking time is provided for each hike. Metric units are used for all measurements in the text. Common abbreviations used are: cm (centimetres), km (kilometres), m (metres), km^2 (square kilometres), m^2 (square metres) and ha (hectares). The distance and hiking times given for loop hikes or circuits are the round-trip totals. The distances and hiking times given from trailhead to destination are one-way totals. Distance and hiking time figures do not include side-trip options.

The trail distances and hiking times are based on figures provided by parks agencies. These were compared to readings taken from a Global Positioning System navigator (GPS) and those provided in other guidebooks. Any discrepancies were field checked.

Some trails are not located in parks and are not shown on any maps. The distances and routes for these were based on readings taken from a GPS. These were then compared to other reference sources.

Round-trip hiking time estimates are given so that you can gauge how long a hike may take. The times are based on a person hiking at an average pace in good conditions. It is estimated that the average person can hike 2.5 km/hour. However, each individual's hiking time will vary depending on ability, pace, weather and trail conditions. Use these time estimates as a guide and factor in any elements that may affect the hike.

The majority of the trails are marked with signs or brightly coloured ribbons. The rocky sections of a trail are often marked by cairns or by markings painted on rocks. Some old park trail signs indicate incorrect distances.

Mountain bike and early season hike indications have been listed in the route information. Thanks to southwestern B.C.'s mild weather, some of the early-season trails can be hiked all year round. This is often dependent on how cold the winter is in a given year.

Ratings

Each trail is rated on a scale of three stars. All of the *Classic* hikes are rewarding and are worthy of being hiked. However, some hikes have more to offer in terms of scenery and scope. These ratings are provided as a guideline to help give you an idea of the hike's qualities. The ratings are as follows:

Three stars: Outstanding
Two stars: Highly recommended
One star: Recommended

The hikes are also rated in terms of difficulty. These are the ratings:

Difficult: Combinations of steepness, length and trail conditions make this trail difficult.

Intermediate: The trail is moderately challenging in terms of steepness, length or trail conditions.

Easy: Little elevation gain, moderate to minimal length and excellent trail conditions make this trail easy. These trails are recommended for small children.

Transportation and Access

Vancouver is the closest major centre to the majority of the *Classic* hikes. The hikes are all within a three-hour drive of the city. The exceptions are the Long Beach and West Coast Trail hikes, which are located in Pacific Rim National Park on Vancouver Island. Victoria

and Nanaimo are the closest major centres to these hikes. Both Vancouver and Victoria are served by international airports.

The main road that accesses southwestern B.C. is the Trans-Canada Highway (Highway 1). From Edmonton, you can also take the Yellowhead Highway (Highway 5). The Alaska Highway (Highway 97) leads south from the Yukon and Interstate 5 leads north from Washington State. For road conditions and maps, call the Ministry of Transportation and Highways at (604) 660-8301 or 1-900-451-4997.

Bus and railway lines service southwestern B.C. and are another option for getting around. There is limited public transportation to some of the *Classic Hikes* trailheads. Ferry service is also available for those travelling to or from Vancouver Island, Alaska or Seattle.

Accommodation

A wide variety of accommodations are available throughout southwestern B.C. Commercial accommodation is available at the major centres of Vancouver, Victoria, Nanaimo, Whistler, Chilliwack and Hope. Limited commercial accommodation is also available at smaller centres.

Low-budget accommodation is available at frontcountry campgrounds and at hostels in Vancouver, Victoria and Whistler. For more information on hostels, contact Hostelling International, B.C. Region at (604) 684-7111, E-mail bchostel@axionet.com, or homepage: www.virtualynx.com/bchostels.

Campgrounds offer facilities for tents and recreational vehicles. Some areas have commercial facilities where private enterprises operate lodges, cabins, ski facilities or restaurants. These areas are: Cypress Provincial Park, Grouse Mountain, Mount Seymour and Manning Provincial Park.

Camping

You must purchase a daily or annual pass when you enter a national park. Campground fees are also charged. Fees vary according to the sites and services that are offered and usually range from $7.25 to $17.50. No camping fee is charged for backcountry users.

Reservations for campground sites can be made at Long Beach and trail access reservations can be made for the West Coast Trail. A reservation fee is charged.

Provincial parks and recreation areas vary widely in the types of services they offer. Overnight fees range from $6 to $15.50. People with disabilities can camp for free by showing a disabled access card. B.C. seniors can camp for a discount of 50 per cent before June 15 and after Labour Day. Backcountry wilderness campsites are usually free. However, the more popular sites may charge a fee. Reservations can be made for some provincial park campsites through the Discover Camping Reservation Service. A reservation fee is charged. Otherwise, try to select your campsite early in the day during the busy summer months so that you can be assured of finding a spot.

Forest Service recreation sites are very basic. They usually offer only minimal services such as water, pit toilets, firewood and picnic tables. No campsite fees are charged for camping in these sites and reservations cannot be made. Most parks can be used all year round, depending on weather conditions.

Climate

The weather in British Columbia is as diverse as its geography. In general, the southern coast has a gentle climate all year round. Autumn and winter are mild, with temperatures in winter averaging 5°C. Winters are characterized by overcast, rainy weather. More rain falls in December than at any other time of the year. It may snow intermittently at low elevations. Higher elevations receive lots of snow. However, temperatures generally remain mild, so it is not uncommon for snow to turn to rain. The ocean ports do not freeze in winter.

It is often possible to hike during the winter months at lower elevations, but be prepared for lots of water or ice on the trails. Trails may turn into raging streams as a result of the abundant rainfall. If it is a cold year, there may be snow.

Summers are usually sunny and mild with temperatures averaging 18°C. There are usually some glorious days in autumn that are perfect for hiking. Indeed, these spells of sunny, dry weather are for many hikers the favorite time of year. The smell of damp leaves, the brilliant colours of the trees and the soothing, warm rays of the sun make hiking a blissful experience.

As a general rule, temperatures drop as elevation increases. When you hike in the mountains, be aware that in summer, the nighttime temperatures can plummet to 15 degrees below daytime highs. The hiking season in the mountain regions usually begins in late May and lasts until early October at lower elevations. Higher up, the season runs from mid-June to mid-September. You may encounter snow at high elevations, even in the middle of summer.

The farther inland you go in southwestern B.C., the drier it becomes. Winters become colder and summers hotter. The southern interior receives half as much rainfall as does the coast. You will notice this climactic transition when you hike in Manning Park. It is much drier and hotter in the summer, and winters are characterized by cooler temperatures with an abundant snowfall.

Hiking in the Rain

Hiking in the rain is a fact of life in southwestern B.C. The western side of the Coast Range has one of the wettest climates in the world; more than 100 cm of rain falls each year. The wettest weather station in North America is Henderson Lake, near Ucluelet on Vancouver Island. It receives an average annual rainfall of 6,550 mm. In many areas, rainfall exceeds a whopping 3.5 m. An ongoing joke here is that people don't tan in B.C., they rust. It is inevitable that if you hike in southwestern B.C., you will eventually be hiking in the rain.

Why does it rain so much along the coast? The abundant rain is a result of the position of the Coast Mountains. Their north-south orientation places them in the path of warm, moist Pacific air. The air is forced upward by the mountain barrier and the air rises to cooler altitudes. When it rises, the air contracts and its water vapour condenses, causing rain to fall in enormous amounts.

11

Gold Creek in Golden Ears Provincial Park

Geographic Area Covered

Classic Hikes takes you through a varied landscape of ocean, beaches, rainforest, extinct volcanos, glacier-covered mountains, forested valleys, fjords and semi-arid mountain ranges. This area has the most concentrated population in the province, however much of it remains wilderness. Vancouver is Canada's third largest city, yet amazingly, 30 km north of it begins a stretch of wilderness that extends all the way to the Arctic.

The area covered in this book starts on the western mainland coastline at the city of Vancouver and stretches upward along a puzzle of inlets, fjords and islands past Powell River to Bute Inlet. The eastern edge starts from the Lillooet area and runs south through the historic corridor of the Fraser River Valley and past the town of Hope. It then diverts slightly east to include Manning Provincial Park. The southern edge of this region runs along the 49th parallel on the United States border. Vancouver Island makes up the westernmost portion of this area. It lies parallel to the B.C. mainland, is 450 km long and covers 3,175,000 ha of ocean beaches, mountains and valleys.

Parks

You may wonder why some parks allow activities such as logging, while others do not. The answer to this question is that not all parks in southwestern B.C. are created equally. The government has various categories for parks.

Parks in B.C. are divided into two main categories: national and provincial parks. National parks are managed by the Canadian federal government. They are operated through the Canadian Parks Service under the Ministry of Environment.

Provincial parks are managed by the provincial government through the Ministry of Parks. Provincial parks are classified according to how they are used.

Class A parks have the highest level of protection and are to be used for recreational purposes only. No industrial or commercial use is allowed. Marine and coastal parks are included in this classification.

Class B parks are used primarily for recreational purposes. However, resource use is permitted if it has been proven that such use will not harm the area.

Wilderness Conservancies are pristine, roadless tracts of land where no development or exploitation of any kind is permitted.

Recreation Areas are park reserves that are being considered for park status, but commercial resource extraction may occur and private operations such as ski facilities may operate.

Forest Service Recreation Sites are areas where the Forest Service works with logging companies to provide camping areas within a forest management area.

It is legal to camp on Crown land in B.C. as long as you do not violate any permit or lease. Be sure that no special restrictions or fire closures are in effect when you camp on Crown land.

Most provincial parks have some degree of ranger patrol or staff supervision, depending on the needs of a particular park. All national parks have ranger patrol and staff supervision. The opening and closing dates of a park vary and may change from year to year. Contact the park office for specific information.

Native Land

Some of the *Classic Hikes* pass through areas of land owned by First Nations people. For example, there are a number of Indian reserves that you pass through when you hike the West Coast Trail. Indian reserves and all of the materials and structures found on the land are private property. Stay on the trail when you are on reserve lands and do not trespass.

If you wish to visit a site on native land, you must request permission from the local band council by letter or phone. B.C. Band addresses can be obtained from Legal and Statutory Requirements, Lands, Revenues and Trusts, Suite 300, 1550 Alberni St., Vancouver, BC V6G 3C5 (666-5132).

Hiking Ethics

Listed below are some ethics that every hiker should be aware of and abide by. It takes little effort to follow these basic rules, and the gains are significant. These practices will ensure that the remarkable landscape and environment of southwestern B.C. are maintained for current and future generations. If anything, remember the most basic rule of "leaving no trace" and treat others as you would want them to treat you.

Here are some guidelines to hike by:

- Conduct yourself in a manner that reflects favorably on hikers.
- Be self-reliant and carry all necessary food, clothing and equipment at all times.
- Leave a trip schedule with a dependable person.
- In a hiking party, the most challenged person sets the limits in terms of speed and distance covered.
- Try to have a minimal impact on the environment. Do not litter, and pack out all of your garbage. If you see litter on the trail, pick it up and pack it out.
- Stay on the maintained trail. Don't take shortcuts or go on trail sections that are undergoing rehabilitation.
- Do not damage, disturb or remove any natural objects.
- Respect wildlife. Never feed or bother wildlife.

Vancouver Island

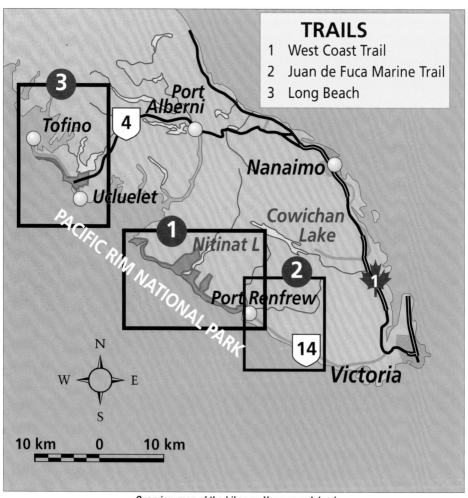

TRANS

TRAILS
1   West Coast Trail
2   Juan de Fuca Marine Trail
3   Long Beach

Overview map of the hikes on Vancouver Island

West coast shoreline of Vancouver Island

Pacific Rim National Park is located on the western coast of the 32,261 km² Vancouver Island. The Island stretches 451 km from Cape Scott to the provincial capital city of Victoria and it is an island of great diversity. Mountains form the spine of the island and they are surrounded by thick forests and approximately 2,000 lakes. The western side of the mountains is rugged, wild, filled with inlets and is populated with small communities. In contrast, almost all of Vancouver Island's major centres are located on its eastern coast.

Pacific Rim National Park is comprised of three separate units. These are Long Beach, the West Coast Trail and Broken Group Islands. Included in this is also 22,300 ha of ocean. The Broken Group Islands are composed of 100 islands and rocks in the centre of Barkley Sound, 12 km west of Bamfield. They are only accessible by boat.

The entire park totals 51,300 ha of breathtaking ocean landscape. The hiking trails are unique in that they encompass a wild shoreline made of sandy beaches, unique geographic formations, lush rainforests, rich marine wildlife and vibrant cultural history.

Park use fees are in effect from mid-March to mid-October.

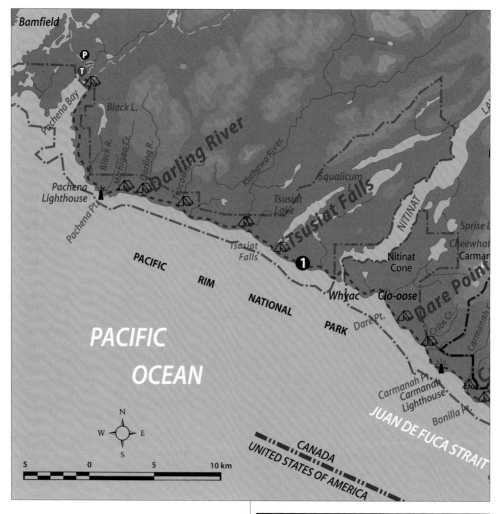

~ 1 ~

West Coast Trail

The West Coast Trail is located between the villages of Bamfield and Nanaimo. The southern trailhead is at Gordon River, just outside of Port Renfrew. The northern trailhead is located at Pachena Bay, near Bamfield. A complete range of supplies, services and

1. Route (see map above)

Distance: 75 km one way; 5-7 days
Rating: *** Intermediate; early season hike
All elevations are at sea level. Hiking times are highly variable and depend on whether a beach route or forest route is taken.

Gordon River	Dare Point: 38 km
Trailhead: 0 km	Tsusiat Point: 48 km
Thrasher Cove: 5 km	Darling River: 61 km
Camper Creek: 13 km	Pachena Bay
Walbran Creek: 22 km	Trailhead: 75 km
Carmanah Creek: 29 km	

Topographical maps: 92C/9, 92C/10, 92C/11, 92C/14

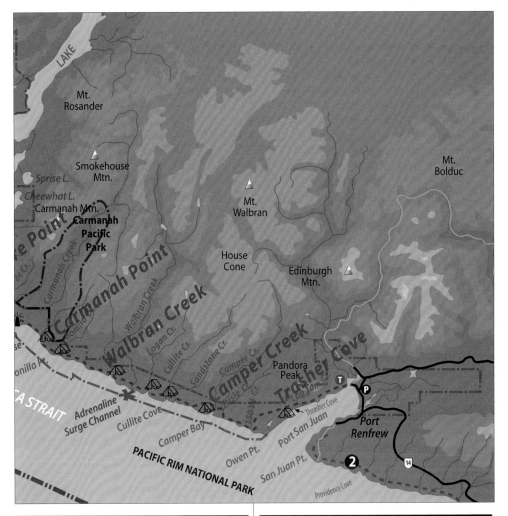

1. Southern Trailhead

Gordon River (South): Take Highway 14 northwest for 113 km from Victoria to Port Renfrew. Other options include the the West Coast Trail Express Bus (ph. 1-800-999-2288). The West Coast Trail Hiker Registration Office is located on Highway 14 at Port Renfrew (ph./fax 250-647-5434).

1. Northern Trailhead

Pachena Bay (North) is located 5 km south of Bamfield. Drive for 94 km on gravel logging roads from Port Alberni. Take the branch in the road just before Port Alberni to Bamfield. Other options are the West Coast Trail Express Bus from Victoria or Nanaimo, and the Alberni Marine Transport Ltd. passenger ferry from Port Alberni (250-723-8313). The WCT Hiker Registration Office is located 6 km south of Bamfield at the trailhead (ph./fax 250-728-3234) at the trailhead.

accommodation is available in Victoria or Port Renfrew and Bamfield.

Park information centres are located at Port Renfrew and Pachena Bay. Wilderness campsites are located along the trail, and commercial campsites are located at the trailheads. There is a hostel in Victoria. Ranger stations and visitor centres are located in the south at Port Alberni and at Pachena Bay in the north.

Registration

Every hiker requires a trail use permit, as a quota system is in place. Permits cost $25 from April 15-30 and October 1-15. They then go up to $70 from May 1 to September 30. To pre-register, call ahead starting March 1. The fee to pre-register is $25 and is non-refundable. If you do not pre-register, admittance to the trail is on a first-come, first-served basis. Be prepared to wait 1-3 days. The maximum group size allowed on the trail is 10. To register, call: Greater Vancouver 663-6000; in Canada and the USA: 1-800-663-6000; outside North America: 250-387-1642

General Information

The cost of the ferry crossing from Port Renfrew to the Gordon River Trailhead is $12.50. It costs $12.50 to cross the Nitinat Narrows by boat. You can buy a waterproof map of the trail with tide table information at the parks registration centre.

For more information, contact Pacific Rim National Park Reserve, Box 280, Ucluelet, B.C. V0R 3A0, ph. 250-726-7721.

Also, check out the WCT home page at http://www.parkscan.harbour.com/pacrim.

This trail lives up to its reputation as one of the world's great hikes. Its variety and scope are simply amazing. There are few places in the world where you can walk a shoreline of this length, beauty and pristine ruggedness. This hike takes you along a magnificent coastline, through lush rainforest, past waterfalls and over creeks and rivers. The beaches alongside it are filled with sand, tide pools, chasms, caves, chiselled sandstone formations, rich marine wildlife and shipwreck relics.

People come from all over the world to the West Coast Trail, giving it a cosmopolitan flavour. Unfortunately, this also means that it is busy. A tip for avoiding hiking with other people is to leave camp later or earlier than others do in the morning. However, don't let

Logan Creek Suspension Bridge

Tide Tables

You will become very familiar with using and reading a tide table when you hike the West Coast Trail. Maps and tide tables are easy to read and are provided with all West Coast Trail reservation packages. They can also be bought at the trailheads, at most marine stores and at the Canadian Hydrographic Service at Department of Fisheries and Oceans, Institute of Ocean Services, 9860 West Saanich Road, Box 6000, Sidney, BC, V8C 4B2 (ph. 250-356-6358).

The tide tables are for the village of Tofino, located north of the trail. When you read the table, add one hour to allow for the distance between the town and the trail.

When planning your day, remember that beach routes are often limited in their use due to high tide levels. It is a good idea to look at the tide table when you are in the planning stages of your trip to the West Coast Trail. By looking at the table, you can time your trip to coincide with low tides. This way, you can maximize your beach walking.

Black bear

the popularity of this trail put you off. There are still plenty of luxuriant rainforest, deserted beaches and secluded campsites to explore. One could spend a lifetime exploring this area, and many people return yearly to do just that.

The weather in this area can vary and change quickly. When it is sunny and hot it may seem like you are hiking in the South Pacific, but if it is rainy and cold, you will know that you are really on the West Coast. Summer temperatures average 14°C. The mornings may be foggy, but the fog usually burns off by

1. Camping, Cycling, Dogs

Camping: Beach camping is one of the most unique and enjoyable parts of this experience. All campsites along the trail are located on the beach to minimize environmental impact. Campfires are allowed and should be made in previously established fire rings. Use only driftwood found on the beach and do not cut wood from the forest.
Mountain biking: Cycling is not permitted.
Dogs: Dogs are not allowed.

afternoon. Winter temperatures average 6°C with frequent, heavy rainfall. The area receives heavy rainfall of up to 300 cm per year.

Be prepared to encounter wet, cold weather while hiking here. If you are inadequately prepared, hiking this trail can be extremely challenging. It is easy to become hypothermic, so bring good rain gear and warm clothing. It is a good idea to use a waterproof cover for your pack to keep it dry. Wrap all your gear in plastic bags and make sure that your tent is waterproof.

This trail is quite demanding, so tackle it when you are fit and be sure to have some backpacking experience. Remember to pack out all your garbage. Use the outhouses or bury human waste at the intertidal zone at the water's edge.

Overall, the trail is quite flat. The high point is on the north side of Port San Juan, where it rises to only 183 m. Most of your travelling will be done along the beach or the 25-m-high cliffs that flank many stretches of the forest. If you start at the south end, remember that Thrasher Cove to Walbran Creek is the most difficult and muddy part of the trail. Once you are past this point, you will be able to cover great distances very quickly. If you start from the north, conserve some energy for the last two days.

Gordon River to Thrasher Cove

The trail is mostly flat with some undulating sections. If it has been raining, the trail will be full of mud and the log crossings over the many small streams will be tricky. This section remains completely in the woods due to impassable cliffs on the shore. This portion is forested and thus provides few, if any, spectacular views. It heads southwest through a second-growth forest, which has dense underbrush not found in old growth forests. Thickets of salmonberry are a common sight and skunk cabbage can be seeing growing in the swampier parts of the trail.

Near the halfway point, the climbs and descents get steeper with the forest opening up in a few places, providing views of Port San Juan and the Olympic Mountains in Washington. The highest point on the West Coast Trail is 183 m and it is located at a viewpoint just before

Log Jam Creek. From there, the trail drops steeply to a small creek and then to a series of ladders which lead down to Thrasher Cove.

Thrasher Cove to Camper Creek

The inland part of this trail is a puzzle of gnarled roots, logs, bridges, boardwalks and mud. This section is a training ground where you will learn how to balance while walking over logs, which can be slimy and slippery when wet. Be ready to negotiate your way over many fallen logs. If your balance is not great, a walking stick or ski pole can help. A rubber-soled, light hiking boot may be better for going over this kind of terrain than a heavier hiking boot. Progress along this stretch is slow, but the old-growth forest is quiet and lovely.

The temperate rainforest is populated with the western red cedar, western hemlock, Douglas fir and Sitka spruce, which form a canopy overhead. The forest floor is resplendent with ferns, salal, skunk cabbage, lichen and decaying

History of the West Coast Trail

The shore between Barkley Sound and Port San Juan on Vancouver Island's coast is often called the "Graveyard of the Pacific" because of the many ships that have foundered here. Bad weather, fog, brutal storms and currents off the mouth of the straits are responsible for many of these shipwrecks.

In 1873, a lighthouse was built at Barkley Sound to help navigation in the area. In 1890, a second lighthouse was built at Carmanah Point and a telegraph line was installed from Cape Beale to Victoria. Despite these improvements, shipwrecks continued to occur along the coast.

A tragedy of tremendous proportions occurred on January 22, 1906. When the American passenger steamer S.S. *Valencia* ran aground at Pachena Point, 126 people died. This incident initiated the placement of new navigational aids along the coastline. A new lifesaving trail was constructed and the Pachena Point Lighthouse was built in 1907.

This area was near the territory of the Nitinat, Ohiaht, and Pacheenaht natives, and the community was very active in fishing and whaling. Before World War One, the community of Clo-oose became the target of a scheme to promote the area as one of the world's great beach resorts, but the plan eventually failed.

The lifesaving trail became obsolete by the 1950s as new radar and radio technologies took over. After 1954, the trail was no longer maintained and it soon became overgrown.

In 1967, the natural beauty of the area attracted renewed interest, and this soon led to the creation of a park around the old lifesaving trail. The trail was reopened in 1969 when the Canadian Parks Department included this region in the development of the Pacific Rim National Park. During this

Pachena Bay Lighthouse

time, conservationists fought a long and hard battle with logging companies over park boundary definitions. The Sierra Club of B.C. played a major role in this fight and it is due to their hard work that the trail exists today. The West Coast Trail officially became a part of the Pacific Rim National Park in 1970, and its beauty draws hikers from all over the world.

Ladders between Walbran and Camper Creeks

matter. Again, there is no view, as this section of trail is surrounded by forest. Before 150 Yard Creek, the route crosses a series of wooden boardwalks that are a relief after the logs. These boardwalks can be slippery, as the wetness combines with moss to form a slick layer over the wood. Some areas of the boardwalks are starting to rot and can break. If you doubt the sturdiness of the boardwalk, place your foot across two boards at once or close to the sides where the boards are nailed in.

The trail runs past a blowdown area just before arriving at Camper Creek. If the tide is below 1.8 m (six feet), there is an accessible beach route from Thrasher Cove to Owen Point. It is slow going, as there are many algae-covered boulders to cross. The stern of a trawler can be seen just before Owen Point. The trail passes by cliffs, two sea arches and a huge sea stack at Owen Point. Sea stacks are picturesque islets of rock that usually have a few trees growing on top. After Owen Point, the shelf is reached and walking becomes smoother and flatter. The route passes by several small beaches. Note that there is a difficult surge channel between 150 Yard Creek and Trisle Creek, where the tide must be below 1.7 m (5.5 feet) in order for you to pass. There is an

impassable headland just before Camper Bay, so take the beach access point back into the forest.

A series of ladders leads down to the Camper Creek, where a great beach campground greets you at Camper Bay. A cable car runs over Camper Creek, but you can easily walk through it if the creek is low. Camper Bay is a fairly rocky beach with some sandy areas. The campsite has its own unique character like all the beaches along this trail.

Camper Creek to Walbran Creek

You can hike along the beach from Camper Creek when the tides are below 1.2 m (four feet). The beach route passes two surge channels, the last one being at Sandstone Creek. There is an impassable headland after this point, so you must leave the beach and walk up Sandstone Creek. Follow the creek, hiking alongside it. If the creek is flooded, your only choice is to embark on a bushwhack up the side slope of the creek. Once you are at the top of the creek, you must climb up a steep slope of loose dirt and gravel on the left side of the bridge. Use the fixed wire cable to pull yourself up.

Alternatively, you can get onto the forest trail from Camper Creek by climbing up some ladders. The hike to Sandstone Creek follows an easy trail surrounded by false lily of the valley, ferns and dwarf dogwood. Dwarf dogwood has small, greenish-white, yellow or purple flowers and bright red berries. The plant is evergreen and grows 5 to 25 cm tall.

The trail from Sandstone Creek to Cullite Creek is easy and can be hiked quickly. A beautiful campsite is located at Cullite Cove on the southeast side of the creek.

The trail from Cullite Creek to Logan Creek passes through a large bog. This section has the most mud and the most ladders of any part of the trail. Progress here is very slow as you work your way through mud pools, tangled tree roots, fallen logs and swamp. If it is hot and sunny, you can see the bog steaming. After a few kilometres, you may give up the battle to avoid getting covered in mud, finding that it is much easier to walk right through it.

Getting caught in a large pool of mud,

Carmanah Lighthouse on Carmanah Point

however, can be tiring. Your boots get sucked in and it is a struggle to get out of the black, cement-like matter. A slip on a root here can throw you thigh-deep into the stuff, so take your time.

Boardwalks have been built over the more sensitive areas of this bog, and they are often waterlogged, covered in moss and tipped sideways. The bog is populated with stunted red cedar, shore pine, bunchberry and sphagnum moss. The fascinating carnivorous sundew plant also lives here.

The infamous ladder section of the trail begins right after the muddy part. The ladders run straight up and straight down, in and out of creek gorges. This is probably the most difficult section of the trail, but take your time climbing these ladders and you will reap the benefits of your efforts. Some recommend starting at the Pachena Bay trailhead so that the ladders can be tackled with a lighter pack. Others prefer to hike the most difficult part of the trail first.

Luckily, the ladders often have little platforms where you can stand and rest before continuing on. A few of these ladders have over two hundred rungs and for the most part, they are very well maintained. However, this is a wilderness trail and it is not uncommon to find ladders that have missing rungs or to find ladders that have been rendered useless because of land slides. Be prepared to slide down dirt cliffs or to negotiate the occasional large gap between missing rungs. Be especially careful on ladders if they are wet, and use careful, methodical foot placement to get you through safely.

A series of steep ladders leads down to Logan Creek, where a 100-m-long suspension bridge has been bolted into the walls of the small canyon. Hikers must walk single file across the bridge, as it is made of a single plank suspended between twin cables that serve as handrails. The walk over the creek offers a superb view of the creek below. A series of steep ladders greets you at the west end of the bridge. A campsite is located on the west side of Logan Creek, and there is a sandy beach where the beachcombing is good.

The trail continues through more bog from Logan Creek to Walbran Creek. Progress through this area is slow and tedious. Watch out for the many huge banana slugs that slither across the boardwalks.

The beach route from Logan Creek to Walbran Creek can be hiked at tides below 2.1 m (seven feet), however you must cross the surge channel at Adrenalin Creek. This is

Sea lions

the most difficult surge channel crossing on the trail, and people have died trying to cross it. Surge channels or chasms are sections where the ocean sweeps up into breaks in the shelf rock. Often, it may only be possible to pass through the head of the channel at low tide if the surge channels have eroded to the base of the shoreline cliffs. The rock surfaces around surge channels are often wet and slippery, so be careful with your footing.

The Adrenalin surge channel can only be crossed if the tide is below 1.7 m (5.5 feet). When the tide is this low, a rock is exposed in the middle of the channel, and you can step on it in order to get across. The rock will be slippery, as a waterfall makes all the rocks slippery here. If you attempt to cross the channel, it is recommended that you unstrap your pack's hipbelt and use ropes in case you are pulled into the channel. Canadian Parks staff recommend taking the forest route through this section.

When you get to Walbran Creek, the campsite on the wide expanse of beach is a welcome sight. There are shallow pools at the end of the creek just before it joins the ocean, and this is a wonderful place to bathe and soak your muscles after having scaled the ladders. At low tide, the shelf is exposed and you can explore the fascinating, sculptured sandstone, tide pools and mini surge channels. The tide pools are teeming with life and you can see crabs, sea urchins, sea anemones, periwinkles and chitons here.

Walbran Creek to Carmanah Point

To get to Carmanah Point, begin hiking west on the beach right from Walbran Creek. However, if Walbran Creek is flooded, take the forest route for 2 km and then drop down to the usual route on the beach. Walbran Creek is the turning point in the trail for those who started at the south end. As the upcoming section of beach hiking is one of the most glorious parts of the trail. The beaches are long, wide and sandy with magnificent views. The hiking is very easy, with Bonilla Point about one and a half hours away.

The Carmanah Lighthouse, established in 1890, is visible in the distance at Bonilla Point. The route passes by some seastacks, one of which is populated with a colony of cormorants. The beach is filled with fascinating discoveries

"Graveyard of the Pacific"

About 60 ships have foundered on this portion of B.C.'s coast since 1854. Here are just a few of the ships that have gone astray in this area:
- At the Surge Channel just before Dare Point, the steamship *Santa Rita* struck a reef and sank in 1923. Metal debris can be seen at low tide.
- The American schooner *Vesta* went down in 1897 just before Tsusiat Point.
- The Russian freighter *Uzbekistan* lost course due to blacked-out lighthouses in 1943. It ran ashore at Darling River. You can still see its engine and boiler at low tide. The shipwreck was kept secret for many years. The crew of 40 survived.

- The iron steamship *Valencia* ran aground in January 1906 just north of Trestle Creek and south of Billy Goat Creek. 126 people perished.
- The *Janet Cowan* crashed ashore in a blinding snowstorm in the same spot in 1895. Seven persons died including Captain Thompson, who froze to death. The wreckage of the four-masted steel barque can be seen at low tide.
- The boiler and propeller shaft of the wooden steamer S.S. *Michigan* can be seen at low tide at Michigan Creek. The wooden steamer ran aground in January, 1893. One crew member died of exposure.

Debris from a wreckage

such as the remnants of a shipwreck, which appears at low tide. There are tangles of bull kelp, various seaweeds and shells. Oyster catchers and sandpipers can be seen searching for food.

There is a glorious campsite with a good water source on the sandy beach at Carmannah Creek. It is surrounded by wide, empty expanses of sand with the ocean waves surging onto shore.

If you hike 1.3 km up Carmanah Creek, you can view the Carmanah Giant, a 95 m, 400-year-old Sitka spruce. This is the tallest tree recorded in Canada and is thought to be the tallest Sitka spruce in the world. Carmanah Valley, now a 10,000 ha provincial park, is an area with an environment ideally suited to growing giant trees, many of which live for over one thousand years. Carmanah Pacific Provincial Park was established in 1990 after the Western Canada Wilderness Committee won a long and hard-fought battle to save the area from being logged.

When gazing into the ocean, look for migrating gray whales that can often be seen swimming by. Nearly 20,000 Pacific gray whales swim past the entire B.C. coast in spring and fall. It is easy to hear them, as the noise they make when they breathe through their blow holes is unforgettable. It is certainly a memorable experience to see and hear whales pass by in the ocean in front of your tent door in the morning.

Carmanah Creek to Dare Point

The sandy beach is your route as you leave Carmanah Creek and head north toward the Carmanah Lighthouse. At the lighthouse, the beach route is passable at low tide but it involves scrambling over large, slippery rocks. The rocks are a great place to poke around for fossils, anemones and starfish. If you are lucky, you will see sea lions on the rocks in front of the lighthouse. These are sea lion haul-out rocks, which are populated with California and Steller's sea lions.

A forest route is accessed just before the lighthouse. Walk up the ladders, around the lighthouse and along a series of boardwalks for about 15 minutes until you reach another beach access point, where you can drop back onto the beach.

Many consider the trail from Carmannah Point to Tsusiat Falls to be the most scenic part of the trail. The hiking is easy along both the beach and forest routes. Cribs Creek is

Wreck of the S.S. *Valencia*

In January of 1906, the S.S. *Valencia*, a three-deck passenger steamer, ran aground seven km east of Pachena Point. The 1,630-ton American steamship was carrying 164 people when it crashed onto the rocks at night during a gale.

Nine people made it to shore, climbed the cliffs and followed a telegraph line and rough trail to a lineman's cabin where they called for help. It took 18 hours for rescuers to reach the scene of the wreck. Once they got there, they did not have adequate rescue facilities and they could only watch helplessly as the heavy seas pounded over the wreck.

Less than a day later, a life raft drifted ashore 33 km from the wreck site on Turret Island in Barkley Sound. It contained three drowned bodies and four survivors.

In all, 126 people died, including Captain O.M. Johnson, who went down with his ship. Tragically, the passengers died, not from injuries sustained in the wreck, but from drowning or exposure. This incident received wide media coverage, and people were outraged by this needless waste of life. The tragedy prompted the government to build the Shipwrecked Mariner's Lifesaving Trail, and the West Coast Trail follows much of the original route. The remnants of the *Valencia* have sunk over the years, and no parts of it are visible.

a good place to fill up your water bottles as water is scarce from here to Tsusiat Falls. The beach route crosses one surge channel and then goes onto "Cribs rocks," a natural breakwater made of tipped slabs of rock.

Make sure it is low tide when you walk over these slabs, as it would be dangerous to be trapped here. The area is characterized by many small surge channels that cut into the sides of the shelf. It is an eerie place filled with strange moaning and groaning wave noises, rock that look like spider webs and Swiss cheese, intricately carved gullies, chasms and rock pools. There is also an abandoned house in the trees. It is a fascinating place to explore.

About three km after Cribs Creek, you may see some wreckage of the steamer *Santa Rita* in a surge channel at low tide.

The trail reaches a difficult surge channel just before Dare Point. The channel is passable at tides below 2.1 m (seven feet), but it is tricky. To pass it, you must slither along a very small lip around the towering walls of the channel. It is a huge surge channel and from above, its walls look like cliffs. Luckily, there is a beach access point right before the surge channel where the trail rises steeply into the trees and across a ridge which bypasses the surge channel. The trail continues along the top of the ridge almost to Dare Point, where it descends back to sea level.

Dare Point to Tsusiat Falls

A beautiful camping spot is located at the south end of the beach at Dare Point, but obtaining drinking water here may be a problem. You will have hiked almost half the trail once you reach Dare Point. Impassable headlands just past Dare Point cause the trail to re-enter the forest. From here, it passes through a beautiful forested area filled with sand dunes. This idyllic part of the trail is very well maintained, mostly flat and easy to hike. Most of it consists of a long series of wooden boardwalks that stretch from Dare Point to Nitinat Narrows.

The trail reaches the Cheewat River, which is a slow-flowing tidal river. *Cheewat* means "river of urine." Aboriginals named it this because of its taste and colour. A small bridge leads over the river and from there, the trail passes through Ditidaht reserve land. Hikers are required to stay on the trail when going through this section. Look for a huge cedar tree to the right soon after you cross the bridge. Animals you may see include river otters, cougar, raccoons, black-tailed deer, black bears and mink.

Soon, the trail passes by the settlement of Clo-oose, which is also on Indian land. The land between the river and the open beach of Clo-oose Bay was once cleared as part of the Clo-oose townsite. It is now overtaken by a second-growth forest. At one time, Clo-oose was permanently occupied, but is now used only on a seasonal basis.

How Tides Work

Over 70% of the earth's surface is covered with water, which is affected by two tidal cycles per day. They produce two high tides and two low tides, and each cycle has a different height. The lowest tides occur during midsummer days and midwinter nights.

Tidal heights change daily and each tide occurs at a later time than it did on the previous day. The best time to go to the seashore is usually 2 hours before and after the predicted low time in the tide table.

Tide pool

Tides occur due to the gravitational pull of the sun and moon. Every 24 hours the moon swings around the earth, creating a bulge of water on the side of the earth that faces the moon. At the same time, a bulge of equal size appears on the other side of the earth. Tides are also influenced by the shape of ocean basins and by enclosed land masses.

Tsusiat Falls

From Clo-oose, the trail climbs to a cliff where it bypasses the old village of Whyac, which is one of the oldest villages on the West Coast of North America. The route continues on to the Nitinat Narrows, where the tidal Nitinat Lake empties and gathers its waters. Every six hours, the sea pushes through the shallow channel leading from Nitinat Lake to the ocean.

The only way across to the west side of this channel is by boat. To get a ride across, wait at the dock until a ferry picks you up and takes you to the other side. The ferry service operates from 9:00 a.m. to 5:00 p.m. from mid-May to October 1st and it costs $12.50. You may want to ask the driver if he has any fish or crabs for sale. If you want to exit the trail, you can do so here via Nitinat Lake by ferry.

From the Nitinat Narrows, the trail enters the forest and then pops out at the top of a cliff. This portion of the trail is especially beautiful as it has sandy beaches, rocky headlands, sea caves and abundant marine life. This is a good place to spend an extra day exploring. A series of spectacular cliff top views start at Tsuquadra Point, where the trail winds over and around headlands, offering a series of breathtaking views east and west of the coastline. Look for bald eagles sitting out on the sea stacks. Salal, shorepine and spruce populate the cliff tops. The trail continues along the cliffs and then moves gently lower until you are once again at beach level. A roomy cave is located beside the trail, just before Tsusiat Falls at Tsuquadra Point. This is a perfect dry place to camp if the weather is bad.

There is a fascinating natural rock arch on the beach at Tsusiat Point called Hole-in-the-Wall. It is possible to walk on top of the arch by

The Best Drinking-Water Sites

The following areas provide an abundance of good, dependable drinking water along the trail. It is recommended that you filter or treat the water before using it. Water is scarce between Cribs Creek and Tsusiat Falls, so fill up at either of these points. The best water is located at:

Gordon River	Tsusiat Falls
Thrasher Cove	Tsocowis Creek
Camper Bay	Darling River
Walbran Creek	Michigan Creek
Bonilla Point	Pachena Light Station
Carmanah Creek	Pachena Bay Trailhead
Cribs Creek	

Treasures On the Seashore

The shoreline along the West Coast Trail may well be one of the most fascinating places you will ever explore. Ranging from expansive sandy beaches to chiselled sandstone riddled with tidal pools, the shoreline is rich with a wide variety of marine life. The following are some of the treasures you will find on the seashore during your hike.

Limpets: Limpets are tiny mollusks that grow to 6 cm and are shaped like tiny hats. They have a single conical shell that does not have spirals. They are found intertidally on rocks, floats and some kelps. Limpets usually position themselves so that they are shaded at low tide, and they feed by grazing on microscopic algae that grow on rock.

Limpets defend themselves against predators by clamping down on the object they are attached to. Try to pick one up, and you will be amazed at the strength of this tiny creature.

Purple sea urchin: These creatures look like round pincushions and are made of many fused plates that come together to make a single, hollow ball. An urchin's teeth and mouth are located on its underside.

Sea urchins feed on bits of seaweed that are trapped on its spines. Tube feet are located between these spines and from here, they pass seaweed along to the urchin's mouth.

Most urchins live for four to eight years. They are found intertidally on exposed, rocky shores in holes worn in the rock. Purple sea urchins often use their pointed, hard spines to grind out small pockets in the soft sandstone tide pools where they live.

Bull kelp: Bull kelp are a large form of seaweed. The stems look like long green whips with a small bulb at the end. Individual fronds are located on the bulb, which acts as a float. By keeping the plant near the water's surface, this frond ensures that the plant can get enough light.

Great kelp beds often act as hosts for smaller organisms, thus providing a support system for other

marine life. The plant may grow to 20 m in length and lives from four to seven years.

Barnacles: Barnacles are shells made of overlapping plates. The opening at the top of the shell is closed by muscles that move the plates. A barnacle shell may be cemented directly to an object by means of a tough, flexible stalk.

Barnacles cannot cope with drying, so they survive at low tide by closing up tightly with a small amount of water inside their shells. A barnacle captures food by kicking out its sticky feet.

Sponges: Sponges form brightly coloured soft and spongy encrusting mats. They come in a wide array of brilliant colours and are often shaped like tubes, cups or branches. A sponge's cells are organized around a network of pores, chambers and canals. Look for them under rocks, on floats and pilings or in crevices. They are eaten by sea stars, some snails and sea slugs.

Anemones: Anemones look like delicate, colourful flowers whose tentacles wave gracefully in the air. They are carnivores, and if you put your finger into their tentacles, you can feel a delicate sticky pull. Once prey is trapped, the anemone pulls the food into its mouth and gut cavity for digestion.

Anemones live an incredibly long time. Scientists believe that they live for over one hundred years. They attach themselves to pilings, kelp, rocks and sometimes buried in sediments.

Starfish: Beach hikers revel in the sight of exquisitely coloured starfish. Starfish have a central disk from which a number of rays (arms) grow outward. A starfish usually has five rays, but there can be as many as 24. They range in colour from pink or yellow to purple and blue.

Starfish have tube feet that form sucker-like tips. They use these feet to dig for and pull prey. Starfish eat shellfish, fishes, anemones and other starfish.

Starfish have a remarkable ability to regenerate. A whole individual can regenerate from a single ray.

a path that leads off the side to the top. You can also walk underneath it at tides below 2.7 m (nine feet) and cross to the other side. The top of the arch is a great place to watch for whales or to take in the scenery.

It is common for gray whales to pass by quite close to shore here. Some biologists believe that a population of gray whales remains year round in the region of Pacific Rim National Park.

From Tsusiat Point, it is an easy beach walk to Tsusiat Falls. Look for a colony of black cormorants sitting on a sea stack just before Tsusiat Falls. The crashing surf on the beaches with ships drifting by on the ocean makes the hiking glorious.

There are superb, sometimes deserted beaches here where you can beachcomb to your heart's delight. Some of the beaches are open and wide with long expanses of sand, while others form secluded little bays surrounded by rocky cliffs and crags. You can see many varieties of red, yellow and black seaweed that resemble paper, leaves and grass. There are also bunches of intertwined giant bull kelp that are washed ashore. When it dries, it becomes white and paper-like.

The campsite at the Tsusiat Falls is one of the most popular ones on the trail, and it will most likely be crowded. You may wish to find a more secluded spot among the cliffs and crags that jut out onto other parts of the beach.

The falls cascade down into pools at the bottom of the beach and are a great place to bathe or swim. There is a splendid view from the waterfalls, where you can see the water collecting into pools that flow into the ocean. The north end of the falls is used to collect drinking water. Some don their bathing suits and stand under the falls to do this. Drinking water should be obtained from the falls and not the pools.

Tsusiat Falls to Darling River

From Tsusiat Falls, you must hike up into the forest along the trail, as the beach is impassable. As you wind through the forest, boardwalks meander around a ridge and then down to ladders that lead to the Klanawa River. A

Darling River

How Whales Breathe

A whale breathes through a blowhole located on the top of its head. Muscles surround this blowhole, which work to seal the entrance to the hole when the animal goes under water. Whales do not breathe rhythmically and involuntarily like humans. They must make a conscious effort to breathe and they breath quickly, blowing air forcefully from their lungs.

Through adaptation, whales have developed a high tolerance to carbon dioxide. This means that they can stay under water for very long periods of time. They also have a huge capacity to store oxygen. Each breath that a whale takes provides it with an 80-90% renewal of air in its lungs. In comparison, a land mammal is provided with only a 10-20% renewal of air in its lungs every time it breathes.

Trestle Creek

cable car takes you over the Klanawa River, which like the Cheewat, is tidal.

You can continue hiking through the forest once you are past the river or drop back down onto the beach. If it is low tide near Trestle Creek, you will see some rusty wreckage and remnants of a ship. The beach hiking becomes more difficult along some stretches where portions of small boulders are mixed with sand.

You must rejoin the forest trail at Trestle Creek, as there is an impassable headland farther up. The forest trail is a very easy and well-maintained trail. It passes by the Valencia Bluffs, which is where the ill-fated ship S.S. *Valencia* went down in 1906.

The trail soon reaches Tsocowis Creek, where you can see the wreckage of a huge barge on the beach. It is possible to walk up on part of the barge and explore the wreck. The trail then passes Orange Juice Creek, which is a good place to fill up on water.

The beach trail from Tsocowis Creek to Darling River runs along a shelf that is passable at tides below 2.7 m (nine feet). Darling River has fine camping located among many washed-up logs that provide shelter from the wind. The beach is covered in small pebbles, boulders and sand that has the texture and

Harbour Seal

Harbour seals are the most common true seal of the West Coast. They are distinguished by their short front and hind flippers. They also have no external ear pinna. When mature, the seal is 156 to 187 cm long and weighs up to 114 kg. Harbour seals like to sleep out of the water for part of the day, so they are often seen on secluded beaches or sandbars.

Harbour seal pups are born in spring or early summer. Each mother bears only one pup, which weighs about 10 kg at birth. They can swim, are fully furred and are weaned by six weeks of age. Harbour seals are devoted and gentle mothers, and often like to play swimming games with their pups.

It is extremely important not to touch a seal pup if you find one lying on the beach. The pups cannot dive as deep as the mothers, so they are often left alone while their mothers go fishing. If a pup is handled by a human, it will likely be abandoned.

Raccoons

appearance of brown rice. An excellent water source is located at the river.

Darling River to Bamfield

From Darling River, the trail runs along the beach to Michigan Creek, which is the last good campsite before the trail's end. The steamer *Michigan* foundered on the rocks of *Michigan* Creek in 1893, and the boiler remains wedged in rock at the mouth of the creek. From this point onward, the trail runs back into the forest where it stays until it reaches the Pachena Bay trailhead.

The trail continues along an old, level, well-maintained road. The 3.6 m-wide road that stretches from the Pachena Lighthouse to Bamfield was constructed in 1907. The Pachena Lighthouse is located two km west of Michigan Creek and it is worth a visit. At the entrance to the lighthouse is a collection of hand-painted signs that say "welcome" in 35 different languages. The lighthouse grounds are filled with gardens, green lawns and white clapboard houses. You are welcome to explore the grounds and fill up on water from tanks located on lighthouse grounds. However, please respect the privacy of the families that live there.

As you continue on the main trail, you will see a path that goes off to the south (left) through the bushes. This path leads to a viewpoint where you can see a sea lion rookery. The sea lions can be seen in early spring and fall.

The main trail continues to be wide, well maintained and easy all the way to the Bamfield trailhead. The trail gradually descends for 10 km around Pachena Bay. As you near Pachena Bay, the view improves and you are treated the sight of sandy Pachena Beach. The trailhead is located at the east end of the beach and camping is available. Remember to sign out as you leave the trail. Bamfield is reached by heading north through the parking lot to the main road.

~ 2 ~
Juan De Fuca Marine Trail

2. Route (map, page 17)

Distance: 47 km one way, 3-4 days
Rating: ** Easy, early season hike
All elevations are at sea level (0 m)
Botanical Beach Trailhead: 0 km
Parkinson Creek: 10 km
Sombrio Beach: 19 km
China Beach: 47 km
Topographical maps: 92C/8, 92C/9,

2. Trailhead

The Juan de Fuca Marine Trail can be reached by the following four trailheads: Botanical Beach, Parkinson Beach, Sombrio Beach, China Beach. The Botanical Beach Trailhead, however, is the most common starting point. Botanical Beach Trailhead: From the town of Port Renfrew, drive southwest along Cerantes Road for 4 km. The road is rough and unpaved. To reach Port Renfrew, take Highway 14 from Victoria and drive northwest for 113 km, at which point you follow the signs to Botanical Beach.

2. Alternative Access Points

The following are alternative starting points for the Juan de Fuca Marine Trail:
Parkinson Creek: From Victoria, take Highway 14 northwest for 103 km.
Sombrio Beach: From Victoria, take Highway 14 northwest for 94 km.
China Beach: From Victoria, take Highway 14 northwest for 75 km.

Opened in the summer of 1995, this new provincial park hugs the shoreline of southwestern Vancouver Island for 47 km. It runs along the Strait of Juan de Fuca from China Beach, just west of the community of Jordan River to just north of Botanical Beach Provincial Park near Port Renfrew. This trail is intended to act as an extension of the popular West Coast Trail. However, the trail is a separate entity and does not provide any access to the West Coast Trail.

Unlike the West Coast Trail, this trail has easy access points along the route, allowing you to hike portions of the trail or all of it. It runs up and down the shoreline, with extended sections of beach hiking. This trail also has marvellous scenery that includes beach camping, rich tide pools and wildlife viewing, shoreline trails and unusual geological features. The best time to hike the trail is from August to September. Beach trail access points are marked by fluorescent orange balls hanging from the trees.

For more information, contact BC Parks, South Vancouver Island District, 2930 Trans-Canada Highway, Victoria, BC, V9B 5T9; ph. 250-391-2300 or the Juan de Fuca home page at http://wlapwww.gov.bc.ca/bcparks/explore/parkpgs/juan_fuc/trailhd.htm

Botanical Beach Trailhead to Parkinson Creek

What sets this beach apart from others is that seldom is such a display of marine life set so high on the intertidal zone. There is an impressive sandstone shelf that has hundreds of clear, deep tide pools, rich marine life and odd sandstone formations. Gray whales and killer whales can often be seen during their migration from Mexico to Alaska during March and April.

The trail heads south from Botanical Beach and passes Providence Cove, where there is a small campground. The area is rich with marine mammals and shore life.

The section ends at Parkinson Creek, one of the four access points to the trail. Camping, parking and information facilities are located here. Parkinson Creek and the Kuitshe Seal Cove are the sites of two unique seal colonies. The seals congregate in a grotto that is a 3,000-m^2 natural cavern in a seaside cliff. It is connected to the open sea by a wide chasm and underwater tunnel. The grotto has two waterfalls and four caves where seals give birth.

Long Beach

About 75 seals congregate in this area every season. This is also a good area to look for eagles, bears and orcas.

Parkinson Creek to Sombrio Beach

This moderately challenging part of the trail passes Kuitshe Creek, where there is a wilderness campsite. It then follows the beach for a stretch near Sombrio River.

Sombrio Beach is another access point to the trail. Information, camping and parking facilities are located at the east end of the beach. The beach has a long, sweeping shore with a creek flowing across one end, and it is considered to be one of the best spots for surfing on the southern part of Vancouver Island. There are also sea caves, pools and tunnels to explore. Wildlife that you may see includes river otters, gray whales, orcas and a variety of marine birds.

Sombrio Beach to China Beach

This section of the trail is challenging, as it crosses a number of creeks and has steeper changes in elevation. Check your tide tables before you leave camp as there is a beach-walk section half a kilometre past Zin Creek that is only passable at low tide. Be ready for muddy sections between Loss Creek and Newmarch Creek.

Loss Creek to Bear Beach is the most difficult section on the trail. Two camping spots are located about two km apart on Bear Beach, but the trail between the two campgrounds can only be hiked at low tide. It is important to check the tide tables before you set out.

The trail ends at the China Beach Trailhead and a campground, information booth and parking are located at this spot. This area features a sandy beach, tidal pools, a waterfall, abundant marine wildlife and exquisite views. You may see gray whales passing by in the spring or fall.

2. Camping, Cycling, Dogs

Camping: Beach and forest sites are available. Group size is a maximum of 10 people.

Mountain biking: Cycling is permitted on roads, but not on trails.

Dogs: Dogs must be on a leash and are not allowed on beach areas.

Driftwood on Long Beach

~ 3 ~

Long Beach Trail

3. Route (map, page 34)

Distance: 20.5 km one way; 8-10 hours, 1-2 days
Rating:*** Easy, early season hike
Schooner Trail Trailhead: 50 m
Long Beach: 1 km
Long Beach Parking Lot: 3 km
Green Point Parking Lot: 6 km
Combers Beach Parking Lot: 7.5 km
South Beach Trail (Wickaninnish Centre): 11 km
South Beach Trail and Wickaninnish Trail: 12 km
Florencia Bay Parking Lot: 50 m, 14.5 km
Willowbrae Trail: 18.5 km
Highway 4 Trailhead: 50 m, 20.5 km
Topographical maps: 92C/13, 92F/4

Long Beach is the most accessible of the three units of the park. It is named for its 11-km stretch of sandy beach, located between the villages of Ucluelet and Tofino. Access by car or passenger bus is via Highway 4. Passenger ferry and air charter flights are also available.

Major centres in the area are Port Alberni and Nanaimo. A complete range of services, supplies and accommodation are available here as well as at Tofino and Ucluelet. An information centre is located on Highway 4, just inside the park boundary. Wickaninnish Centre, an interpretive facility, is located near the information centre. Walk-in and drive-in campsites are situated in the park. Commercial campgrounds are operated outside park boundaries. There are no hostels.

This is the most decadent of all the *Classic Hikes*. The hike takes you along six expansive

3. Trailhead

The trail is located between the towns of Ucluelet and Tofino on Vancouver Island, 195 km from Nanaimo and 305 km from Victoria. From Nanaimo, drive west on Highway 4 to the Ucluelet-Tofino T junction. Turn north on Highway 4 (right) and drive for three km for the Pacific Rim Park Information Centre and eight km for the Wickaninnish Centre. Schooner Trail is located 14.8 km north of the Information Centre. You will need to leave a car or arrange for transportation at either trailhead.

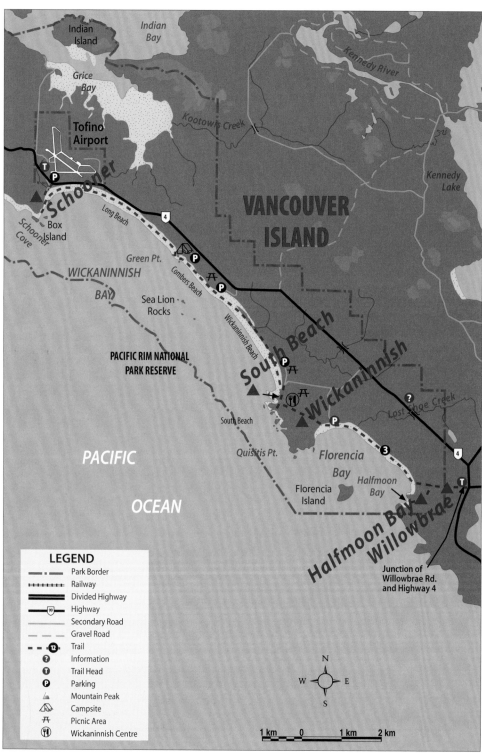

LEGEND

— · — · —	Park Border
┼┼┼┼┼┼	Railway
▬▬▬▬	Divided Highway
▬ 99 ▬	Highway
———	Secondary Road
– – – –	Gravel Road
· · · 12 · · ·	Trail
❓	Information
❶	Trail Head
℗	Parking
▲	Mountain Peak
⛺	Campsite
𝍏	Picnic Area
🍽	Wickaninnish Centre

Indian Island

Indian Bay

Grice Bay

Tofino Airport

Schooner Cove

Box Island

Schooner

Long Beach

WICKANINNISH BAY

Green Pt.

Combers Beach

Sea Lion Rocks

PACIFIC RIM NATIONAL PARK RESERVE

Wickaninnish Beach

South Beach

Quisitis Pt.

South Beach

PACIFIC OCEAN

Florencia Bay

Florencia Island

Wickaninnish

Halfmoon Bay

Lost Shoe Creek

Halfmoon Bay

Willowbrae

Junction of Willowbrae Rd. and Highway 4

Kennedy River

Kootowis Creek

VANCOUVER ISLAND

Kennedy Lake

N
W — E
S

1 km 0 1 km 2 km

beaches and to isolated coves that are joined together by lush rainforest trails. The ocean scenery is breathtaking, the surf is huge and there is ample opportunity to beachcomb or explore the marine wildlife. The hiking is on glorious, hard-packed sand along long stretches of wide beaches. The hiking is so delightfully easy that you can do most of it in your bare feet!

The Long Beach Unit of Pacific Rim National Park encompasses 8,100 ha that includes a wild, extraordinary 30 km stretch of shoreline from Cox Point in the northwest to Wya Point in the south. The park features 20 km of sandy beaches, the longest being an 11 km stretch of sand on Long Beach.

This area was settled just after the turn of the century and was once called Long Bay. Before Highway 4 was paved in the early 1970s, this area was only accessible via a treacherous dirt road from Port Alberni. In the 1960s and early 70s, Florencia Bay was a popular gathering spot for artists, drifters, writers and hippies who lived in makeshift shacks and shanty communities on the beach. The squatters left when Long Beach became part of Pacific Rim National Park in 1971.

The trail begins in the north at Schooner Cove and goes to Half Moon Bay at the south end of the park. Several short forest trails link the trailheads to the beaches, and Wickaninnish Beach is linked to South Beach by two short forest trails that cross Quisitis Point. The route is accessible from many points along Highway 4, allowing you to do either the whole hike or parts of it.

Schooner Trail to Long Beach

From the Schooner Cove Parking Lot, take the one km Schooner Trail southeast into the forest. The trail passes by a salmon-spawning stream, and as you near the beach, the cedar-hemlock forest is gradually taken over by Sitka spruce. These tough trees have evolved so that they can withstand the harsh winter gales that bombard them with sand and sea salt. They thrive on magnesium-rich soil and form the Sitka spruce fringe, which skirts the entire coast of Vancouver Island, Queen Charlotte Islands and open coastal sections of the B.C. mainland.

As you hike toward the beach, the sound of the pounding surf leads you onward until the trail emerges from the forest and onto the

Half Moon Bay Trail

This 500 m trail branches off at the junction on the Willowbrae Trail. Alternatively, you can start from the Willowbrae trailhead and hike to the junction.

Heading southwest over a headland between Florencia Bay and Half Moon Bay, the trail leads to a small cove south of Florencia Bay. The route goes through a cedar and hemlock forest to a wooden boardwalk, where it passes through skunk cabbage, salal and sword fern. From the boardwalk, you descend steeply to the beach of Half Moon Bay.

This is the southernmost beach of the Long Beach Unit and it provides a fantastic view of Florencia Bay to the north. Look for California sea lions in the winter on an islet near Wya Point at the south end of the bay.

northwest end of Long Beach. Schooner Cove is located 700 m southwest and faces Box Island, just around the point. These first breathtaking views of the open expanses of beaches and billowing, massive waves rushing to the shore will probably stay with you forever.

Long Beach to South Beach Trail

To reach the South Beach Trail, head south on Long Beach along the 11-km stretch of sand after which the park is named. This area is known as the surfing capital of Canada, and you can see surfers, windsurfers and surf kayakers playing in the waves. It is also a popular area for kite-flying.

Two ships were wrecked on Long Beach. In 1866, a three-masted barque called the *Mustang* ran aground on the beach. Another ship called the *William G. Irwin* also ran aground here in 1887 after it was abandoned at sea.

The landscape along this coastline is magical, the endless spaces and the sound of the waves create a relaxing, meditative environment. The sand on the beach is flat, hard and smooth, making it perfect for hiking. There are many tangled bunches of bull kelp on the beach, while sea grass grows closer to the forest. Driftwood that has been thrown ashore piles up in front of the sea grass. Beachcombers like to poke around in the driftwood, looking for treasures that have washed up during the ferocious winter storms. For many, the ultimate find is a Japanese glass float that miraculously makes it to shore after having been carried along on the ocean currents.

You soon reach Green Point, where there is

Whale watching

Whale watching is a very popular pastime at Long Beach. Every year, Pacific gray whales pass the southern coast of Vancouver Island as they migrate from Baja, California and Mexico to the Gulf of Alaska. The whales pass by from late February to May, and some whales pass by just a few kilometres from shore. The whales leave their northern feeding grounds to migrate south between late September and early October, averaging about 185 km per day.

When you are watching for whales, look and listen for them blowing through their blow holes. This blast that can shoot up to 5 m in the air. The best time to view them is at Long Beach is in the early morning. April is the peak migration time.

Pacific gray whales were once hunted almost to extinction during only 18 years of whaling on the West Coast. Atlantic gray whales were eliminated decades ago, leaving only the Pacific gray whale. Pacific gray whales were protected in the 1940s by international agreement, and remain protected today by Canadian and American law. They have miraculously replenished their population and there are now approximately 20,000 Pacific gray whales.

Wickaninnish Centre

Sea Otters

Almost everyone falls in love with these delightful creatures. Sea otters have cute, animated little faces lined with whiskers. Fine, dense brown fur coats their long bodies. They are characterized by a long neck, short legs and short, flat tail. They have no blubber on their bodies and their average weight is 23 to 45 kg.

Sea otters often swim and eat on their backs. They may eat up to 25% of their body weight daily. Otters congregate in groups of 30 or more and are found in rocky areas. They also frequent kelp beds. Sea otters were once hunted almost to extinction for their fur, but they are making a comeback.

a parking area and a campground. Combers Beach is reached 1.5 km farther on, where a sea lion haul-out rock is located directly in front of the parking lot. This is one of four year-round haul-outs for Steller sea lions on the west coast of Vancouver Island.

Just after you pass the sea lion rocks, you have to wade across a rip current to get to the other side of the beach. Rip currents are present when sandbars are located just off the shoreline or there are slight depressions in the shore that extend into the water. A rip current occurs when large volumes of water that are trapped between the sandbar and the shore return to the ocean through a channel in the sandbar. Use caution when crossing a rip current.

The Wickaninnish Centre is located at the south end of Wickaninnish Beach. Its name comes from a powerful Nootka Chief who was leader of the Clayoquot Indians in the 1800s. The centre is an interpretive facility that has displays, films, exhibits and a restaurant. The centre is open from March 15 to October 15 (ph. 250-726-7706).

South Beach Trail to Wickaninnish Trail

The 700 m-long South Beach Trail begins at the Wickaninnish Centre and enters the forest as it crosses Quisitis Point leading toward South Beach. The trail passes through a forest of Sitka spruce, where some short side trails lead to coves that are surrounded by headlands. One of these coves is named after Group of Seven painter Arthur Lismer, who was a regular visitor here. Lismer Beach has tide pools that you can explore at low tide. From Lismer Beach, a boardwalk goes up to the top of the headland towards South Beach. The trail is surrounded by dense walls of salmonberry and salal, and there are superb views of Lismer Beach and Long Beach.

From here, the trail leads to a junction with the Wickaninnish Trail. If you want to go to South Beach, take the south (right) trail along the boardwalk past moss gardens and more Sitka spruce. The boardwalk ends at South Beach, where a double sea-arch and some massive surge channels in the rocky bluffs are located to the north. A hike on the beach of polished gravel leads southward to several small, secluded coves.

Wickaninnish Trail to Willowbrae Trail and Trailhead

To hike this 2.3 km trail, turn east (right) at the junction on the South Beach Trail. The Wickaninnish Trail once linked the villages of Tofino and Ucluelet until a road was built in 1942. About halfway along the trail, part of the original path is still visible in a mat of sphagnum moss. When the trail was first built, hand-cut slabs of cedar were laid across it in a corduroy pattern.

The carnivorous sundew plant can also be seen in the sphagnum moss. This plant lures insects with the smell and colour of its tiny green leaves, which are covered with tentacles. Insects

Salal

become trapped by red, gluey droplets on the tentacles, which bend around the insect, making escape impossible.

The trail continues through the sphagnum bog where stunted, twisted shorepine live and ends on the west side of the Florencia Bay Parking Lot Trail. To continue to Florencia Bay, head southeast on the trail that begins just to your left (north) at the Florencia Bay Parking Lot to a set of stairs that leads you down to the beach. Florencia Bay was named after a Peruvian brigantine that was wrecked in the bay in 1861. This cove was known as Wreck Bay until 1934.

At the south end of the Florencia Bay, the Willowbrae Trail goes east and climbs to where it intersects with the Half Moon Bay Trail. The Half Moon Bay Trail runs southwest (right), while the Willowbrae Trail continues southeast (left).

The Willowbrae Trail crosses a small bridge and is lined with salal, bracken and deer fern. Like the Wickaninnish Trail, this trail was also originally covered with slabs of cedar and was

3. Camping, Cycling, Dogs

Camping: A campground with 94 campsites is located at Green Point Campground, 10 km north of the information centre. Phone-in reservations are taken for sites. A fee is charged, and reservations are recommended (ph.1-800-689-9025). Many commercial campsites are located outside the park boundary.

Mountain biking: Bikes are not permitted.

Dogs: Dogs are allowed, but must be kept on a leash. They are not allowed on beach areas.

used by locals to carry supplies between Tofino and Ucluelet. It was originally wide enough for a horse-drawn wagon, but is now overgrown.

The trail widens and opens up as it nears the trailhead. It emerges from the forest on the outskirts of the park onto Highway 4, two km south of the Ucluelet-Port Alberni T intersection.

~ 4 ~

Cape Scott

4. Route

Distance: 23.6 km one way to Cape Scott, 2-3 days
Rating: *** Easy to intermediate; early season hike
San Josef Bay: 2.5 km, 3/4 hours
Fisherman River: 9.3 km, 3 hours
Hansen Lagoon: 14.7 km, 5 hours
Cape Scott: 23.6 km, 8 hours
Topographical maps: 102I/16

4. Trailhead

Take Highway 19 to Port Hardy, and drive 64 km over a rough road past Holberg to a parking area near the park's southeast boundary. The trail is open year round.

4. Camping, Cycling, Dogs

Camping: Wilderness camping areas are located near San Josef Bay, Nels Bight, Nissen Bight and Guise Bay. Camping is on the beach. Commercial vehicle campgrounds are located on the road before the park entrance at Eric Lake.
Mountain biking: Bikes are not permitted.
Dogs: Dogs are allowed, but must be kept on a leash. They are not allowed on beach areas.

This magnificent, 21,847 ha rugged wilderness park is located at the northwest tip of Vancouver Island. This provincial park offers 40 km of hiking trails. It is rich in marine life, has rugged shorelines, a lighthouse and archaeological sites.

Attempts were made by pioneers to settle this area in the 1700s, in 1897 and in 1910. However, the harsh environmental conditions forced them to abandon their settlements. Remnants of these fledgling settlements can still be seen in the Hansen Lagoon area.

There are nine beaches in the park that total 23 km in length. Many of the beaches, like the fine-textured, white-sand beach at Nels Bight, are sandy.

This area is famous for its violent storms, strong winds and heavy rainfalls, so caution is advised if you are doing this hike early in the season. Be prepared for rough, muddy trails and follow designated beach routes. Drinking water may not always be available. A variety of wilderness camping spots are located in the park. Supplies and garbage must be packed into and out of the park, as there are no facilities here.

Surfing

With its huge surf and long beaches, Long Beach has become known as Canada's surfing capital. Surfers, windsurfers and surf kayakers come from all over the world to enjoy conditions that, except for the chilly water, rival those found in southern California.

You can often see surfers practicing in the waves, and competitions are held regularly in the area. Most surfers wear full wet suits to protect themselves from the cold water that averages 7 °C in winter and 12 °C in summer. Wet suits also increase a surfer's ability to float. Ask at the park information centre for recommended surfing locations.

The North Shore

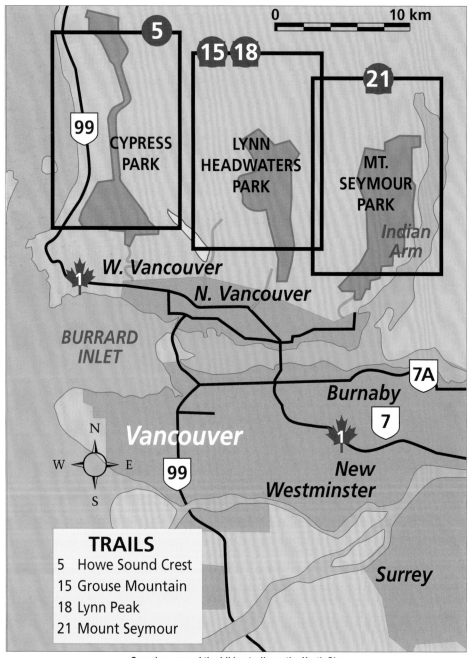

5

0   10 km

15 18

21

99

CYPRESS
PARK

LYNN
HEADWATERS
PARK

MT.
SEYMOUR
PARK

*Indian
Arm*

W. Vancouver

N. Vancouver

1

*BURRARD
INLET*

7A

Burnaby

7

N

Vancouver

1

W   E

99

*New
Westminster*

S

TRAILS
5 Howe Sound Crest
15 Grouse Mountain
18 Lynn Peak
21 Mount Seymour

Surrey

Overview map of the hiking trails on the North Shore

View from Howe Sound Crest Trail of Bowen, Boyer, Gambier and Vancouver islands

Located on the northern shore of Burrard Inlet, the North Shore Mountains and the twin peaks of the Lions dominate the view from the city of Vancouver. Vancouverites have taken advantage of this superb area so close to their homes since the early 1900s. During the twenties

and thirties, a fleet of ferries would transport people from Vancouver across Burrard Inlet so that they could hike and ski. Today, the area is just as popular. The main recreation areas that people visit on the North Shore include Mt. Seymour Provincial Park, Cypress Provincial Park, Grouse Mountain and Lynn Headwaters Regional Park. The hiking trails in these areas are generally rugged, taking you into fairly isolated wilderness areas. The scenery along the trails is characterized by ocean, canyons, ski terrain, lush rainforest, alpine wilderness, mountains and spectacular views of Vancouver.

Despite this area's close proximity to Vancouver, it remains remote and wild. This is, in part, due to the Greater Vancouver Water District watershed. The watershed is located between Grouse Mountain and Cypress Provincial Park, and the boundaries around the watershed are off limits to the public.

The main centres in this area are Vancouver, North Vancouver and West Vancouver, and access is gained via Highways 1 and 99. A full range of accommodations, supplies and services are available here.

Park information kiosks are located at provincial and regional park trailheads. Wilderness campsites are located at all the provincial parks. Camping is not allowed at Lynn Headwaters Regional Park. Hostels are located in Vancouver at Jericho Beach and downtown.

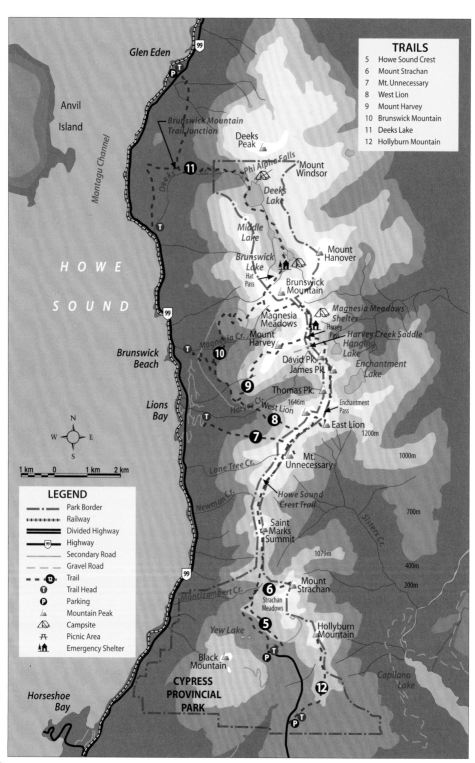

TRAILS

5	Howe Sound Crest
6	Mount Strachan
7	Mt. Unnecessary
8	West Lion
9	Mount Harvey
10	Brunswick Mountain
11	Deeks Lake
12	Hollyburn Mountain

LEGEND

	Park Border
	Railway
	Divided Highway
	Highway
	Secondary Road
	Gravel Road
	Trail
	Trail Head
	Parking
	Mountain Peak
	Campsite
	Picnic Area
	Emergency Shelter

Glen Eden

Anvil Island

Montagu Channel

Brunswick Mountain Trail Junction

Deeks Peak

Phi Alpha Falls

Mount Windsor

Deeks Lake

Middle Lake

Brunswick Lake

Hat Pass

Mount Hanover

Brunswick Mountain

H O W E

S O U N D

Magnesia Meadows

Magnesia Meadows Shelter

Harvey Pass

Mount Harvey

Harvey Creek Saddle

Hanging Lake

David Pk.

James Pk.

Enchantment Lake

Brunswick Beach

Thomas Pk.

1646m

Enchantment Pass

Enchantment Lake

Lions Bay

Harvey Cr.

West Lion

East Lion

1200m

Lone Tree Cr.

Mt. Unnecessary

1000m

N W E S

1 km 0 1 km 2 km

Newman Cr.

Howe Sound Crest Trail

Sisters Cr.

700m

Saint Marks Summit

1079m

400m

Montizambert Cr.

Mount Strachan

200m

Strachan Meadows

Yew Lake

Hollyburn Mountain

Black Mountain

Capilano Lake

Horseshoe Bay

CYPRESS PROVINCIAL PARK

~ 5 ~
Howe Sound Crest Trail

5. Route (map, page 42)

Distance: 29 km one way, 2-4 days
Rating: *** Difficult
Cypress Provincial Park Trailhead: 900 m
St. Mark's Summit: 1,460 m, 5.5 km
Unnecessary Mountain: 1,520 m, 8.4 km
West shoulder of the Lion: 1,646 m, 10.5 km
James Peak: 1,460 m, 12.22 km
Harvey Creek Saddle: 1,460 m, 13.62 km
Magnesia Meadows Hut: 1,480 m, 14.32 km
Brunswick Mountain Trail Junction: 1,500 m, 16.56 km
Hat Pass: 1,500 m, 18.06 km
Brunswick Lake: 1,160 m, 19.06 km
Deeks Lake: 1,097 m, 22.17 km
North Trailhead/Hwy 99: 61 m, 29 km
Topographical maps: 92G/6, 92G/11

5. Trailhead

The southern trailhead is located at Cypress Provincial Park. From downtown Vancouver, drive 12 km via the Lions Gate Bridge to West Vancouver and continue along the Upper Levels Highway (Routes 1 and 99). Take the Cypress Provincial turnoff (exit #8) and continue to the Upper parking lot near the lift ticket wicket.

The Howe Sound Crest trail can also be accessed at the trailhead just south of Porteau Cove. From the village of Lions Bay, drive north on Highway 99 for 10 km beyond the village of Lions Bay. The trailhead is located just after Bertram Creek on the east side of the road. Park at the parking lot on the west side of the highway. You must leave a car at the far end of the trail or arrange for transportation back.

The trail is marked with orange markers. For more information on Cypress Park, call (604) 926-6007 (summer) or (604) 926-5612 (winter).

The rugged Howe Sound Crest Trail rivals the West Coast Trail in scope and beauty. The trail traverses the ridge of the Pacific Coast Mountains, which is visible on the northern skyline of Vancouver. Amazingly, this hike is located only 20 minutes from downtown Vancouver. Few alpine areas on the continent are so accessible from a major city.

This is the most difficult of all the *Classic Hikes*, but it is also one of the most rewarding. The hike takes you over three mountain peaks and passes close by 10 others. It goes through four mountain passes, along five lakes, three waterfalls and many other small lakes, streams, meadows and tarns. There are panoramic views of ocean, islands, mountain ranges and valleys along most of the route.

The trail starts at Cypress Bowl in the south and runs north along the mountain peaks that parallel Highway 99. It ends just south of Porteau Cove Provincial Park. The route runs over and past St. Marks Mountain, Mt. Unnecessary, the West and East Lions, Thomas Peak, James Peak, Mt. Harvey, Brunswick Mountain, Hat Mountain, Brunswick Lake and Deeks Lake. This hike links these well-known mountain peaks in a continuous route that runs northward, overlooking the waters of Howe Sound.

There are also individual routes up these mountains, which are considered to be classics. The wonderful part of this trail is that it can be done in a variety of ways. You can do the entire hike or parts of it as a day hike.

When hiking the entire trail, it is recommended that you start from Cypress Bowl in Cypress Provincial Park. It is much longer and more difficult if you start from Porteau Cove due to the uphill grade.

This is a rugged, demanding hike and you should be comfortable hiking over rocky mountain ridges, up steep mountain slopes and over loose rock. The trail is very rough and isolated in the section between the Lions and Harvey Creek Saddle. It is recommended that only advanced hikers tackle this section. The trail is well marked but a topographical map and compass are musts. If you are hiking either early or late in the season, be aware that a small amount of snow can obliterate the trail markers in some sections. Bring plenty of water as there are few water sources between Cypress Bowl and Magnesia Meadows, unless you

Small tarn on Mt. Unnecessary

are prepared to treat pond water.

There is a lot of bear activity along this trail, so you should make noise frequently as you hike.

Cypress Park to St. Marks Summit

From the Cypress Bowl parking lot, walk west along the Yew Lake trail and turn north (right) at the first signed intersection. After crossing a road, take a path that goes uphill along the forest. Continue through a small ravine and a stretch of upper road to the forest on the west side of Mount Strachan. The trail heads through the forest for about 40 minutes, after which it branches again at a small bridge at the Strachan Meadows. The narrow trail to the east (right) heads up Strachan Mountain.

Continue straight ahead up switchbacks to a knoll before St. Marks Summit. At the top, you can see Howe Sound, the Sunshine Coast and the islands through the trees. From this knoll, the trail switches back steeply up St. Marks Mountain. At the top are rocky bluffs from which you can see Howe Sound, Bowyer Island, Vancouver Island, and the islands beyond.

St. Marks Summit to Mt. Unnecessary (South Peak)

From St. Marks peak, the trail descends steeply down on the way to Unnecessary Mountain. The trail is rough and scattered with rocks and roots. Grouse inhabit the area, so keep an eye out for them. The trail meanders in and out of the forest with alternating views to the left of the Howe Sound archipelago. About 15 minutes after leaving St. Marks, the trail enters a

5. Camping, Cycling, Dogs

Camping: Wilderness camping is allowed beyond the alpine and nordic ski areas at higher elevations and along the Howe Sound Crest Trail. There are no designated sites, so choose locations carefully to avoid environmental damage. Recommended sites are located at Magnesia Meadows, Brunswick Lake and Deeks Lake. Emergency shelters are located at Magnesia Meadows and Brunswick Lake. Open fires are not permitted. Drinking water sources may be limited.

Mountain biking: At Cypress Park, mountain biking is allowed on the main paved road and on designated trails.

Dogs: Dogs are allowed, but must be kept on a leash.

little clearing where there is a little pond. Beside the pond are a chair and some letters of the alphabet that have been chainsawed out of wood. This is a nice, small camping spot and the view is fantastic. The pond is stagnant, so you will need to treat the water if you use it for drinking.

When you get down to the valley between St. Marks and Mt. Unnecessary, you will see a sign that says "Improved trail ends." From here, the trail starts to climb very steeply, and you must scramble straight up Mt. Unnecessary. When you near the top, the trail leaves the forest and the grade starts to level off. A sign near the top indicates that it is a half hour walk to the peak. As you continue along the ridge, you will pass quite a few stagnant ponds that can be used for drinking water if treated.

The panoramic view is revealed as the trail winds to the very top of Mt. Unnecessary, and continues all the way to Brunswick Lake. From the south peak of Mt. Unnecessary, you can see Howe Sound and Sechelt Peninsula to the west. To the north are the Lions, the Tantalus Range, Mt. Garibaldi and Mamquam Mountain; to the east is the Greater Vancouver watershed and the Cascade Mountains; and to the south is Vancouver, Mount Baker, Vancouver Island and the San Juan Islands. The Greater Vancouver watershed is out of bounds and no one is allowed into this area.

Mt. Unnecessary (South Peak) to Base of the West Lion

The trail continues northeast on the ridge and then goes down the north side of Mt. Unnecessary, offering a superb view of the Lions. You can see the village of Lions Bay, logging scars on Mt. Harvey, the islands in Howe Sound and some pretty little lakes to the east.

As you descend, there is a rope to help lower yourself down one short, steep section. Continue on to where you encounter another steep downhill section. Make sure you follow the markers and be careful along this rough scramble.

The Lions (Binkert) Trail from Lions Bay intersects the Howe Sound Crest Trail on the ridge. From there, you continue along in the open, up several slab knolls until you reach the base of the West Lion. At the intersection at the base of the West Lion, you can head west (straight) if you want to climb the West Lion or turn east (right) if you want to continue on to James Peak.

West Lion to James Peak

From the base of the West Lion, head down the trail and then northeast (left), where you can either cross the rocky face of the West Lion or go below it. If you do not want to cross the ledge, which is mildly exposed, follow the rock face along the bottom and up the gully until it joins the trail. Do not dawdle at this spot as rocks can fall from the West Lion, especially if people are climbing it. Continue on the trail and it will go up the bump between the two Lions.

The trail then descends off the bump between the Lions and north towards Thomas Peak. The ascents and descents are very steep on this part of the route. It is very rugged with thin ridges and loose rock, so progress is very slow. The trail continues to be well marked but the markers can disappear in the snow, so be sure to have a map of the area.

Continue following the trail as it skirts around the east side of Thomas Peak and down to Enchantment Pass. It descends an open slope covered with large, loose boulders. Unlike any other *Classic Hike*, this part of the hike feels very remote, as though you are in isolated wilderness. This is particularly unique considering how close the trail is to Vancouver.

After you have reached the bottom of the slope, the trail climbs to Enchantment Pass and follows the southern ridge leading up to the summit of James Peak. The climb is very steep and demanding. It requires some confidence to move over steep rock. Once you reach the top, the trail continues along the summit ridge. A chain and a rope strung between the most narrow and exposed parts of the ridge can be used as a handrail.

James Peak to Harvey Creek Saddle

The trail continues down the northwest side of the James Peak and drops down to a meadow in the col between James Peak and David Peak. From there, it continues to switchback down toward Hanging Lake. It passes through a gully where the hiking becomes demanding due to loose rock. The trail skirts around the cliffs on the east side of David Peak, staying above Hanging Lake while passing it on its west side. At the north of David Peak, the trail heads up a gully to the Harvey Creek Saddle.

Harvey Creek Saddle sits between David Peak and Harvey Pass. As you approach the saddle, you enter an open slope that has been logged and burned. From there, traverse the slope leading northwest and upward through the slash toward Harvey Pass.

The north face of Mount Harvey

Harvey Pass to Magnesia Meadows Emergency Shelter

The Mount Harvey Trail from Lions Bay intersects the Howe Sound Crest Trail from the west as you go through Harvey Pass. This is also where the developed trail begins again, growing wider and clearer as it goes downhill. Soon, you reach Magnesia Meadows, which is a

Cypress Provincial Park

This 3,000 ha park sits on the western end of Vancouver's North Shore Mountains. The original trails in the area were created by people of the Squamish Nation. Then, in the 1870s, Moodyville loggers came to cut the enormous stands of fir, cedar and hemlock trees that grew here. The trails used today are remnants of the network of logging skid roads that wound through the area at that time.

Cypress officially became a park in 1975. The park is known for its outstanding panoramic views and wildlife such as black bears, cougars, lynx, blacktail deer, raptors, merlins, hawks and pika. In winter, Cypress is a popular spot for downhill and nordic skiers. The downhill ski area has several chairlifts, a double rope tow, a ski school, ski rentals and a restaurant.

Nordic skiers have a long history of skiing the trails in the Hollyburn Ridge area of the park. There are more than 26 km of groomed tracks and the trails are lit for night skiing. Backcountry skiers can ski to the top of Hollyburn Mountain.

The historic Hollyburn Lodge is located on Hollyburn Mountain. The lodge opened in 1927 and has been a popular gathering place ever since. In summer, hikers used to trek up from West Vancouver to sleep in the lodge on beds made of cedar boughs and matting. In winter, skiers could leave their skis at the lodge, where they would be maintained and looked after for the whole season.

Hat Pass

beautiful, open sub-alpine area that has a little creek running through it. This is a good place to get water.

From there, the trail quickly reaches the Magnesia Meadows emergency shelter, where there are a lovely sub-alpine meadow and a small lake. This is a great spot to camp, and the shelter can accommodate four people. The area is surrounded by mountains except for the

Porteau Cove Provincial Park

This park is located near the northern trailhead of the Howe Sound Crest Trail. To reach the park, drive 35 km north from Vancouver on Hwy 99 or 8.5 km south of Britannia Beach. This popular park is open year round and offers oceanfront camping with more than 50 campsites. Unfortunately, the train tracks are only two m from the campsites and you may be subject to noisy awakenings. The park is located on the waters of Howe Sound. The Sound is a coastal fjord that was formed by the action of glacier ice. The ocean at Porteau Beach has moderate depths and minimal currents, making it very popular with divers. In fact, two ships were sunk in the cove in 1980 and 1985 to provide an interesting experience for divers.

west side, which looks out onto Sechelt and the waters of Howe Sound. A creek north of the hut is another excellent water source. The most challenging sections of the trail are now behind you, as the trail is mostly downhill from here.

Magnesia Meadows Emergency Shelter to Brunswick Mountain Trail Junction

As you leave Magnesia Meadows, the trail heads north through open sub-alpine forest, going steadily uphill as it traverses the southern and western slopes of Brunswick Mountain. The trail levels off as you move around the west side of Brunswick Mountain and the views of Horseshoe Bay and Bowen Island are spectacular.

Continue through the forest along the west side of the mountain to where the trail meets the Brunswick Mountain Trail junction. The trail to the left (west) is the Brunswick Mountain Trail from Lions Bay.

Brunswick Mountain Trail to Hat Pass

Hat Pass is just a 10-minute hike from the

Brunswick Mountain

Brunswick Mountain Trail junction, while Brunswick Lake is an hour away. Hat Pass is another lovely sub-alpine area filled with many tarns and streams that are surrounded by mountain peaks. The trail skirts around the eastern side of Hat Mountain (1,540 m). If you wish to climb up to the peak of Hat Mountain, it is an easy, short jaunt up the open eastern slope to the top.

Hat Pass to Brunswick Lake

The trail goes downhill from this point to Porteau Cove. The trail switches back, sometimes steeply down a long descent through the west side of the gully leading to Brunswick Lake. It passes through pretty, sub-alpine meadows and there are splendid views of Deeks Lake Valley, Brunswick Lake, Brunswick Mountain to the northwest and Mt. Hanover to the northeast.

The trail passes the Brunswick Lake emergency hut, which can sleep up to five people, and continues down to the shoreline of the beautiful azure lake. This is a beautiful spot where you can camp right along the shoreline in the sub-alpine meadow. A picturesque little pond sits to the west side of the lake and a waterfall cascades down at its south end.

Brunswick Lake to Deeks Lake (Outlet)

To reach Deeks Lake, continue north on the trail as it follows the creek that connects Brunswick Lake with Deeks Lake. The route goes down the middle of the valley through mature forest toward Middle Lake. You will soon pass a small, cascading waterfall that feeds into the creek flowing to Middle Lake. Cross over this waterfall outlet and continue through the forest. You will see Middle Lake about 15 minutes after you leave Brunswick Lake.

Just before the trail reaches Middle Lake, it passes by another waterfall that cascades down a cliff and into the lake. You must cross the creek by walking over some logs. Then continue down to and around the west side of Deeks Lake. At the west end of the lake, the trail drops steeply down to the outflow stream and across a log jam. Some camping spots are located at the cleared area by the outflow stream.

Deeks Lake (Outlet) to Highway 99

Please note that you can also access Deeks Lake from a separate trailhead off of Highway 99. See hike # 11.

As you leave Deeks Lake, the trail continues steeply downhill. You pass another waterfall and continue down through the trees to where it connects with an old logging road. The narrow route is fairly rough, as it is littered with tree roots and rocks. You will reach an intersection where you must leave the logging road and turn right (east) onto an upper route. This bypass route avoids a dangerous slide area. It is 4.5 km to Porteau Cove from this intersection.

The bypass route joins back onto the wide logging road after 1.5 km. Keep right at all forks except the last signed one as you go down the road. Stay on the main, well-used sections of the trail if you are in doubt.

As you near Porteau Cove, the trail passes a small pond where a side trail leads off to the west (left). This trail lets you exit by the steep trail down Deeks Creek and to the bridge on the highway, which is located five km south of the Porteau Cove trailhead. Continue straight ahead for the Porteau Cove trailhead.

The trail soon meets a signed intersection at which you turn left (west) for Porteau Cove. The trail descends and comes out at some rocky bluffs by a power line. Continue down, passing by a little creek and soon, you will emerge at the trailhead on Highway 99.

~ 6 ~
Mt. Strachan

6. Route (map, page 42)

Distance: 5 km one way, 4.5-6 hours, day hike
Rating: * Intermediate
Trailhead: 900 m
Mt. Strachan: 1,445 m, 5 km
Topographical map: 92G/8

6. Trailhead

The trailhead is located at Cypress Provincial Park. From downtown Vancouver, drive 12 km via the Lions Gate Bridge to West Vancouver where Route 1 and Route 99 from the west (Upper Levels Highway) join the park access road. The trail starts at the Upper parking lot near the lift ticket wicket.

The trail is marked with orange markers. For more information on Cypress Park, call (604) 926-6007 (summer) or (604) 926-5612 (winter).

6. Camping, Cycling, Dogs (see pg 44)

This trail leads you along fairly rugged terrain to the peaks of Mt. Strachan, where fantastic panoramic views await you. It also lets you explore the sub-alpine ski terrain that is found around Cypress Provincial Park. This trail is located just on the outskirts of Vancouver, which makes it a popular day hike for locals.

From the parking lot, follow the Howe Sound Crest Trail northward through a lovely forest of hemlock and cedar. Continue past a couple of viewpoints of Howe Sound and then over Montizambert Creek until you reach the Strachan Meadows. Once you are at the meadows, continue along the trail as it crosses a small bridge and turns eastward (right) into the meadows. Filled with Indian Hellebore, moss and grass,

Red squirrel

Mt. Strachan

the meadows are a good place to look for wildlife such as deer, squirrels, hares or weasels. Bears frequent the meadows too, so be sure to make noise when you are here.

From the meadows, the trail continues steeply up a rocky gully. In the winter, Cypress Bowl offers some of the most challenging skiing in Vancouver. Sometimes, skiers seeking an extra thrill end up in this out-of-bounds area, which can be dangerous as it is prone to avalanches. The gully may be covered in snow until mid-July, so you may wish to hike it later in the season if you are uncomfortable on steep snow.

As you continue climbing upward, you will find that the gully becomes narrower. If you find the route too narrow for your liking, there is an alternate route in the trees. Just follow the taped markers for 15 to 20 minutes, after which you can rejoin the gully. Continue following the gully upward as it narrows and steepens until it reaches the pass between Mount Strachan's two peaks. The north summit has the best view, so turn north (left) at the pass and continue on to the north summit. Once you are at the top, you can take in the panoramic views of Howe Sound to the west,

the Sechelt Peninsula to the northeast and the twin peaks of the Lions to the north.

From here, you can either hike back down along the same route that you took on the way up or go down an alternate, easier route, which runs down the south side of Mt. Strachan along the Cypress Bowl ski trails. To take the alternate trail down the mountain, hike back to the pass between the two summits. Continue southward along the easy climb up to the rocky south summit. At the top of the summit, you will see ski lifts and snow fences, which are a reminder of the ski activity that takes place here in the winter.

To continue down the mountain, head south and follow the orange painted rocks and markers. The trail continues left (east) past the chairlift and into the forest. From there, it follows a steep, well-defined trail downward. Soon, you will come to a meadow and pond, where you can hook up with the wide ski run that lies just to the west (right). Continue following the ski run down and it will eventually take you back to the trailhead where you began.

~7~

Mount Unnecessary

7. Route (map, page 42)

Distance: 4.7 km one way, 5-6 hours, day hike
Rating: * Difficult
Route: Trailhead: 215 m
Mt. Unnecessary: 1,520 m, 4.7 km
Topographical map: 92G/6

7. Trailhead

Trailhead: Drive north for 11 km from Horseshoe Bay on Highway 99. At the village of Lions Bay, turn east (right) at the Oceanview Road Exit, which is the second exit into Lions Bay. Continue up Oceanview Road until it ends at a gate by a water tower. Walk up the road to the No Trespassing sign. The trail begins here and is marked with orange squares. Note that Mt. Unnecessary can also be accessed from the Howe Sound Crest Trail.

7. Camping, Cyclng, Dogs (see pg 44)

Beginning near the oceanside community of Lions Bay, this steep trail ascends directly up the western side of Mount Unnecessary to its south peak. What makes this hike so popular is the reward you get once you are at the top. On a clear day, you are treated to a breathtaking panoramic view of the ocean, islands and mountains. The trail is also popular with day hikers from Vancouver, as it offers a fairly quick and direct route up to the gorgeous summit and surrounding vistas. Pick a sunny, clear day to do this hike and you won't be disappointed. This hike gains altitude quickly, so be prepared to hike up a steep trail on the way up.

The beginning of the trail is rough and passes through a deep gully filled with fallen trees and steep sections. The grade of the trail steepens after the gully and the hike becomes a scramble upward and northward through the forest. After much climbing, you will emerge from the trees onto a ridge. From here, the trail continues to undulate up and down along the ridge. The forest becomes sparse and you can see some dramatic views of Mount Unnecessary, Howe Sound and the islands below. When you near the top, the grade of the ridge eases. However, you still have to get through a final steep section. Once you are through this last steep part, the trail joins up with the Howe Sound Crest Trail. From here, continue along the ridge over rocky outcrops and past tiny pools of still water. Soon, the panoramic scenery will become increasingly spectacular as you near the south peak of Mt. Unnecessary.

Once you have reached the summit of the south peak, you will be able to see Howe Sound and Sechelt Peninsula to the west. To the north are the Tantalus Range, Mt. Garibaldi and the Lions. To the east are views of the Greater Vancouver watershed, which is out of bounds to the public. The city of Vancouver, Vancouver Island and the San Juan Islands to the south complete the show.

~8~
The West Lion

8. Route (map, page 42)

Distance: 7.5 km one way, 7 hours, day hike
Rating: * Intermediate
Trailhead: 275 m
Base of West Lion: 1,575 m, 7.5 km
Topographical map: 92G/6

8. Trailhead

Drive north for 11 km on Highway 99 from Horseshoe Bay to the village of Lions Bay. Then turn east (right) at the Oceanview Road Exit, which is the second exit into Lions Bay. Turn left on Cross Creek Road, go over Harvey Creek, then turn right on Centre Road. Turn left on Bayview Road and drive for 1.1 km. Turn left on Mountain Drive, then left on Sunset Drive and park at the gate. The trail is marked with orange and pink markers.

8. Camping, Cycling, Dogs (see pg 44)

The famous landmarks of the Lions are so enticing when viewed from a distance that it is almost impossible to resist the urge to hike to them. This is a popular route as it provides easy access to the two cone-shaped peaks and the magnificent scenery that surrounds them. The trail to the Lions goes up a ridge, where it joins the Howe Sound Crest Trail. From there, you can follow it to the base of the Lions. Once you are at the base, you can decide whether you wish to climb to the top of the West Lion. The East Lion is in watershed territory, which means that it is out of bounds.

This trail is also known as the Binkert Trail, in reference to Paul Binkert. Binkert cleared and improved the trail in 1971, making the route much more attractive to hikers. Before this, hikers used to access the Lions by a much longer

trail via Mount Unnecessary, which took them about two hours longer than it does today.

The trail starts at the old logging road by the yellow gate that is marked with a sign that reads "Watershed." From here it heads up the wide gravel road and into the lush rainforest of ferns, moss, second growth cedar and maple. The trail is a former skid road that was once used for logging. You can still see logging cables and the huge stumps of old logged trees. After about 15 minutes of relentless uphill hiking, the trail reaches an intersection from which you have a great view of the north face of Mount Harvey and Brunswick Mountain. Continue on the southeast (right) trail for the Lions. Stay right at all of the forks after this point.

The trail continues upward and becomes steeper as it gains altitude. After another 20 minutes, the trail comes to a junction where an orange marker is nailed to a tree. The trail that goes northeast (left) is the Brunswick Mountain Trail. Continue south (right) to the Lions Trail. Soon after the junction, the steepness of the trail begins to ease up until it becomes level and the hiking becomes easier. The forest begins to open up and you can see Mount Unnecessary and the ridge below the West Lion. As you continue across a rockfall area, there are more views through the trees of Horseshoe Bay, Howe Sound and the Gulf and San Juan Islands to the southwest.

Continuing on, you soon reach another T intersection, where the left fork leads northeast to the north face of Mount Harvey. Keep going on the southeast (right) fork and about five to 10 minutes later, you will reach yet another intersection. This intersection is marked with three huge rust-coloured boulders and a rock cairn marked with orange tape. The fork northeast (left) leads to Mount Harvey. Continue on the south (right) fork past a couple of waterfalls and a tiny wooden bridge. Keep traversing along the rocky, narrow trail as it heads up a creek bed. When it looks like you could follow the stream upward, take the southeast (right) fork and continue down into the dark, damp valley. Follow the trail until it peters out and goes into Harvey Creek. Cross Harvey Creek and continue on the trail as it heads steeply upward through the trees. Use the pink, orange and silver markers to guide you up through the

The Lions

cedar, fir hemlock and Douglas fir forest. The trail winds over rocky slopes, blow-down areas, tree roots and some wet sections. After this, it comes to a viewpoint, where you can see Howe Sound and the islands below.

Continue along the switchbacks as they lead upward and then across the final steep slope. The slope becomes even steeper as you climb over tree roots and mud. After about 40 minutes of continuous climbing, the trail levels off before taking you up a final short section to the ridge between Mt. Unnecessary and the West Lion. From there, continue following the trail markers to the where the trail intersects with the Howe Sound Crest Trail. At the intersection, go northeast (left) and continue upward to the base of the West Lion.

At the base, you can decide whether you want to climb the West Lion. The higher peak of the West Lion should only be climbed by those who are experienced and confident on steep rock with exposed sections. Fatal accidents

First Ascent of the Lions

The first ascent of the East Lion was made in 1903 by the Latta brothers: William, John and Robert. The seven-day journey took the trio up along Capilano Creek, past Capilano Lake and up Sisters Creek to the base of the Lions. With almost no climbing experience and using rudimentary climbing gear, the brothers were successful in climbing the peak of the East Lion. When they got to the top of the peak, they realized that they were the first ones to climb it.

After conquering the peak, the brothers began to make their way back to Vancouver. On the way back, John was become increasingly concerned about the state of his clothes. His pants and shoes were so worn that they were disintegrating and had to be tied together with string. His coat got burned

on the sixth night of the trip when he slept too close to the campfire. John's shoes finally fell apart on the fourth day and he replaced them with some buckskin moccasins. As the brothers hiked through Capilano Creek, his pants literally fell apart. Luckily, he was able to buy a pair of trousers for 50 cents from a Swede at a logging camp they passed along the way.

By the time they neared the north shore, John's moccasins had completely worn away. He entered Vancouver barefoot, wearing pants that went up to his armpits and were tied with string. Who would have guessed that this strange-looking man was in fact a victorious climber who had just climbed one of Vancouver's landmarks?

have occurred here, so proceed with caution and at your own risk. The rock also becomes very slippery when it is wet. To climb up to the top of the peak, you must first cross an exposed gap that runs over a steep gully. Once you are across the gap, traverse eastward across a downward sloping ledge. The ledge leads to a bush-lined, marked route beyond, which you can follow upward to the top. Watch your footing on the descent and try not to displace any loose rocks, as others may be below you.

~ 9 ~

Mount Harvey

9. Route (map, page 42)

Distance: 6.25 km one way, 7 hours, day hike
Rating:** Difficult
Route: Trailhead: 240 m
Mt. Harvey: 1,705 m, 6.25 km
Topographical map: 92G/6

9. Trailhead

Drive north for 11 km on Highway 99 from Horseshoe Bay to the village of Lions Bay. Then turn east (right) at the Oceanview Road Exit, which is the second exit into Lions Bay. Turn left on Cross Creek Road, go over Harvey Creek, then turn right on Centre Road. Turn left on Bayview Road and drive for 1.1 km. Turn left on Mountain Drive, then left on Sunset Drive and park at the gate. The trail is marked with orange and pink markers.

9. Camping, Cyclng, Dogs (see pg 44)

It seems amazing that a trail that is so close to the sprawling urban core of Vancouver can access such a remote and rugged mountain peak in so little time. Although it is steep and demanding, this is a very rewarding hike that leads up to the alpine summit of Mount Harvey. The trail climbs to an open ridge that you

follow upward for about one km to the peak. At the summit, there are exceptional panoramic views of ocean, mountain peaks and valleys. It also offers relatively quick access to Harvey Pass and the exquisite alpine terrain of the Magnesia Meadows. The area around Magnesia Meadows is popular with bears, so keep an eye out for them.

The trail begins at the same wide gravel logging road and yellow gate as the Lions Trail. The road heads eastward into the forest and makes its way to the Harvey Creek Valley. After about 15 minutes of uphill hiking, the trail comes to a forked intersection, where you get good views of Brunswick Mountain and Mount Harvey. Ignore the trail that goes southeast (left) and keep going on the fork that heads south (right). The trail becomes even steeper as it continues upward through the forest. After another 20 minutes, you will reach another intersection where an orange marker is nailed to a tree. Again, stay on the south (right) trail, as the northeast (left) fork leads to Brunswick Mountain.

Soon after the intersection, the steepness of the trail eases up slightly and becomes fairly level. The forest begins to open up and you can see Horseshoe Bay, Howe Sound and the islands below. Very soon, you will come to a T intersection with a glorious view of the blue ocean and mountain to the south (right). The left fork at the intersection leads northeast to the north face of Mount Harvey; this is not the correct trail. Continue heading southeast (right) and in about five to 10 minutes, you will come to another intersection. This important intersection is marked with a rock cairn that has an orange marker tied to it. Three rust-coloured boulders also mark this intersection. On the northeast (left) side of the trail you will see a path that is marked with orange markers. This trail leads to the summit of Mount Harvey, so leave the road and follow the narrow trail as it winds steeply upward through the rocks and into the trees. The trail will reach a gully, enter the forest and begin to switchback to a wide basin.

Continue eastward from the basin to the main ridge, which is an ugly, stark area that a fire blazed through years ago. Keep following the trail along the ridge, where there are open views of the surrounding peaks and where vari-

Brunswick Lake

Crest Trail, continue directly east from the summit of Mt. Harvey and drop down to Harvey Pass. The trails will intersect at Harvey Pass, where you can either continue northward on to Magnesia Meadows or southward toward the Lions past David, James and Thomas peaks.

~ 10 ~
Brunswick Mountain

10. Route (map, page 42)

Distance: 7.25 km one way, 7 hours, day hike
Rating: * Intermediate to difficult
Trailhead: 235 m
Brunswick Mountain: 1,785 m, 7.25 km
Topographical map: 92G/6

10. Trailhead

Drive north for 11 km on Highway 99 from Horseshoe Bay to the village of Lions Bay. Then turn east (right) at the Oceanview Road Exit, which is the second exit into Lions Bay. Turn left on Cross Creek Road, go over Harvey Creek, then turn right on Centre Road. Turn left on Bayview Road and drive for 1.1 km. Turn left on Mountain Drive, then left on Sunset Drive and park at the gate. The trail is marked with orange and pink markers.

10. Camping, Cycling, Dogs (see pg 44)

ous heathers and wildflowers bloom when they are in season. After about one km, the trail pops out onto the rocky peak of Mount Harvey, where you can enjoy a scramble over the rock. From the summit, you can enjoy dazzling panoramic views of Howe Sound and the Sechelt Peninsula to the west. Also across the water, you can see the rugged mountains and glaciers of the Tantalus Range. You can see the Howe Sound Crest Trail across Mount Harvey's eastern ridge as it meanders over to the Magnesia Meadows.

To join up with the Howe Sound

This trail leads to the top of Brunswick Mountain, where you can enjoy glorious panoramic views. If you have ever been tempted to try mountaineering, this trail is a good one to tackle as it gives you a taste of what the sport has to offer. The upper part of this trail is steep with rough, open sections. You should keep this in mind if you wish to go all the way to the top. These sections can be dangerous in snow or poor weather and corniced, steep snow can

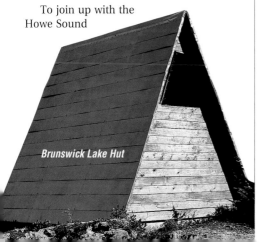

Brunswick Lake Hut

sometimes be found on the trail until July. If you are going to tackle the top section of the trail when it is covered in snow, you should take an ice axe and know how to use it.

Don't skip this trail altogether if you don't want to tackle the top part of this mountain. The trail up to the ridge (near the Howe Sound Crest Trail junction) provides a spectacular view and is a rewarding hike in itself.

The trail follows the same wide, gravel logging road as the Lions Trail, which begins at the yellow gate. The winding road heads uphill through the forest and after about 15 minutes, it reaches an intersection. Ignore the left (northeast) trail and continue on the path that heads right (southeast). Follow the trail as it climbs even more steeply. In about 20 minutes, you will reach another intersection where an orange marker is nailed to a tree. Take the left (north) trail, as this is the route that leads to Brunswick Mountain. The right trail (southeast) continues on to Mount Harvey and the Lions. After the junction, the trail crosses Magnesia Creek, from which you can see Mount Harvey and Howe Sound. The creek is the last reliable water source, so fill up your water bottle here if you need to.

A little less than half a kilometre later, the trail comes to another fork. Take the steeper branch, which goes right (northeast). From here, the trail steepens even more as it winds around hairpin turns up the old logging road and the logged mountainside. The forest gives way to small brush and spectacular views of the surrounding area. When the road ends, the trail steepens even more and continues to zigzag through the trees to the shoulder of Brunswick Mountain. Finally, the trail reaches a ridge that offers fabulous views of Howe Sound, the Sechelt Peninsula, and Gambier, Keats and Bowen islands. The Howe Sound Crest Trail junction is just beyond this point.

Continue heading east on the trail if you wish to hike up to the summit of Brunswick Mountain, which is now just under a kilometre away. The trail up this final section is steep and rough with exposed sections, drop-offs and loose rock. Be extremely careful here, especially if there is snow on the ground. The trail continues up the rocks and stays just to the right of the crest. The west peak of Brunswick Mountain is now visible just above. As you hike

Brunswick Mountain view

into the open, keep to the left of a very steep, open slope of loose rock. Exercise particular caution when you are heading back down.

At the summit ridge, you will see a fork in the trail. For the best views, take the easier West Peak Trail by going left over the rock and then following the paint markings up a gully to the pointed summit. The view here of steep rock faces, desolate boulder-filled gullies and remote, jagged mountains in the distance is breathtaking. Here, you also see ocean, islands, glaciers, valleys and rows of razor-edged mountain peaks. Keep back from the north edge as it is often corniced and can be dangerous. Remember to watch your footing when you are ready to tear yourself away from the view and head back down.

~11~

Deeks Lake

11. Route (map, page 42)

Distance: 6.8 km one way, 7 hours, day hike
Rating: * Intermediate
Trailhead: 61 m
Deeks Lake: 1,097 m, 6.8 km
Topographical map: 92G/11

11. Trailhead

From the village of Lions Bay, drive north on Highway 99 for 10 km. The trail is located just after Bertram Creek on the east side of the highway. This is also the northern trailhead for the Howe Sound Crest Trail. The trail is marked with orange markers. You can also begin at the Deeks Creek pullout on Highway 99, which is located 6 km north of the village of Lions Bay.

11. Camping, Cycling, Dogs

Camping: Wilderness campsites are located at the west side of Deeks Lake beside an outflow stream.
Mountain biking: Cycling is not allowed.
Dogs: Dogs are allowed.

This hike is a refreshing day's outing that takes you through lush rainforest terrain to Deeks Lake. This trail is popular due to its close proximity to the city of Vancouver and because it can be combined with other trails that make up part of the Howe Sound Crest Trail. The Deeks Lake Trail begins with wonderful ocean views of Howe Sound and the surrounding islands. From there, you enter a rainforest filled with bubbling creeks and rocky, rugged terrain. The trail continues along sections of an old logging road, past a waterfall and finally ends at the pristine alpine lake. Deeks Lake has a very secluded, rugged feel to it, which is often hard to find in day outings.

To begin the hike, cross Highway 99 to the west side, where the trailhead and map are located. Be very careful when crossing the highway; cars drive through here at a breakneck speed. Follow the trail as it meanders steeply upward alongside a small creek. The trail will level out soon, as it reaches a power line and some rocky bluffs.

Continue upward from the bluffs and soon you will come to a signed intersection. Turn right (south) at the intersection and keep going southward up a wide logging road. After about half an hour of hiking up the logging road, you will pass a small pond where a side trail leads off to the right (west). This is an alternate route that climbs steeply alongside Deeks Creek. It begins at the Deeks Creek pullout, which is located on Highway 99, six km north of Lions Bay.

As you continue upward, you will notice many minor side trails that wander off to the sides and into the forest. Ignore them and stay on the well-used logging road. Keep left at all forks if you are in doubt.

After about three km, you will reach a junction where you must leave the logging road and turn left (east) onto an upper route. This bypass route avoids a dangerous slide area, and lasts for about 1.5 km. Follow the orange markers and red tape to where the trail joins back up to the logging road.

From here, the trail continues steeply upward along a narrow route that is fairly rough in places. You will be clambering over many tree roots and rocks, some of which may be wet and slippery. Be particularly careful of these areas when you head back down the trail. Soon, you will reach the picturesque Phi Alpha Falls, which are on your right. This is a good place to take a break before you resume climbing up the trail's switchbacks. After about a kilometre, you will emerge from the forest above Deeks Lake.

Deeks Lake was created in 1910 when a wooden dam was built on Deeks Creek by the Deeks Sand and Gravel Company. The water was used by the company. The lake is named after John Deeks, the owner of the company. Surrounding the lake are the summits of Deeks Peak to the north and Mount Windsor to the east.

Once you are at the lakeshore, you can continue right (west) to where you must cross over a series of chained logs that sit over an outflow

View of Black Mountain from Hollyburn Peak

of water. Some camping spots are located at the cleared area by the outflow stream. The trail continues along the west side of the lakeshore until it reaches the southern end of the lake. From there, it continues up to Middle Lake and eventually, Brunswick Lake. This section makes up part of the Howe Sound Crest Trail. Refer to the section of the Howe Sound Crest Trail (hike # 5) for alternate return routes for this hike. Otherwise, you can head back down along the same trail you took to get here after you have finished exploring the lake.

Blueberry Shrubs

If you hike the Holly-burn Peak trail in autumn, you will find yourself surrounded by delicious blueberries. Blueberry shrubs are low, matted deciduous shrubs that grow up to 30 cm tall. Their green leaves are one to three cm long, oval in shape and smooth-edged. They produce white to pink flowers that are five to six mm long and are shaped like tiny urns. The shrubs grow in low-elevation bogs, subalpine meadows or heath and rocky alpine tundra.

These shrubs are sought after for the edible, sweet blue berries they produce. These berries, measuring five to 10 mm across, were once a very important part of the diet of coastal and northern native peoples of Canada and Alaska. The berries were eaten fresh or dried into cakes. Sometimes they were harvested with a comb-like device made of either salmon backbone or wood. Today, blueberries are grown commercially and are widely available. However, there is nothing like feasting on fresh, sun-warmed wild blueberries when you come upon them unexpectedly on a hike.

~12~

Hollyburn Mountain

12. Route (map, page 42)

Distance: 4 km one way, 4 hours, day hike
Rating: ** Easy
Trailhead: 900 m
Hollyburn Peak: 1,325 m, 4 km
Topographical map: 92G/6

12. Trailhead

Take the Upper Levels Highway (Routes 1 and 99) to West Vancouver. Continue to the Cypress Provincial Park turn-off (exit 8) and drive up the Cypress Parkway. Take the right-hand turn-off (east) for Hollyburn Ridge Cross-country Ski Area and continue to the parking area.

12. Camping, Cycling, Dogs

Camping: Wilderness camping is allowed beyond the alpine and Nordic ski areas at higher elevations and along the Howe Sound Crest Trail. There are no designated sites, so choose locations carefully to avoid environmental damage. Emergency shelters are located at Magnesia Meadows and Brunswick Lake. Open fires are not permitted.
Mountain biking: At Cypress Park, mountain biking is allowed on the main paved road and on designated trails.
Dogs: Dogs are allowed, but must be kept on a leash.

This trail takes you past streams, ponds and tiny lakes to the top of Hollyburn Mountain, where spectacular panoramic views grace the skyline. Although it is only minutes away from Vancouver, this trail begins at the high-elevation Hollyburn Ridge Cross-country Ski Area in Cypress Provincial Park. Almost immediately,

the trail enters lovely sub-alpine terrain and in no time, you can access the fabulous views at the top of Hollyburn Peak.

From the parking lot, follow the wide Powerline Road Trail as it begins a steep but short ascent northeastward along the power line. The rocky path is lined with mountain hemlock, yellow cypress and blueberry shrubs. As you continue upward, stop and turn around to take in the view of the ocean and islands to the south. The trail forks as you near the top of the climb. Follow the right-hand trail. Although both trails will meet up again, this is a more pleasant route. The grade of the trail levels off as it continues, and you will soon reach an idyllic little lake called Fourth Lake. The lake is surrounded by blueberry shrubs, the leaves of which turn a warm red colour in autumn. Immediately after the lake, you will come to an old cabin that is used as a warming hut in winter for cross-country skiers. There is a signed intersection (1,093 m) right below the cabin, where you take the left path that leads northward.

The hundreds of blueberry bushes on Hollyburn Mountain make it a very popular trail with bears in autumn. The density of the shrubs sometimes makes it difficult for hikers to watch for bears. Bear warning signs are posted when bears are in the area, and you should be careful to make noise while you are on the trail so that bears know you are there.

As the trail heads north from the warming hut, it runs past tiny Fourth Lake and continues upward into the forest. Although the path is riddled with tree roots and rocks, it is very well maintained and the pungent aroma of sub-alpine plants fills the air. The trail soon passes to the left of another pond called Fifth Lake and meanders upward through the forest over small wooden bridges and tiny creeks.

Then the trail reaches another intersection at which you take the right-hand fork that continues north. The left fork is the Baden-Powell Trail, and it heads northwest for 40 minutes to the Cypress Bowl parking lot. From there, it continues on up to the top of Black Mountain. For Hollyburn Peak, continue upward at a moderate grade through a few muddy sections. About 15 minutes later, you get a view of the ocean through the trees to the right, after which the trail gets slightly steeper.

59

The trail begins switching back for a short while as it continues through sparse forest along the ridge. Here, the trail levels off briefly as it goes over patches of granite rock. This section offers a partial view through the trees of the blue ocean waters. The trail continues upward around the northwestern edge of the ridge, switching back occasionally. Farther on, there are views to the east and south of Mount Baker, Vancouver, Greater Vancouver and the Fraser Valley. At a viewpoint that is located a few metres off the trail there is a small wooden bench. There are great views here of The Camel and Crown, Goat, Dam and Grouse mountains.

After another 10 minutes of hiking upward, the trail leaves the forest behind and emerges onto a picturesque rocky tarn. In this lovely spot, small ponds surrounded by little streams and heather rest among slabs of granite. The trail continues past two more small ponds on the tarn before it leads you to the last ascent to the peak.

On this steep but short climb, you have to scramble over granite, tree roots and rocks. On your way along this section, take a moment to take in the view to the south and behind you of tarn, forest, ocean and islands. Keep climbing and soon you will come to some rocky bluffs. Keep going all the way to the top of the bluffs, where you will find another little tarn and spectacular panoramic views. To the south lie Mt. Baker, Washington, the city of Vancouver and Vancouver Island. Looking west, you can see Howe Sound, Bowen Island and the Sechelt Peninsula. To the north are Mt. Strachan and the twin peaks of the Lions, with Mt. Garibaldi and Mamquam farther behind them. To the east and northeast are Capilano Valley, Crown, Goat and Grouse mountains. The distinctive Camel sits beside Crown Mountain.

~13~
Capilano Canyon

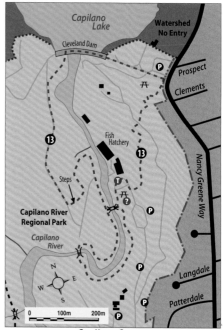

Capilano Canyon

13. Route (see map above)

Distance: 4.2 km loop, 1.5 hours, day hike
Rating: * Easy, early season hike
Trailhead: 40 m
Cleveland Dam: 90 m, 1 km
Trailhead: 40 m, 4.2 km
Topographical map: 92G/6

13. Trailhead

From Highway 1, take the Capilano/Grouse exit #14. Continue north on Capilano Road. Turn left (west) on Capilano Park Road and continue north to the parking area.

Salmon

13. Camping, Cycling, Dogs

Camping: No camping is allowed except at Camp Capilano (reservations are required, call (604) 432-6352 for information).
Mountain biking: Cycling is only allowed on the commuter cycling path that passes over the Cleveland Dam.
Dogs: Dogs must be on a leash.

Capilano River Regional Park is a rugged, 160 ha wilderness area located between the districts of West Vancouver and North Vancouver. The park was created in 1926 and is one of the most popular in the Lower Mainland, attracting over one million visitors yearly. This hike skirts the steep-walled Capilano Canyon and winds through a lush, green rainforest that is filled with towering trees. It runs past the Cleveland Dam and Capilano Lake, and provides spectacular views of the Coast Mountains. A fish hatchery museum is also open for public viewing. Be sure to carry a map, as there are a number of trails in the park. Many of the forks and intersections are not marked so it is very easy to get disoriented.

The hike begins on the Pallisades Trail (#4), which is located on the northeast side of the parking lot, opposite the Capilano River Hatchery. Before you head out on the trail, you may want to explore the informative display at the fish hatchery. The hatchery, which opened in 1972, is operated by the Department of Fisheries and Oceans. Steelhead trout, chinook and Coho salmon and sometimes chum salmon are raised at the hatchery and then released into the river. For more information about the hatchery, call (604)666-1790.

From the fish hatchery, cross to the northeast side of the parking lot to where the Pallisade Trail leads you over a series of wooden bridges that cross bubbling brooks. Continue

Cleveland Dam and Capilano Watershed

The impressive **Cleveland** Dam was built in 1954 by the Greater Vancouver Water District. It holds back the Capilano River, which in turn forms Capilano Lake. The dam can hold 75 million cubic metres of water. The dam, which is 5.6 km long, 79 m deep and 90 m high, was named after Dr. Ernest Cleveland, the first Water Commissioner.

Capilano Lake was formed when the Capilano Dam flooded the Upper Capilano River Valley. Before the flood, the valley contained forest, squatters shacks and fish-spawning beds, which are now under water. Early mountaineers used to cross

through the Capilano Valley on their way to climb The Lions and other peaks. However, this area is now off limits to the public, as it is one of three watersheds that contribute to the drinking water supply for the western sector of the Greater Vancouver area. Since the upper fish-spawning beds were flooded by the dam, the fish are now diverted by a weir to the hatchery.

The water in the dam is collected from rain and snowmelt streams that flow into the Capilano River. The lake can reach a maximum elevation 146 m above the ocean.

View from Grouse Mountain of Vancouver, the Strait of Georgia and the islands

up a series of wooden steps into the lush, green rainforest. Although tree roots and rocks make the trail quite rough, it is used often and is very well-maintained. The trail heads upward, climbing fairly steeply for 0.5 km past beautiful groves of ferns, moss and skunk cabbage. Soon, the trail reaches a wide gravel service road and from this point, it is only another 0.5 km to the dam. From here, the trail levels off slightly and continues northward and upward. Stay left (west) at the fork. Take the right (east) trail at the next two forks, continuing the gradual climb up the service road. Once you are at the top, turn left (west) and continue on the path that leads over the 90 m Cleveland Dam.

At the top of the dam, there are panoramic views of Mt. Strachan, Unnecessary Mountain, the Lions, Crown and Grouse Mountains and Capilano Lake (Watershed and Reservoir). The dam created Capilano Lake and now controls the lower section of the Capilano River. As you proceed west over the dam, you are confronted with a view of the massive amount of water that spills from it into the Capilano River and canyon.

Once you have crossed the dam, turn southwest (left) and stay to the left by continuing on the Capilano Pacific (#2) Trail. This trail is a wide gravel service road that heads southward into a forest filled with fir, cedar and hemlock trees, salal, salmonberries and bunchberry. Soon, you will reach the Giant Fir (#6) Trail, which begins with a series of wooden

steps that descend into the forest to your left (east). Follow the trail and it will lead to a massive Douglas fir tree that measures over 61 m in height and 2.4 m in diameter. This tree, known as Grandpa Capilano, is the largest old-growth Douglas fir in the park. It is important to stay behind the fences when you look at it so that the roots of the tree are not damaged. Too many footprints close to the tree can also cause the soil to become compacted, which can disrupt groundwater flow.

The Giant Fir Trail soon forks with the Second Canyon Viewpoint (#10) Trail. Take the right (south) fork and continue south along the Second Canyon Viewpoint Trail. The trail passes the Cable Pool Bridge, after which it turns into the Coho Loop (#3) as it continues southward. Follow the Coho Loop southeastward to the Pipeline footbridge. This is a popular area for those who wish to try their luck fishing for coho, chinook, steelhead and chum salmon. From May to December, salmon and trout make their way through the Capilano River as they prepare to spawn. If you want to watch them go up the fish ladder or see them in sorting and holding ponds, a trip to the Capilano River Hatchery's display area makes for an informative visit.

Walk over the footbridge and then turn left (southeast), continuing upward over wooden steps. There is a good view of the canyon to the left. Follow the sign to the Coho Loop and Fish Hatchery. Soon, you will pass the Cable Pool

Grouse Mountain

Bridge again. This is a good spot to take in views of the chiselled granite walls of the canyon and the trees, moss and ferns that cling precariously to its sides. There is a also a small, picturesque waterfall that tumbles down alongside the bridge. From the bridge, the trail leads back to where you began at the parking lot and fish hatchery.

Grouse/Goat/Crown Mountains

This rugged mountain wilderness setting is only a 15 minute drive from downtown Vancouver. The area has a long history of recreational use that predates the 1890s. The mountain was given its name in 1894, after a party of hikers shot and killed a blue grouse on the mountain.

In January of 1910, the BC Mountaineering Club obtained land on Grouse Mountain. They built a cabin which became the weekend haunt of many of its members. Using this hut as their focal point, members began trips farther into the backcountry, exploring up Howe Sound towards Garibaldi and east toward Golden Ears.

A highway that led to the top of the mountain and a log chalet was built in 1924. Many hikers used the chalet as a rest stop. Grouse Mountain was sold in 1945 and construction began on an aerial tram in 1965. Development on the mountain kept expanding from then on.

The area surrounding Grouse Mountain continues to be a popular hiking spot. It offers a wide range of enticing hikes to various mountain peaks. You can also hike to the Lynn Headwaters trails via Hanes Valley, exiting at Lynn Headwaters Regional Park.

~14~
Crown Mountain

14. Route (map, page 64)

Distance: 3.8 km to Crown Mountain one way, 5-6 hours, day hike
Rating: ** Intermediate
Grouse Alpine Area Kiosk: 1,260 m
Dam Mountain Jct: 1,300 m, 0.6 km
Goat Mountain Jct: 1,280 m, 1.8 km
Crown Mountain: 1,501 m, 3.8 km
Topographical map: 92G/6

14. Trailhead

From downtown Vancouver, cross the Lion's Gate Bridge and take the North Vancouver exit to Marine Drive. Turn left on Capilano Road and drive for 4 km.

14. Camping, Cycling, Dogs

Camping: Grouse mountain is private property and camping is not allowed. Sections of the trail are within the boundaries of Lynn Headwaters Regional Park. Wilderness camping is only allowed outside these boundaries.
Mountain biking: Bikes are not allowed on Grouse Mountain unless you are registered with special tour groups.
Dogs: No dogs are allowed on Grouse Mountain.

Trail to the Kiosk

It is 1 km from the Chalet to the Grouse Alpine Area Kiosk. To reach the Kiosk, hike from the Chalet to the Peak Chair. From there, go west (left) to the road and hike to the right side of the bottom of the Paradise Rope Tow. Continue along the wide gravel road (Whistler Pass) that skirts around the west side of Grouse mountain. The kiosk is on the left, where the trail starts. The trail is well signed and is marked with red and white dots and green posts.

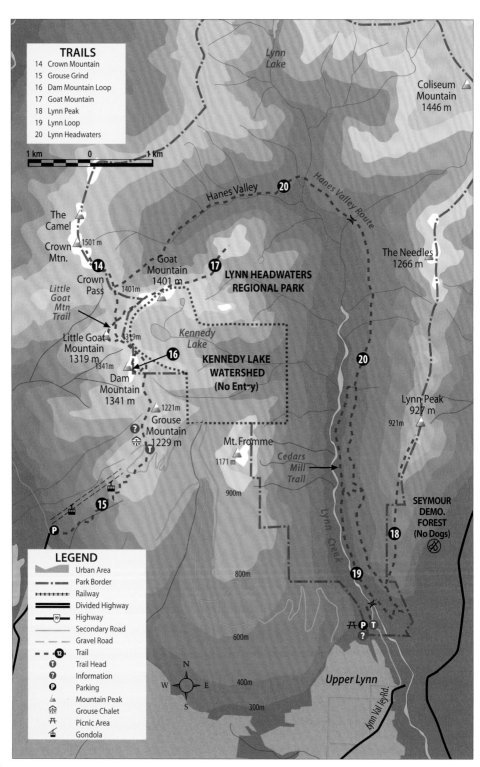

TRAILS

14 Crown Mountain
15 Grouse Grind
16 Dam Mountain Loop
17 Goat Mountain
18 Lynn Peak
19 Lynn Loop
20 Lynn Headwaters

1 km   0   1 km

Lynn Lake

Coliseum Mountain 1446 m

Hanes Valley

20

Hanes Valley Route

The Camel 1501 m

Crown Mtn.

14

Crown Pass 1401m

Goat Mountain 1401 m

17

LYNN HEADWATERS REGIONAL PARK

The Needles 1266 m

Little Goat Mtn Trail

Little Goat Mountain 1319 m

1319m

Kennedy Lake

16

1341m

Dam Mountain 1341 m

KENNEDY LAKE WATERSHED (No Entry)

20

Lynn Peak 927 m

921m

1221m

Grouse Mountain 1229 m

Mt. Fromme

?

15

1171m

Cedars Mill Trail

900m

SEYMOUR DEMO. FOREST (No Dogs)

18

P

800m

19

Lynn Creek

600m

P **T**

?

LEGEND

	Urban Area
	Park Border
	Railway
	Divided Highway
99	Highway
	Secondary Road
	Gravel Road
12	Trail
T	Trail Head
?	Information
P	Parking
⛰	Mountain Peak
🏠	Grouse Chalet
⛱	Picnic Area
🚠	Gondola

N
W   E
S

400m

Upper Lynn

300m

Lynn Valley Rd.

southern part of the Little Goat Mountain loop. Stay to the northwest (right) for Crown Mountain and continue slightly downhill. From here, there are good views of Goat and Crown Mountains. The trail then starts to climb again, continuing north toward Little Goat Mountain. Keep to the north (right) fork at the next intersection as the west (left) fork is the northern section of the Little Goat Mountain loop.

At the next junction, take the left fork northwest for Crown Mountain as the trail to the right goes northeast to Goat Ridge and Goat Mountain. As you continue along the route, you will come to a viewpoint from which you can see Hanes Valley and Crown Mountain. From here, the trail drops down the slope to Crown Pass. The slope is fairly steep and you have to scramble through roots, rocks and muddy terrain that can be slick when wet.

When you reach the bottom of the slope, the trail traverses a rockfall and passes through a forest, which features a small grove of huge Douglas fir trees. Take the left fork northwest at the junction in the forest to continue to Crown Mountain. The trail to the right runs northeast to Hanes Valley. If you continue down Hanes Valley, you can go out by the Headwaters Trail in Lynn Headwaters Regional Park. If you take this route, it is a good idea to call Lynn Park Headquarters beforehand at (604) 985-1690 to find out if Lynn Creek is passable. In this case, you will have to arrange for transportation at the park. Taxis and a bus service are available at the park entrance area.

Soon after it runs along Crown Pass, the trail begins to climb through a forested area up the southeast side of Crown Mountain. The trail narrows and steepens as it continues upward, but it remains well defined and marked with pink flags. The trail then becomes very steep and you must scramble over roots, big boulders and slabby granite sections. There are good views of Goat Peak and Hanes Creek Valley to the right.

The trail traverses along a short, steep section of rough granite. Be careful here, as there is a drop-off to the left. Then continue climbing through the steep forest until the trail levels off as you near the top of Crown Mountain. As you turn a corner, you are treated to fantastic views of the ocean and mountains to the west. The terrain is now sub-alpine and the ground is

Crown Pass

The challenging Crown Mountain hike takes you over ridges, through a valley and up the steep, jagged peak of the mountain. From Crown Peak, you get close a view of the Camel, a rocky, outcropping on the shoulder of Crown.

The trail is rough and rocky but very well defined. As you leave the kiosk, the trail starts to switch back fairly steeply north up the hillside and over a series of wooden steps. Soon, it reaches a signed fork. To the west (left) is the south end of the Dam Mountain loop. Continue straight ahead for Goat and Crown Mountains and for Hanes Valley via Crown Pass.

The trail continues to climb over more roots, wooden steps and rocks. At the next intersection, take the northwest fork (right). The trail to the southwest (left) is the northern section of the Dam Mountain loop. Soon you will be able to get a view of the northeast. The trail begins to level off slightly as it winds along a ridge with Dam Mountain to the west.

After this flat section, the trail reaches another intersection. The west trail (left) is the

covered in shrubs of heather.

Continue up a rockfall using the red and white dots and cairns to guide your way until you reach a rocky ridge. Scramble carefully along the ridge as it has steep drop offs on either sides. Be very cautious on this section. The views from of the ocean, Vancouver, western mountain ranges, Howe Sound and eastern mountain ranges are outstanding. The final stretch takes some climbing up jagged rock to the peak. Be very careful here.

Once you are on the top of Crown peak, you will find yourself standing on pointed, jagged slivers of rock. Crown Mountain was first climbed in 1895 by G. Edward, Knox, Musket and R. Parkinson. To the north side of Crown's highest summit is The Camel, a massive chunk of rock which was once a popular rock-climbing practice area. Today, you can still see climbers attempting various routes to the top. If you look closely, you can see rappel slings attached to the rock.

~15~

Grouse Grind

15. Route (map, page 64)

Distance: 2.9 km one way, 2-3 hours, day hike
Rating: * Intermediate
Trailhead: 280 m
Grouse Mountain (Grouse Chalet): 1,221 m, 2.9 km
Topographical map: 92G/6

15. Trailhead

From downtown Vancouver, cross the Lion's Gate Bridge and take the North Vancouver exit to Marine Drive. Turn left on Capilano Road and drive for 4 km.

15. Camping, Cycling, Dogs (see pg 63)

Grouse Grind is a hike that heads straight up the face of Grouse Mountain. This hike has become very popular in recent years. This is probably due to the fact that it is only 15 minutes from Vancouver, relatively short and offers a fantastic view of the surrounding area. These factors make it a perfect workout for those who are interested in getting fit in an outdoor setting.

The rugged trail climbs steeply for 853 m through the forest and ends at the Grouse Chalet, which sits at the top of the mountain. Once you reach the Chalet, you can either hike down the same trail or take the gondola down. Parts of the descent can be as steep as 45 degrees, so those with bad knees may want to avoid hiking down. If you are planning on taking the gondola down, be aware that there is now a $5 charge for the ride.

Keep in mind that this trail is usually packed with people on weekends or after working hours, especially during the summer months. It is not a hike for those seeking solitude. Also, since most of the hike runs through deep forest, there are no vistas along the way except at the top, near the Grouse Chalet.

To hike the trail, start at the lower parking lot and hike along the Baden Powell Trail to the Grouse Grind Trail intersection. Then, turn left (north) and hike for approximately 15 minutes until you reach a second junction. Turn left again and continue over a log bridge. Be prepared for muddy sections on the trail; roots and rocks add to the challenge. If you are very lucky, you may see a grouse in the forest along the way.

Options for Going Up Grouse Mountain

A gondola goes up to the Chalet on top of the mountain, and it costs $14.95 + GST for a round trip. Call Grouse Mountain at (604) 980-9311 for more information.

Alternatively, you can hike up the Grouse Grind or BCMC Trail to the top of Grouse Mountain. The 3.5 km BCMC Trail goes up the face of Grouse paralleling the Grouse Grind, which is to the north (left). This is the original trail was built in 1900 by the BC Mountaineering Club. It is similar to the Grouse Grind, except that it has some steeper sections. The trails are accessed from the Baden Powell Trail at the east end of the parking lot. The hike up will add about an hour to your hiking time.

The Camel

Continue on the trail, as it ascends steeply through the trees in a direct line up Grouse Mountain. After you have hiked for about half an hour, you will get an idea of how high you are as the trail nears the skyride and you can hear and see it overhead. Continue along the trail as it zigzags steeply upward and eventually, you will emerge on the rocks just below the viewing deck of the Grouse Chalet. At the top, you will have a wonderful view of the Lower Mainland, the North Shore and the ocean.

Every year a popular hike/race takes place up the Grouse Grind, where people challenge themselves and each other by seeing how fast they can hike up the trail. Many people make a tradition of the race and participate in it year after year. People can register to hike the trail in various categories including Team, Family or Individual. For more information, call Grouse Mountain at (604) 980-9311.

~16~
Dam Mountain Loop

Trythall's Cabin

In the early days, the hike up Grouse Mountain was an arduous, three-day journey. Typically, it took one day to get from the ferry landing to Trythall's cabin, a second day to reach the summit and a third day to get back down to the ferry.

Not counting loggers' cabins, Trythall's cabin was the first mountain cabin on the North Shore mountains. It was built in 1908 and was located beside Mosquito Creek Falls. The cabin and the surrounding 40 ha of land were owned by W.J. Trythall. The family used the cabin for vacations, but for the rest of the year, they graciously left it open for hikers and climbers to use.

The cabin was a popular gathering point where people could camp, replenish their water supplies and rest. It also functioned as a first-aid post. In 1954, the Grouse Mountain double chairlift was built near the cabin, and eventually, the cabin was abandoned.

16. Route (map, page 64)

Distance: 1.5 km from Grouse Alpine Area Kiosk one way, one hour, day hike
Rating: * Easy
Route: Grouse Alpine Area Kiosk: 1,260 m
Dam Mtn: 1,341 m, 1.5 km
Topographical map: 92G/6

16.Trailhead

From downtown Vancouver, cross the Lion's Gate Bridge and take the North Vancouver exit to Marine Drive. Turn left on Capilano Road and drive for 4 km.

16. Camping, Cycling, Dogs (see pg 63)

If you find yourself on Grouse Mountain and are looking for a short and easy hike that offers great views, hike to Dam Mountain (1,341 m). A trip up on the gondola makes this hike easy, and you can still experience the wilderness and mountain environment that attracts so many people to this area. You may also want to explore this loop trail on your way to other destinations in the Grouse area. Although the trail is short, keep in mind that it is riddled with tree roots and loose rock. Bears also frequent the area, so be sure to make plenty of noise and take heed of any posted bear warning signs.

To get to Dam Mountain, go to the registration kiosk (see box, page 63) and begin hiking on the Goat/Crown Mountain Trail. Don't let the initial appearance of the rough zigzagging trail put you off. This section of wooden steps and tree roots does not last long. Soon, you will reach a signed junction for Dam Mountain, where you take the west (left) turn.

The trail continues west through a lovely alpine meadow filled with blueberry bushes and alpine flowers. It veers around the south side of Dam Mountain and as you wind around it, there are great viewpoints to the west and south of the ocean, city and mountains. From there, the trail winds at an easy grade up the south side of Dam Mountain. At the top, there are rocky bluffs where you can take a break while you admire Vancouver, Vancouver Island, the Strait of Georgia and the mountains of Washington.

To return to the registration kiosk, either retrace your steps or take the trail that heads downward, leading northwest from the bluffs. This trail will soon emerge onto the main Goat/Crown Mountain Trail. Once it does, follow it south as it heads downward and back to the kiosk.

~17~

Goat Mountain

17. Route (map, page 64)

Distance: 2.9 km one way from Grouse Alpine Area Kiosk, 4 hours, day hike.
Rating: * Intermediate
Route: Grouse Alpine Area Kiosk: 1,260 m
Goat Mountain: 1,401 m, 2.9 km
Topographical map: 92G/6

17. Trailhead

From downtown Vancouver, cross the Lion's Gate Bridge and take the North Vancouver exit to Marine Drive. Turn left on Capilano Road and drive for 4 km.

17. Camping, Cycling, Dogs (see pg 63)

This hike shows off the rugged wilderness that is so close to Vancouver, and yet seems so untouched and remote when you are actually hiking through it. It has superb views of the Coast Mountain Range and the Capilano Watershed. If you take the gondola up, this trail requires a minimal amount of climbing. However, the trail is rough and riddled with tree roots and rocks, so wear sturdy footwear.

From the hikers' registration kiosk (see box, page 63), follow the signs for Goat Mountain. The trail zigzags steeply northward, going upward and over a series of wooden steps. It passes a fork that leads west to Dam Mountain. Continue straight ahead over more rocks and steps. At the next fork, take the northwest (right) path. Here, the trail levels off for a short section as it skirts along a ridge.

Goat mountain was named after two goats that were shot here by the first party that climbed this peak in 1894. In those days, people who wanted to climb the peaks around Grouse Mountain had to hike in via the Capilano Valley, as it was the only accessible route

Lynn Peak Trail

Once you are at the summit, you can see Sky Pilot to the north, Mount Baker and Indian Arm to the southeast, the Lower Mainland, the ocean and islands to the southwest and Lynn Peak and Mount Seymour to the east.

~18~
Lynn Peak

18. Route (map, page 64)

Distance: 3.6 km one way, 4 hours, day hike
Rating: * Intermediate, early season hike
Trailhead: 200 m
Lynn Peak/Lynn Loop Junction: 300 m, 2 km
Lookout: 921m, 3.6 km
Topographical map: 92G/6

18. Trailhead

From Second Narrows Bridge or Lion's Gate Bridge in Vancouver, take Highway 1 to Lynn Valley Road (exit #19) in North Vancouver. Follow Lynn Valley Road east for four km to the park entrance.

18. Camping, Cycling, Dogs

Camping: No camping is allowed in this area.
Mountain biking: You can cycle in the adjacent Seymour Demonstration Forest, but not on the trails in Lynn Park.
Dogs: Dogs are allowed, but must be on a leash.

to this area. Today, the Capilano Valley and watershed are closed to the public, as they supply drinking water for Greater Vancouver.

A little farther on, you will come to a wooden bench that overlooks the eastern side of the ridge. Here, you can sit and take in a fine view of Goat and Coliseum mountains. As the trail continues, it comes to another intersection. Take the northwest (right) trail and continue heading north. You will soon meet up with yet another intersection, where you take the north (right) fork. Down below, you can see views of Kennedy Lake, which is part of the Greater Vancouver water supply. At the next junction, take the northeast (right) trail for Goat Mountain.

The trail leads around the southeast slope to Goat Ridge. After you have hiked up the steep part, you have a choice of going either to Goat Ridge (right) or finishing the climb to Goat Mountain (left). The ridge, which also features a lovely panoramic view, is a pleasant spot to take a break.

To continue to the peak, turn left at the intersection and continue upward along the trail.

Lynn Peak is located in the rugged, 4,685-ha Lynn Headwaters Regional Park. Amazingly, this wilderness park is just minutes from the north edge of the District of North Vancouver. The park has 20 km of developed forest trails. Located between Seymour and Capilano Watersheds, it is characterized by dense rainforest, the turbulent Lynn Creek, mountain peaks, debris chutes and cascading streams.

From 1929 to 1983, Upper Lynn Creek supplied the City of North Vancouver's drinking water and the area was closed to the public. In

Lichen

October, 1981, a series of severe storms washed out the water intakes, altered the course of Lynn Creek and destroyed part of the road on the east side. Replacement of the intakes was judged to be too expensive, so the water supply was shifted to the existing Capilano and Seymour watersheds. This resulted in the watershed being open to the public. The park officially opened in June of 1986. Lynn Valley was originally known as "Shaketown" because of its production of cedar shakes and shingles. "Lynn Creek" is named after John Linn of Edinburgh, a member of the Royal Engineers. He came to B.C. in 1859 and built a home on the east bank of Lynn Creek.

This is a refreshing hike that will get your heart racing and lungs pumping. You will enjoy walking under the canopy of trees and among a variety of lichens, ferns and mosses in this rich, temperate rainforest environment. The trail starts at the footbridge that crosses over the boulder-filled Lynn Creek at the park entrance. Lynn Creek is the only watershed along the North Shore that is not controlled by a dam. The amount of water flowing in the Creek fluctuates from a trickle in dry summer to up to 10,000 times this volume after a long rainfall. The area around the bridge is dense with skunk cabbage, salmonberry bushes, ferns and lichen hanging from the trees.

Cross the bridge and turn right onto a wide gravel road. At the end of the road is a kiosk that welcomes you to the Seymour Demonstration Forest. Turn left here and take the trail called the Lynn Valley Loop Trail.

Here, a narrower, well-developed pathway

Stinky Skunk Cabbage

There is one way to tell if you are hiking near skunk cabbage. Breathe in through your nose. The odour of this plant really does smell like a skunk. It has waxy leaves that can grow up to one m long and a half metre wide, making it the largest native plant in the country. The leaves were used for lining berry baskets, berry-drying racks and steaming pits by the northwest coast peoples. Greenish-yellow flowers grow on a spike, which is hooded by a bright yellow bract. They appear in early spring.

Unlike humans who find its odour repulsive, insects such as beetles are actually attracted to the plant's odour. They lay their larvae on the cabbage and so doing, they pick up pollen and carry it to other flowers.

leads into the fern-filled rainforest. The trail meanders upward, curving at a moderate grade. It leads over a wooden bridge to another trail intersection. Turn right at the intersection onto the Lynn Peak Trail. The Lynn Loop Trail is the one that continues straight ahead.

Yellow metal markers on the trees show the way up the trail. The route is rocky and full of big roots. It alternates between steep sections and more moderate ones. You will notice huge tree stumps along the trail and in the forest. These are haunting reminders of the logging operations that once went on here. Also, look for nurse logs along the route, where new trees take root in the thick, nutrient- and moisture-rich dead wood of a fallen tree. They often thrive in a patch of light. It is interesting to look at mature trees with buttressed bases. These trees have grown and now completely surround the crumbling nurse log.

Be prepared for some wet climbing if you hike this trail in the spring. In May, it often turns into a creek bed with water cascading down it. Apparently, the creek dries up once spring runoff is finished. The trail switches back up, leading through an area where big trees have been uprooted.

Soon afterward, you gain the first viewpoint to your right. There is a view of Mount Seymour and the Seymour Demonstration Forest in the valley below. The trail is much drier as it continues upward until it reaches a plateau point. Just after the first lookout is a small stand of original trees that managed to escape the logging operations. This area is called "The Enchanted Forest." The trail soon levels off and starts to descend. It narrows and passes through a young forest of Douglas fir trees. After this brief respite, the trail starts to go up again.

As it meanders right, you will come to a second lookout. Then the trail continues upward and curves around to the left. The second growth forest opens up slightly at this point. Soon, the trail reaches a rocky bluff and the third lookout. There is a good view of Grouse Mountain from here.

Continue on and very soon you will come to a sign that says Lynn Peak. Turn to your right. At the top, you are rewarded with fantastic views of the Seymour Demonstration Forest, Vancouver, Vancouver Harbour and Burrard Inlet.

~19~
Lynn Loop

Logging

Logging began in the Lynn Valley in the late 1890s. In 1907, Julius Fromme bought the Hastings Shingle Company. He renamed it the Lynn Valley Lumber Company and built a second mill at Lynn Valley Road and Mountain Highway. The company focused its logging operations on the west bank of Lynn Creek.

In 1917, Cedars Ltd. constructed a large mill on the east bank of Lynn Creek. The remains of a plank road can be seen on the upper section of the Lynn Headwaters Trail between Debris Chute and Norvan Creek. Several logging camps were established in the upper valley. Evidence of their past can still be found today. Artifacts from abandoned workcamps, rusting machinery and remnant corduroy roads can be seen throughout the park. The Cedars Ltd. mill shut down in 1929 because the area was given watershed designation.

19. Route (map, page 64)

Distance: 5.7 km loop, 3-4 hours, day hike, early season hike
Rating: * Easy
Lynn Loop (Headwaters) Trailhead: 240 m
Lynn Loop Trailhead (beside creek): 240 m, 5.7 km
Topographical map: 92G/6

19. Trailhead

From Second Narrows Bridge or Lion's Gate Bridge in Vancouver, take Highway 1 to Lynn Valley Road (exit #19) in North Vancouver. Follow Lynn Valley Road east for four km to the park entrance.

Located on the edge of North Vancouver, Lynn Valley Regional Park is characterized by remote mountain slopes, debris chutes, cascading waterfalls and the turbulent Lynn Creek. The Lynn Loop is a nice jaunt that takes you through second-growth rainforest and alongside picturesque Lynn Creek. This fairly level, easy hike is a good one for those looking for a short, relaxing trek through this rugged valley. The trail can be hiked year round and is especially pretty in the autumn, when leaves are changing colour. The terrain in this park is surprisingly rugged and the weather can change abruptly, so make sure you are adequately prepared when you hike in this area.

To begin the hike, cross the old flood-control bridge that goes over Lynn Creek. Continue to the hikers' registration sign board and turn right. Hike up the gravel road to the yellow metal gate. This gate marks the boundary between Lynn Headwaters and the Seymour Demonstration Forest. From here, take the trail marked "Lynn Loop." After about 300 m you will come to a junction where the trail for Lynn Peak forks to the right. Continue straight ahead through the forest, which is filled with ferns, western hemlock, western red cedar, aspen, lichen, coltsroot and Sitka spruce.

As you hike along, you will pass many massive tree stumps. These stumps, which are about 100 years old, are all that remains of the gigantic trees that once made up the forest in Lynn Valley. In the mid-1880s, many of the trees in this valley were logged. The area was also mined for lead and copper between 1914 and 1918. If you keep an eye out as you hike, you can see various artifacts from these activities along the trail. These articles were left behind by workers who lived in logging camps in the upper Lynn Valley. Watch for rusted logging machinery, pieces of dishes and glassware, boot soles and remnant corduroy roads. Please don't pick up the artifacts.

Ferns

After about 45 minutes, you will pass a sign that indicates a point of interest. This short side trail leads to some huge boulders. The Lynn Loop Trail continues through the forest and soon comes to a signed junction that has a map of the area. To continue on the Lynn Loop Trail, take the trail that drops to the left (west) and follow the path as it zigzags down to Lynn Creek. Then turn left again and continue hiking south as you head back to the trailhead.

The hike along the banks of the creek provides some good views of Lynn Creek, Lynn

19. Camping, Cycling, Dogs

Camping: No camping is allowed in this area.
Mountain biking: You can cycle in the adjacent Seymour Demonstration Forest, but not on the trails in Lynn Park.
Dogs: Dogs are allowed, but must be on a leash.

B.C. Mills House

At the trailhead in Lynn Valley Park, you will see a historic house beside the caretaker's home. This small house was moved from the city of North Vancouver to the park in 1993. The house was built in 1908 and was once a private residence. It was one of the earliest prefabricated homes to be sold in a catalogue, and it provided affordable housing to people of the day. Today, the building houses displays, photographs and artifacts that recount the history of the park and the surrounding area. It also hosts nature programs that are presented by the Greater Vancouver Regional District. For information about the programs and to register, call the Regional Parks at (604) 432-6359.

Valley and Mt. Fromme. Depending on what time of year you hike, the creek can vary from being calm to positively turbulent. The clear clean waters of Lynn Creek once supplied drinking water to the City of North Vancouver . Then, Vancouver decided to join the Greater Vancouver Water District system. In turn, Lynn Valley was opened to the public.

As you continue southward for 1.7 km, the trail will arrive once again at the registration kiosk near the trailhead. From here, you can cross the bridge again and return to the parking lot. If you signed in, as you are asked to do, remember to sign out as you pass by the kiosk.

~ 20 ~

Lynn Headwaters

20. Route (map, page 64)

Distance: 13.4 km loop, 5-6 hours, Dayhike
Rating * Easy, early season hike
Route: Lynn Loop Trailhead: 240 m, 0 km,
Junction with Cedar Mills Trail: 350 m, 4.75 km
Norvan Falls: 375 m, 6.7 km
Lynn Headwaters Tailhead: 240 m, 13.4 km
Topographical map: 92G/6

20. Trailhead

From Second Narrows Bridge or Lion's Gate Bridge in Vancouver, take Highway 1 to Lynn Valley Road (exit #19) in North Vancouver. Follow Lynn Valley Road east for four km to the park entrance.

20. Camping, Cycling, Dogs

Camping: No camping is allowed in this area.
Mountain biking: You can cycle in the adjacent Seymour Demonstration Forest, but not on the trails in Lynn Park.
Dogs: Dogs are allowed, but must be on a leash.

This is a good outing for those seeking a creek-side hike through lush rainforest, rugged mountains, cascades and rock-debris chutes. The hike takes you out along the Lynn Loop Trail and continues north on the Cedars Mill Trail. It then returns on the Headwaters Trail. This is a very accessible all-season hike along fairly level terrain, which is especially good for beginner hikers or families. Autumn is a particularly beautiful time to hike this trail, when the richly coloured leaves have fallen. Keep in mind that the trail can be wet and fairly rough, with roots and rocks underfoot.

At the trailhead (where you can get a good view of the Lynn Valley, Mount Fromme, and Lynn Creek), cross the old flood-control bridge and turn left (north) immediately. Continue into the forest along a wide, well-maintained road. This is the Lynn Loop Trail. It follows the banks of Lynn Creek, taking you through a lush forest filled with aspen, western red cedar, ferns, coltsroot, lichen and moss. Depending on what time of year you visit the park, Lynn Creek may either be raging with torrents of water or it may be a placid, idyllic creek. Early in 1983, after violent storms and flooding damaged water intakes, North Vancouver stopped controlling the creek as a watershed. Consequently, the area was opened to the public as a park.

In 1.7 km, the path becomes the Cedars Mill Trail. The trail takes its name from the Cedars Ltd. Sawmill, which once sat on Lynn Creek's eastern bank. A road was built out of planks to Norvan Creek so that trucks could haul out the logs that were cut down. As you hike along, you will notice various logging paraphernalia such as rusty plates and cups, broken pieces of bottle, kettles, pieces of logging machinery and boot soles at the trail side. These remnants were left behind by workers who lived at logging camps in the upper Lynn Valley. The mill was shut down in 1928 when the area was closed so that it could be used as water supply for North Vancouver.

As the trail continues northward, it passes by a debris chute and a second debris clearing. This is where the trail joins the Headwaters Trail. Continue north from this junction on the Headwaters Trail. If you want to turn back early, continue southward on the Headwaters Trail.

Few people venture along the last this section of the trail, so you will find it much quieter

73

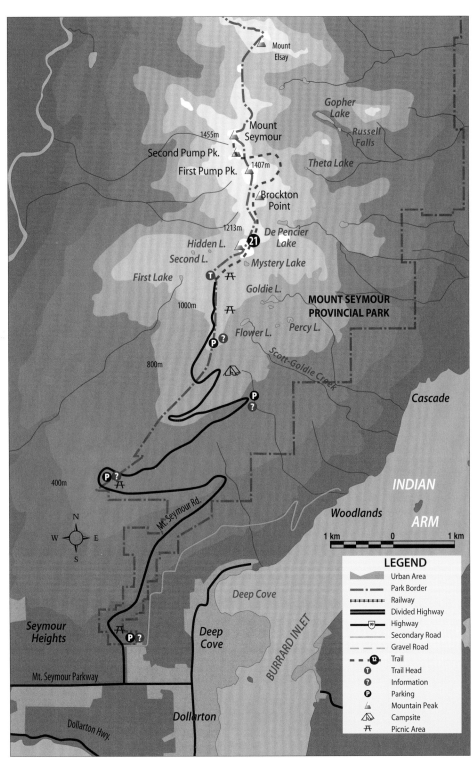

Mount Elsay

Gopher Lake

Russell Falls

1455m

Mount Seymour

Second Pump Pk.

1407m

First Pump Pk.

Theta Lake

Brockton Point

1213m

Hidden L.

Second L.

De Pencier Lake

21

First Lake

Mystery Lake

Goldie L.

1000m

MOUNT SEYMOUR PROVINCIAL PARK

Percy L.

Flower L.

800m

Scott-Goldie Creek

Cascade

400m

INDIAN

ARM

Mt. Seymour Rd.

Woodlands

1 km   0   1 km

N
W   E
S

Deep Cove

Seymour Heights

Deep Cove

Mt. Seymour Parkway

BURRARD INLET

Dollarton

Dollarton Hwy.

LEGEND

	Urban Area
	Park Border
	Railway
	Divided Highway
99	Highway
	Secondary Road
	Gravel Road
12	Trail
T	Trail Head
?	Information
P	Parking
▲	Mountain Peak
⌂	Campsite
⯅	Picnic Area

View from Mount Seymour of Indian Arm

~21~

Mount Seymour

21. Route (map, page 74)

Distance: 4.5 km one way, 5 hours, day hike
Rating: ** Intermediate
Trailhead: 1,058 m
Brockton Point: 1,160 m, 2 km
First Pump Peak: 1,200 m, 3.5 km
Second Pump Peak: 1,400 m, 4 km
Mount Seymour: 1,455 m, 4.5 km
Topographical map: 92G/7

than the first section. Continue along the old road to where it ends at the bridge by Norvan Creek. From here, you can either continue to Norvan Falls, Hanes Valley or Crown Pass. You can reach Norvan Falls quickly by turning right (east) where the trail forks and heading upstream for 300 m. You can still see some evidence of past mining activity around the creek area. Zinc and copper deposits located just south of the creek were mined in the early 1900s, and some old shafts and tunnels are still here, just below the forest floor.

Norvan Falls is the turn-around point for this hike, so when you are ready to return, retrace your steps southward along the Headwaters Trail and hike past the junction with the Cedars Mill Trail. Before the forest was logged in the mid-1880s, it was home to truly gigantic trees. Today, our only reminders of these giants are the huge tree stumps that can be seen at intervals in the forest along the way.

The trail soon passes the first debris chute and passes a viewpoint where a short zigzagging side trail leads west and downward. Here it connects with the Lynn Loop Trail. Continue following the trail straight ahead and past the turnoff for the Lynn Peak Trail, which forks off to the left (northeast). From there, the trail leads back to a yellow gate that sits on the boundary between Lynn Headwaters Park and Seymour Demonstration Forest. At the gate, walk along the gravel road back to Lynn Creek and cross the bridge. The area around the bridge is a pleasant spot to take a break before you head home.

21. Trailhead

The park entrance is north of Mount Seymour Parkway, 15 km northeast of downtown Vancouver via the Second Narrows Bridge and the parkway. Follow the main paved highway up from the park entrance. The trail starts at the north end of Parking Lot 4 by the information kiosk. Weather permitting, the Mystery Peak Chairlift operates seven days a week to the 1,200 m level. The trail is flagged with orange markers.

21. Camping, Cycling, Dogs

Camping: Alpine camping is allowed north of Brockton Point. A group campground is located near Parking Lot 1 (reservations are required; call (604) 986-2666 Mount Seymour Resorts.
Mountain biking: Cycling is only allowed on the main paved highway that accesses the park. It is also allowed on the designated horse trail that goes from Mt. Seymour Parkway to the Park Office.
Dogs: Dogs are allowed, but must be on a leash.

Located a mere 30 minutes by car from downtown Vancouver, Mount Seymour Provincial Park is the closest provincial park to the city. This park is a 3,508 ha semi-wilderness area that has an extensive system of trails leading to lakes, subalpine forests and lookouts on Seymour (1,006 m), Elsay (1,418 m) and Bishop (1,508 m) mountains. The hiking around Mount Seymour is some of the best in the North Shore Mountains. It offers quick entry into alpine terrain that is dotted with pools, bluffs and highlighted with spectacular panoramic views.

The park has seen many generations of use and enjoyment. The Alpine Club of Canada once rented land on the mountain, but the depression years forced it to drop the lease. In 1935, the Alpine Club and other organizations pressed for the preservation of the park. Mount Seymour was established in 1936, with an area of 274 ha. Mount Seymour was first climbed in 1908 by a party from the BC Mountaineering Club.

The rocky, wide and well-maintained trail to the top of Mount Seymour is moderately graded throughout with a few short, steep sections. The trail is quite rugged considering its proximity to Vancouver. Many accidents and mishaps have occurred here, and it is very easy to lose your way when fog or mist closes in. The weather can change with amazing quickness, resulting in soupy "whiteout" conditions. Make a note of trail markers and cairns as you hike and take particular care to note landmarks at the top of Mt. Seymour, as it is very easy to get turned around. Always carry a map and a compass.

The trail heads north from the parking lot, going alongside the west side of the wide road, which is a ski run in winter. As you hike upward, you pass a dam to the right. The trail then reaches a junction where the west (left) fork leads to the Dinky Peak loop. The main trail continues north along a small, placid creek, and after about 50 m, the trail forks again. The west (left) fork goes to First Lake and then on to Dog Mountain.

As you continue straight ahead, the trail is lined on both sides with blueberries, copperbush, false azalea and red huckleberry. The surrounding subalpine forest is populated with huge amabilis fir, mountain hemlock and yellow cedar. The yellow cedar is a native of coastal slopes and mountains of B.C. It grows extremely slowly, and some of the trees in the park may be among the oldest trees in Canada. Notice that the trunks of some trees are curved. This is caused by the weight and downslope creep of deep snow.

Northwest side of Second Pump Peak

Yellow Cedar

The yellow cedar can be found growing in moist to wet areas. It grows to 50 m and often has a slightly twisted trunk with bark that is dirty white to greyish-brown. The flattened branches of a cedar hang vertically and look like they are limp. The bluish-green leaves have sharp, spreading tips that grow tightly bunched together and are scale-like.

The wood of the yellow cedar was highly prized for its tough, straight-grained qualities. Coastal native people made extensive use of the wood, and it became a mainstay in their daily lives. It provided them with clothing, tools, shelter and canoes for transportation. They also used it to make totem poles, dishes, storage containers, masks, cradles, combs, fish clubs, ceremonial drums, harpoon shafts, paddles and many other things.

Bouldering in the Mt. Seymour area

The trail eventually emerges onto a road where you continue heading northeast until you go over the crest of the hill. At this point, turn north (left) and descend back onto a smaller road, continuing for about 20 m. Then turn north (left) onto the main trail for Mt. Seymour and continue past some granite bluffs and a series of small ponds.

Brockton Point, a rocky outcrop on Mt. Seymour, is the first lookout you reach. Volcanoes rose from the sea to form the mountains in this area 100 to 140 million years ago. There is a

Skiing

The skiing terrain around Mt. Seymour was first explored in 1929 by members of the Alpine Club of Canada. In 1930, the club applied for a 21-year lease of over 274 ha of land covering the main ski area. A 20-person cabin was built on the mountain in 1931 and used as a base for skiing and hiking.

Today, Mt. Seymour is a popular and developed ski area. There are four double chair lifts and two rope tows for alpine skiers. A variety of slopes and ski runs suit every level of ability. The hill is lit for night skiing and the orange lights can be seen from Vancouver. A ski school, rentals, nordic skiing and snowshoeing are also offered. A cafeteria is located at the top of Mystery Peak. Call 604-986-2261 for more information.

band of whitish volcanic ash near Brockton Point that is believed to have been deposited in water. The trail meanders among rocky bluffs to a viewpoint of the waters of Indian Arm, the Coast Mountains and part of the Fraser Valley.

Continue past the viewpoint along the east side of the ridge, descending slightly and then going over some big boulders. Follow the trail as it winds upward over the exposed roots of some massive Douglas fir that grow here.

Continue past First Pump Peak to a signed fork in the trail. Seymour Peak is 1.7 km to the northwest (left), while the trail to the right goes northeast for seven km to Elsay Lake, the largest in the park. As you go left up a steep ridge, you get views of Indian Arm, the Fraser Valley, Vancouver and the ocean.

Soon, the trail comes out onto granite blocks and alpine terrain. The granite bluffs around this area are ideal for the sport of bouldering, and you may want to bring your rock-climbing shoes along on the hike for this purpose. This is a great spot to take a break and enjoy the panoramic view. To the north is Second Pump Peak, southwest is Vancouver and southeast is Indian Arm. The Canada jay is a frequent visitor to lunch spots, so keep a lookout for them. Other indigenous birds include blue grouse, mountain chickadees, eagles, ravens and thrushes. Chipmunks can be seen running in and out of the rocks. Occasionally, pika and black bears can also be seen around Mt. Seymour.

From this point, the trail descends to the north and then rises up to Second Pump Peak through a small, steep gully between the trees on the west and the rock face on the east.

To continue to the top of Mt. Seymour, skirt the summit of the Second Pump Peak to the west by going left and slightly downward. This section has a steep drop-off to the left, so be extremely careful—especially in bad weather. A walking stick or an ice axe is advisable if there is snow.

The terrain is rocky and you must scramble down a jumble of roots. You then come out onto smooth granite bluffs, and from here it is an easy walk to the top of Mount Seymour (1,455 m). At the top, you can see the Coast Range Mountains, Indian Arm, Vancouver, the ocean, and the North Shore peaks.

Squamish to Whistler

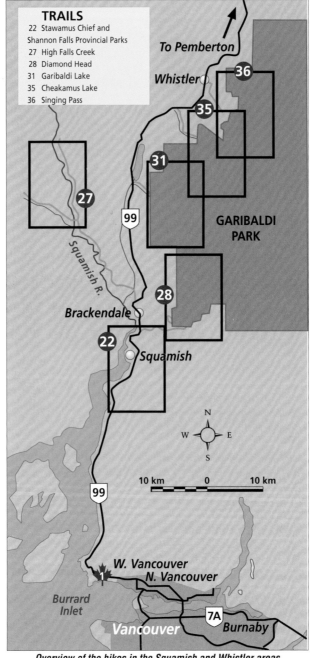

TRAILS
22 Stawamus Chief and
Shannon Falls Provincial Parks
27 High Falls Creek
28 Diamond Head
31 Garibaldi Lake
35 Cheakamus Lake
36 Singing Pass

To Pemberton

Whistler

36

35

31

GARIBALDI
PARK

99

Squamish R.

28

Brackendale

22

Squamish

N
W E
S

10 km   0   10 km

99

W. Vancouver
N. Vancouver
1
Burrard
Inlet
7A
Vancouver   Burnaby

Overview of the hikes in the Squamish and Whistler areas

View of Squamish, Howe Sound and the Tantalus Range

The area from Squamish to Whistler is located along the 100-km corridor of the Cheakamus River Valley. It begins at the at the town of Squamish, which is located at the head of Howe Sound, 64 km north of Vancouver. This area is dominated by the high, glaciered peaks of the steep coast Mountains. Located on the east side of this corridor, Garibaldi Provincial Park (194,904 ha) is one of the province's most outstanding and dominating parklands. It has 196 wilderness campsites, over 85 km of hiking trails, four overnight alpine shelters and three day-use shelters. The park starts just north of Squamish and extends northeast of Whistler and south of Pemberton.

The park is known for its spectacular scenery, which includes volcanic features, glaciers, and alpine meadows and mountain peaks. Garibaldi Park boasts four of the most popular recreational areas in southwestern British Columbia: the Diamond Head, Black Tusk/Garibaldi Lake, Singing Pass and Cheakamus Lake.

Located 106 km north of Vancouver directly west of Garibaldi Provincial Park, Whistler Village is known for its outstanding setting. Special legislation in 1976 created the Whistler Resort Municipality, the first of its kind in British Columbia. It was formerly known as Alta Lake.

Today, it is a four-season, world-class resort community that is dominated by two magnificent mountains, Whistler (2,182 ha) and Blackcomb (2,287 m).

You can access this area by Highway 99. The major centres along this route are Squamish and Whistler. The town of Squamish (pop. 11,709) is the largest community close to Garibaldi Provincial Park. Services, accommodation and supplies are all available at these areas. Access by train, car, passenger bus, charter air flights and ferry are all possible. Park information kiosks are located at the trailheads in each area.

Wilderness campsites are located at all recreational areas. Overnight shelters are located at Elfin Lakes (Diamond Head) and Russet Lake (Singing Pass). A hostel is located in Whistler.

Ranger and information stations are located at Garibaldi and Elfin Lakes (Diamond Head) and at Alice Lake Provincial Park.

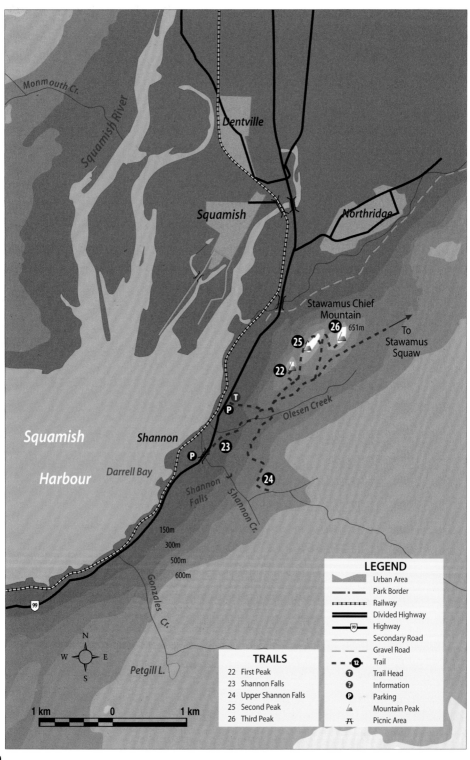

Monmouth Cr.

Squamish River

Dentville

Squamish

Northridge

Stawamus Chief
Mountain
26 651m

25

To
Stawamus
Squaw

22

Squamish

Shannon

T

P

Olesen Creek

23

P

24

Harbour

Darrell Bay

Shannon
Falls

Shannon Cr.

150m

300m

500m

600m

Gonzales Cr.

99

N
W · E
S

Petgill L.

1 km   0   1 km

LEGEND

	Urban Area
	Park Border
	Railway
	Divided Highway
99	Highway
	Secondary Road
	Gravel Road
12	Trail
T	Trail Head
?	Information
P	Parking
▲	Mountain Peak
⚲	Picnic Area

TRAILS

22 First Peak
23 Shannon Falls
24 Upper Shannon Falls
25 Second Peak
26 Third Peak

Stawamus Chief

~ 22-26 ~

Stawamus Chief Provincial Park

The Stawamus Chief is a quintessential West Coast hike that features waterfalls, lush rainforest, thundering creeks and dazzling views from three peaks. The Chief is located in a 100-km corridor that lies beyond the inlet of Howe Sound and is surrounded by spectacular forests, mountains and glaciers.

22-26. Camping, Cycling, Dogs

Camping: A camping area in front of the Chief has been developed into a 40-unit day-use parking lot area with 45 walk-in campsites and 15 vehicle campsites. BC Parks campgrounds are also located at Alice Lake, 12 km north of the Chief and at Nairn Falls, close to Green River Bastion. Commercial campgrounds are located in the Squamish area.

Mountain biking: Cycling is not applicable here.

Dogs: Dogs are allowed and must be kept on a leash except on Chief Peaks Trail.

At 671 m, the Chief is the second largest piece of granite in the world, the first being the rock of Gibraltar. It rises vertically over 541 m from the waters of Howe Sound and oversees the town of Squamish (population 12,000). The Stawamus Chief is a 600 ha Class A Provincial Park. Development of the area began in the winter of 1995 and continued in the summer of 1996. The Stawamus Chief is named after a sleeping Squamish Indian, which it is supposed to resemble in profile.

This popular trail ascends the back side of the Chief along a main trail that branches off at four side trails. These trails access the three main peaks of the Chief and Upper and Lower Shannon Falls. Be prepared to see many other hikers on this trail. It is extremely busy on weekends, especially during summer. Autumn is a better time to hike these trails as it is less crowded and the trails are dry.

Be aware that a small amount of rain can turn the exposed granite slabs on this hike into dangerous areas.

Bridge over Olesen Creek

~ 22 ~

First Peak

22. Route (map, page 80)

Distance: First Peak is 1.5 km one way; 3 hours, day hike
Rating: ** Intermediate, early season hike
Trailhead: 97 m
First Peak: 610 m, 3 km
Topographical map: 92G/11

22. Trailhead

Follow Highway 99 north from Vancouver for 50 km. Turn off at the Chief viewpoint, 1.3 km north of Shannon Falls or 1.5 km south of Squamish. Cross the viewpoint parking lot and turn south (right) onto a road. The road leads to a parking lot and the campground. The trail starts east of the parking lot.

The main trail takes you to First Peak. Four side trails intersect with the main trail along the hike, allowing you to choose different destinations. To reach First Peak, stay north (left) at every intersection. The trail is steep and climbs relentlessly, but don't despair. It takes you very quickly to the top, where you will be treated to a superb view. Take your time and pace yourself, and you will soon find yourself at the top.

The trail begins with a 50-m climb through rainforest along a well-maintained wooden staircase. The first side trail intersects the main trail at the top of the first set of stairs. This side trail leads south (right) to Lower Shannon Falls.

As you continue to the first peak, the trail ascends another set of wooden stairs that leads onto a trail of roots and rock. This is where it enters the steep and boulder-filled South Gully. The boulders in the gully were left behind by glaciers from the last ice age as they sheared off the huge walls of the Chief. The trail moves slowly away from Olesen Creek and passes by some tall cedars. It then passes a second side trail on the right that leads south to Upper Shannon Falls. It takes about one hour to hike to Upper Falls from here.

As you continue on the main trail, keep left and stay close to the steep granite wall as you climb. Soon, a third side trail intersects with the main trail. This is the junction where you can go west (left) to the first peak along the first gully or you can turn east (right) to the second gully leading to the second and third peaks by the Lower Trail. The summit of First Peak is about 45 minutes from this junction. Second Peak takes 50 minutes and Third Peak, one hour and 10 minutes.

As you head to First Peak, the trail passes under an arch made by a boulder leaning against the granite wall. Soon after this, there is a scenic spot to the south (right) where you will find a bluff with a large boulder on it. From the bluff, you can look out over the valley and see the top of Shannon Falls to the southwest.

A fourth side trail intersects the main trail on your right at 426 m, and leads south to the second peak. Stay left for First Peak and continue heading north, climbing up the boulders and huge tree roots until you emerge onto an open granite slab. Granite is a rock composed largely of light-coloured minerals such as quartz and potassium-rich feldspar with an overall hardness of steel. The granite slabs are very smooth, and it may feel as if you are going to slide off, but you won't. Follow the red paint marks along the granite slabs all the way to the top.

It is an exhilarating feeling to reach the top. On a clear day, the view is breathtaking and you can see the town of Squamish to the northwest. Looking back toward Horseshoe Bay, you can see mountainous islands sitting placidly in the ocean. Across the water is a spectacular view of the snow-capped Tantalus Range and to the north, the whole valley opens up.

It is important to be cautious while you are up on top of the peak. Try to keep back from the edge of the cliffs as it is a long and steep fall down. Be extremely careful not to kick any rocks or debris over the edge, as rock climbers may be below and anything falling over the edge is a serious potential hazard to their safety.

Rock Climbers

The towering granite walls of the Stawamus Chief are regarded by rock climbers all over the world as a dream come true. Its famous walls offer a wide variety of quality rock-climbing routes, thus making it one of the most popular climbing destinations in North America.

The mingling of hikers, rock climbers and the nearby townsite of Squamish gives the area a heady atmosphere; excitement seems to buzz in the air. Hikers will sometimes catch the strange sight of climbers scuttling down the trails in their rock shoes after having scaled the Chief's enormous granite walls, or they will hear the metal clink of a carabiner or climbers calling out to

each other when standing close to the ledge on top of the first peak.

A good place to watch the climbers at play is on the Grand Wall. This sheer wall of granite rises over 500 m and is easily seen at the Chief viewpoint alongside Hwy 99. The younger granodiorite rock is sparsely fractured, offering superb climbing. To find the climbers, look for bright patches of colour on the smooth granite face. Once you have focused on a climber, it is easy to watch her/his progress. In fact, it can be downright addictive. Some climbers will spend the night on the face in bivy sacks and hammocks that they have anchored to the wall.

Two hundred and eighty climbing routes have been established up the face of the Chief. It was first climbed by Jim Archer and Hank Mather in 1957. The Grand Wall was climbed in 1961 by Ed Cooper and John Baldwin using 140 bolts that were drilled into the rock.

There are two main climbing areas that are popular on the Chief. "The Apron" features long slab climbs, while the "Grand Wall" offers multi-pitch crack and face climbs. The "Smoke Bluffs," just north of the Chief, are also a popular climbing area. A two-m-wide dike runs up the Chief and is a classic route for big wall climbers. It can take several days to complete.

~ 23 ~
Shannon Falls

23. Route (map, page 80)

Distance: 1.5 km one way, 1 hour, day hike
Rating: * Easy, early season hike
Trailhead: 97 m
Shannon Falls Junction: 152 m, 0.6 km
Shannon Falls: 30 m, 1 km one way
Topographical map: 92G/11

23. Trailhead

Follow Highway 99 north from Vancouver for 50 km. Turn off at the Chief viewpoint, 1.3 km north of Shannon Falls or 1.5 km south of Squamish. Cross the viewpoint parking lot and turn south (right) onto a road. The road leads to a parking lot and the campground. The trail starts east of the parking lot.

At 335 m, the lovely Shannon Falls is the third highest waterfall in British Columbia after Della Falls on Vancouver Island (425 m) and the Hunlen Falls in Bella Coola (352 m).

The hike to Shannon Falls runs along a pleasant, undulating trail that provides occasional glimpses of Howe Sound. The trail is located at the first intersection that leads south (right) off the main trail. Follow the trail across a wooden bridge over Olesen Creek and then back into the forest. The trail continues under moss-covered granite bluffs until it reaches a monument of a 1925 Steam Donkey. This contraption was once used to haul logs. The Falls are located just beyond this monument.

Once you have passed the Steam Donkey, continue southeastward on the well-maintained trail and you will find yourself following the bubbling waters of Shannon Creek up to the falls.

Shannon Falls

~ 24 ~
Upper Shannon Falls

24. Route (map, page 80)

Distance: 3 km one way, 3 hours, day hike
Rating: * Intermediate, early season hike
Trailhead: 97 m
Upper Shannon Falls Jct: 275 m, 1.2 km
Upper Shannon Falls: 488 m, 3 km one way
Topographical map: 92G/11

24. Trailhead

Follow Highway 99 north from Vancouver for 50 km. Turn off at the Chief viewpoint, 1.3 km north of Shannon Falls or 1.5 km south of Squamish. Cross the viewpoint parking lot and turn south (right) onto a road. The road leads to a parking lot and the campground. The trail starts east of the parking lot.

Icicles on the Upper Shannon Falls trail

This hike gives those who wonder what is at the top of Shannon Falls the opportunity to find out. This trail is often avoided in favour of the more popular trails that go up the Chief. Although it doesn't have the panoramic views that the Chief offers, the close-up view of Shannon Creek and Shannon Falls is quite breathtaking. This trail is a quieter alternative to the more popular trails, which can sometimes be very congested. The trail takes you to the top of B.C.'s third-highest waterfalls. Instead of looking up at the falls, you look down at them and the view of Squamish and Howe Sound. This well-laid-out trail runs through a forest filled with bubbling creeks, ferns and towering cedar and Douglas fir trees.

The trail begins at the

Stawamus Chief trailhead and follows the main trail upward. Climb to the top of the first set of steep wooden stairs to where you will see a fork in the trail. This side trail (right) leads south to Shannon Falls. Continue straight ahead by going up the next set of stairs and then over tree roots and rock, heading steeply upward into the tree-covered South Gully. As you continue, the sound of water rushing down Olesen Creek will fade as the trail meanders slowly away from it. Continue upward through this rugged, lush landscape to a second intersection in the trail. Take the right fork that leads into a grove of hemlock trees toward Upper Shannon Falls. Walk a few paces and then take the southeast (left) trail at the fork.

Continue up some small steps and over a log bridge. The trail undulates through the forest until you reach a steep hillside climb. Do not let the steepness of the trail intimidate you as it is not as difficult as it looks and only takes about 10 minutes to climb. There are many well-placed roots and stone boulders within reach that make climbing up the hillside fun. If the weather is wet, watch out for slippery tree roots when you come down. At the time of this writing, this section of the trail was being upgraded by BC Parks. At the top, turn right (southwest) and you will come upon a fine view of Howe Sound and Squamish.

The trail levels off here and you soon pass through a tranquil forested area of granite cliffs and a bubbling creek. This secluded forest of fern, moss, boulders and cedars sits between granite walls and it has a very peaceful feel to it, so you may want to take your time through this section and enjoy it.

In the colder months, water freezes while dripping down from these cliffs, forming extremely long icicles that look like a white curtain that is draped across the side of the cliffs. Interestingly,

Second Peak Trail

~ 25 ~
Second Peak

25. Route (map, page 80)

Distance: 4.5 km, 4 hours, day hike
Rating: ** Intermediate, early season hike
Trailhead: 97 m
Second Peak: 652 m, 4.5 km
Topographical map: 92G/11

25. Trailhead

Follow Highway 99 north from Vancouver for 50 km. Turn off at the Chief viewpoint, 1.3 km north of Shannon Falls or 1.5 km south of Squamish. Cross the viewpoint parking lot and turn south (right) onto a road. The road leads to a parking lot and the campground. The trail starts east of the parking lot.

Shannon Falls keeps flowing even in the winter months and because of the mild West Coast climate, it rarely freezes. However, once every four to five years it becomes cold enough that it does freeze. When this happens, ice climbers rush madly out to climb it before the waterfall begins to flow again.

After this interlude of easy hiking, you will reach the last sustained climb to the top of Shannon Falls. The final climb runs along a series of well-groomed log steps that lead to a viewpoint. Continue upward, following the trail into the narrow gully. Here, you can hear the roar of the falls and get glimpses of the rushing water through the trees. There are some short side trails leading off the main path to viewpoints of Shannon Creek and the waterfall. Be very careful when you are near the creek edge; a slip here could lead to a fatal fall over the falls. If you hike up past the falls for approximately 10 minutes, the trail will peter out at peaceful spot beside Shannon Creek. This is a nice place to take a rest and explore the creek before you head back down.

This hike takes you up the Stawamus Chief's second and highest peak, which sits in the centre between the first and third peaks. Although the view at the top of this peak is spectacular, fewer people head up this way. However, come prepared for crowds if you hike here on a summer weekend. This trail also connects to the Third Peak Trail, thus giving you the option of descending along another route. You should avoid this hike if the weather is bad, as the slab areas can be slick or icy and the drop-offs are steep.

From the trailhead, follow the main trail upward over the stairs and stay left; the right fork goes to Shannon Falls. Continue upward through the forest, where fungi, moss and ferns grow among the huge boulders and rugged forest floor. Go left when the trail reaches the second fork, as the right path goes to Upper Shannon Falls. At the next fork, go left; the right-hand trail leads to the Stawamus Squaw. At 426 m, take the right-hand fork at the final intersection.

You will pass a sign that says "Rocky Passage and Crevasse" as you continue up

left: Second Peak

The three peaks of Stawamus Chief

through the forest and boulder-filled gully. After some climbing, the trail pops out onto a slab ledge at the top of the South Gully. Turn east (right) here and walk across an exposed ledge. Take particular care if the ledge is wet. Once you are past the ledge, you enter a narrow rock slot where there is room for only one person to scramble through at a time. Be careful with your foot placements when you go through the slot, as there are some exposed openings in the rock that form a crevasse. If you look down, you can see through some of the gaps in the crevasse.

At the end of the slot, there are a metal ladder and two ropes that you can use to pull yourself up onto a granite slab. Despite the ladder's decrepit look, it is surprisingly secure and sturdy. More care is needed when you walk across the slab as it is exposed and can be very slippery if it is wet or icy. Follow a cable across the smooth slab rock and continue north, following the orange markers up to the top of the peak. The panoramic view at the top is spectacular and well worth the effort it takes to get there.

On your return, you can either retrace the trail you took to get up or you can continue on to Third Peak by heading northeast across the granite slab. Follow the painted markers down the slab and into a forested area. As you walk through this area, you will come upon a stunning view of the upper part of North Gully. Continue past the intersection (right)

and follow the markers to the Third Peak. From there, you can take the Third Peak Trail down and back to the trailhead.

~ 26 ~

Third Peak

26. Route (map, page 80)

Distance: 5.5 km one way, 5 hours, day hike
Rating: ** Intermediate, early season hike
Trailhead: 97 m
Junction to North Gully (Second and Third Peaks): 396 m, 2.2 km
Third Peak: 640 m, 5.5 km
Topographical map: 92G/11

26. Trailhead

Follow Highway 99 north from Vancouver for 50 km. Turn off at the Chief viewpoint, 1.3 km north of Shannon Falls or 1.5 km south of Squamish. Cross the viewpoint parking lot and turn south (right) onto a road. The road leads to a parking lot and the campground. The trail starts east of the parking lot.

View of Squamish River and Tantalus Range, High Falls Creek

The third and most northern summit of the Chief is reached by the Third Peak Trail. This route has the same marvelous views as the other two peaks, but it is usually quieter than the main and Second Peak trails. The trail goes up the steep North Gully and pops out onto granite slabs, where panoramic views await you. The Third Peak Trail also joins up with the Second Peak Trail, thus giving you the option of returning by an alternate route.

To hike up to Third Peak, go to the trailhead and begin climbing up the steep wooden staircase and into the forest. Stay left at the first and second forks. At the third intersection (396 m), turn right and continue east. From here, the trail enters a dense forest of short alder and cedar trees, most of which measure about 5 cm in diametre. After about 20 minutes of hiking, you reach a fork where the east (right) trail leads to the Stawamus Squaw. It takes about two hours to hike to the Squaw, which is a smaller granite peak that sits to the east of the Chief.

To reach Third Peak, continue north (left) through the forest until you reach the steep North Gully. The trail up the gully is shaded by huge Douglas fir trees and proceeds over boulders, logs and tree roots. When the climb steepens, the trail begins switching back and you gain altitude very quickly. The climb is relentless, however there are many spots where you can stop to take a break and enjoy the view behind you. Keep going and soon enough, you will reach the top. Once you are at the top, turn east (right) at the fork toward Third Peak and continue along the ridge of the gully. If you want to go to Second Peak, head west (left) at the fork and follow the markers.

The forest soon leads out onto open slabs of granite, where the dramatic view unfolds. Keep following the red markers until you reach the top, where a small pond rests in the smooth slab rock. On a sunny day, the panoramic view from Third Peak will simply take your breath away. The glimmering ocean and the Tantalus Range spread out endlessly to the west. The mighty glaciered peaks of Garibaldi and Atwell mountains shimmer in the blue sky to the north. To the east looms Mount Mamquam and to the south rise the ice-capped spires of Sky Pilot Mountain and Crown Mountain.

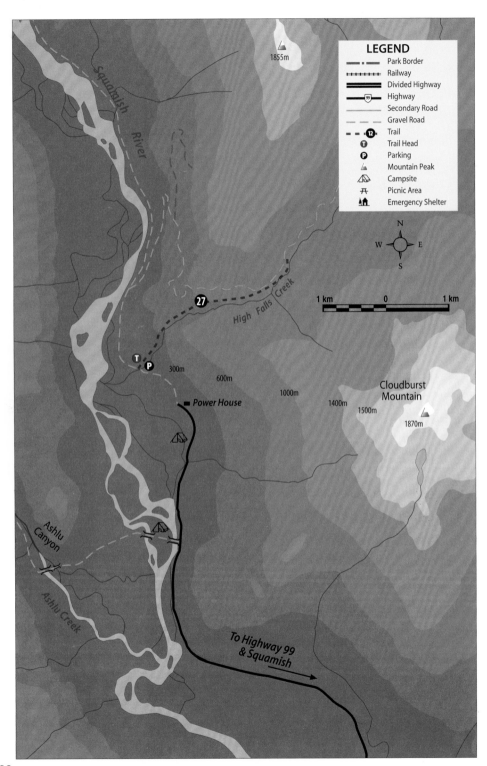

~ 27 ~
High Falls Creek

27. Route (map, page 90)

Distance: 6 km one way, day hike, 4 hours descending via the logging road.
Rating: * Intermediate, early season hike
Trailhead: 80 m
Waterfalls lookout 487 m, 1 km
Logging road: 640 m, 6 km
Topographical map: 92G/14

27. Trailhead

Drive north on Highway 99 until you reach the Alice Lake Park sign, 13 km north of Squamish. Turn left at the sign for the Squamish Valley/Paradise Valley turnoff. If you are driving south, turn at the Tenderfoot Fish Hatchery sign. Drive for 23.4 km. Follow the road through the settlement of Cheekeye. Then veer left where the road divides after the bridge. High Falls Creek will appear 1 km after a Powerhouse. Park just before the creek. Cross the bridge and the trailhead, marked by a wooden sign, will appear to your right. The trail is marked by orange ribbons.

27. Camping, Cycling, Dogs

Camping: No designated campsites exist here.
Mountain biking: Cycling is not appropriate here.
Dogs: Dogs are allowed on the trail.

This is a well-maintained and nicely laid out trail that features outstanding views of the Tantalus Mountain range, a waterfall and moss-covered bluffs. It is a trail of contrasts; the open bluffs and ridges lead into a luxurious old growth forest which ultimately ends at a barren clear cut and a small rockslide. It seems that you come upon a new view almost every minute when you are on this trail.

Soon after you enter the forest, you will come to some bluffs. Climb up these bluffs heading to the right. The climbing is steady and quite steep. Three braided ropes have been placed in the more difficult areas to help you pull yourself up. As the trail moves upwards you can hear the roaring High Falls Creek to your right. Once the trail gains the ridge, a big drop off will appear to your right. Keep away from the edge. Follow the ridge crest all the way to the top. The terrain levels off at this point. You will come upon some lovely, rolling, moss-covered bluffs that lead upward. This is the first of a series of moss gardens on this trail.

After about one km of hiking is a view of a waterfall cascading straight down the cliff. Sometimes a rainbow can be seen in the waterfall area. There are some nice handholds to grab onto as you proceed up the steep part of the cliff after the first waterfall viewpoint. As you scramble up this ridge, another viewpoint will open up to your left. There are views of the Squamish River, Pelion Mountain and Ossa Mountain. Mount Tantalus is barely in view to the left. Continue up and you will soon reach another lookout to the right of the falls of the Squamish River and valley. The Squamish

Nature's Carpet

Look in a rainforest and you will see that moss covers fallen logs and rocks, and hangs like lace curtains from trees. Moss does not have roots, so it has great adaptability. It is able to live on almost anything. Instead, thin hair-like rhizoids act like roots and anchor the plant in place. Moss also manufactures its own nutrients, as it contains chlorophyll. It thrives in wet places like rainforests, absorbing water from the outside.

Moss spreads by releasing airborne moss spores. The spores settle in a favorable place, absorb water and begin growing. Moss can hold many times its own weight in water. It also reduces erosion by cushioning the fall of rain.

River is the second largest in B.C., the Fraser being the largest.

Another moss-covered bluff area will appear soon after this point. The area around this second bluff is very open and offers a panoramic view. You can see Zenith Mountain and the ridge that leads to Tantalus Mountain from here.

After these mossy bluffs, you leave the waterfall behind and enter a forest. A fork in the trail will appear where a sign reading "Viewpoint. No Exit" points to the right. To continue on the trail, take the left fork. Take the right turn in the fork if you want to walk to the viewpoint. It is a short, five-minute walk to the viewpoint and the scenery is thrilling. There are more views of the glaciered Tantalus Range and the thundering waterfall blasting down into a gorge.

Continuing on the trail, you tuck around a corner and go up into the High Falls Creek basin towards Tricouni Park. The trail winds through a mature, peaceful forest where towering Douglas fir grow. Other trees include yellow cedar, mountain hemlock and amabilis fir. As the trail moves downward, it passes through the moss-strewn, moist, shady, forested valley. The mulch trail is very soft and pleasant to walk on. This part of the trail provides a nice contrast to the rocky bluffs of the first part. You will begin to hear the High Falls Creek again soon after you pass the huge Douglas fir. Soon, the trail leaves the forest and emerges onto another moss-covered bluff. As you stand up on the bluff, you will hear the creek gushing by below. The trail continues in a northwest direction and heads along a ridge.

Elfin Lakes, Old Lodge, Ranger Station and Hut at Diamond Head

The Legend of King Tantalus

The Tantalus Range, which you see from the High Falls Creek Trail, was first ascended in 1914. Many of the mountain peaks in the range, such as Lydia Mountain, Mount Dione and Ossa Mountain, were named after the legend of King Tantalus. King Tantalus, a mythical king of the ancient empire of Lydia, was condemned to stand chest-deep in a pool of water with fruit-laden boughs hanging above him. Whenever he tried to grab the fruit, the bough would rise out of his reach. When he bent down to try to drink, the water level would recede. Early climbers seemed to relate to King Tantalus' frustration. Naming the range after the King Tantalus legend may be a commentary on how they felt when the peaks of this spectacular area continued to elude them.

How the Chief was Formed

The Chief was created by natural forces when the Juan de Fuca plate slid under the North American plate 94 million years ago. In its developing stage, the Chief was merely a lump of molten magma that lay 25 km below the surface of the earth. The magma was less dense than the surrounding rock, and this caused it to cool gradually and rise over time until it lay about 10 km below the surface.

For millions of years, the forces of weather, wind and earthquake eroded the earth around the mountain. As this happened, the Chief kept rising from the bowels of the earth until it almost reached surface level. When the last ice age began, glaciers started to sculpt and chisel away at the Chief. The glaciers cut away at the mountain, scraping the walls and deepening the gullies. Debris such as large boulders was deposited at its base.

About 9,500 years ago, the Chief made its first appearance above the earth's surface, although it was still surrounded by icy glaciers. When the glaciers finally receded, the Chief was left behind, where it sits today beside the waters of Howe Sound.

Suddenly, the trail leaves the forest and enters an empty logged area. It is a jarring transition from an old-growth forest into a slash area. Small conifers, snags and stumps are a dramatic contrast to the lush undergrowth and huge trees of the old-growth forest. It is, to say the least, an interesting contrast. Soon after the slash, the trail goes through a rockfall area. Look for orange markers and cairns to guide you across the rocks. The trail ends at a logging road right above the rock face. At the trail's end, you will see a small tree with an orange marker and a cairn in front of it.

At this point, you can return to the trail or walk back along the logging road. To walk back on the road, turn right and go back past the slash along the road heading south. There is some potential for bouldering on granite cliffs along the road. The panoramic view of the Squamish Valley is quite spectacular as you walk down. At the junction with the main road,

Eagles on the Squamish River

Besides being the second largest river in B.C., the Squamish River is also well known for attracting bald eagles. The Squamish River runs northeast down from the Coast Mountains, where it empties into Howe Sound. Salmon come home to spawn in this area every year. Bald eagles come to the river in autumn to follow salmon runs. The eagles come from as far away as Alaska. The birds feed on the banks of the Cheakamus, Cheekeye, Mamquam and Ashlu Rivers. However, 80 per cent of the eagles congregate at a nine km stretch between the Cheakamus and Mamquam rivers. Huge flocks of eagles can be seen near the community of Brakendale, which is 10 km north of Squamish on Highway 99.

In 1994, a new record was set when 3,700 Bald eagles were counted in this area. The previous record was 3,426, set in the 1980s at Alaska's Chilkat River.

During spawning season, an eagle eats nearly a tenth of its own body weight in fish every day. The feast lasts until February. Look for the bald eagles if you are driving to the High Falls Creek hike.

turn left and walk for about 1.5 km to the parking area. It takes about two hours and 20 minutes of easy hiking to get back to the parking area along the logging road.

~ 28 ~
Diamond Head

28. Route (map, page 96)

Distance: 11 km one way, 5-8 hours, day hike
Rating:* Intermediate
Trailhead: 914 m
Red Heather Campground: 1,310 m, 5 km
Elfin Lakes: 11 km one way, 5 to 8 hours
Little Diamond Head (Saddle Lake) junction: 1,432 m, 12.5 km
The Saddle: 1,768 m, 13.5 km
Topographical map: 92G/14, 92G/15

28. Trailhead

From the town of Squamish, follow Highway 99 north for four km. Turn east onto Mamquam Road and drive for 16 km along a rough gravel road to the parking lot.

This accessible trail leads to a scenic subalpine area in southern Garibaldi Provincial Park that has been a popular recreational area since the early 1900s. Roads and trails leading to the area were built back then, and now approximately 22,000 people visit Diamond Head each year. The area's dramatic landscape features volcanoes, glaciers, mountain peaks, valleys and is dotted with idyllic lakes and ponds. It is also an excellent area for backcountry skiing in the winter.

A variety of optional hikes lead out from the Elfin Lakes area. You can hike to the Saddle, Little Diamond Head, Opal Cone or Mamquam Lake. If you are hiking the Opal Cone Trail, you

Cycling on the Diamond Head Trail

may wish to check with park wardens to make sure that Ring Creek is low enough to cross.

The trail starts at an old gravel road that was built in the 1940s to shuttle people to the Diamond Head Lodge at Elfin Lakes. While it is very wide and well groomed, it is rocky. The trail can be used by both cyclists and hikers. Hikers will find the grade of the trails throughout the Diamond Head area to be moderate. Cyclists heading up to Elfin Lakes should be prepared for a long and challenging ride over rocky terrain. However, if you cycle, you will be able to enjoy a fast descent from Elfin Lakes that takes less than an hour.

The trail starts to climb north as soon as it leaves the parking lot. After you have been on the trail for about 15 minutes, you will see a side trail leading uphill to the east (right). This is the original trail and you can cut three km off your hike if you take this route. The trail comes out just after the Red Heather Campground, where it joins the road. If you go this way, you will miss out on some viewpoints, and the trail is steeper than the route along the road.

As you continue on the road, the area starts to open up into sub-alpine terrain just before it reaches the Red Heather Campground. There are spectacular views of the Tantalus Range to the west, Diamond Head to the north, Atwell

Peak and Mount Garibaldi. Mount Garibaldi was first climbed in August, 1907 by a party of six. The journey to the peak took eight days. The party had to take the steamship *Brittania* to the town of Squamish, from which point they embarked on a gruelling hike to base of the peak.

The trail soon arrives at the Red Heather Day Shelter. The shelter contains a wood-burning and propane stove, sink, rescue sled, two picnic tables and benches. Plants to look for while taking a break include blueberry, huckleberry, red and white mountain heather

28. Camping, Cycling, Dogs

Camping: Camping and shelters are located at Red Heather Campground and Elfin Lakes Campground. The cost at the Elfin Lakes Shelter is $10 per person, per night. The Red Heather Shelter is for day use only. There is camping only at Mamquam Lake. The park brochure is incorrect as there is no overnight shelter at Mamquam Lake.

Mountain biking: Cycling is permitted from the parking lot to Elfin Lakes only. It is a challenging, rocky, double-track trail.

Dogs: Dogs are not allowed.

Red Heather Shelter

and partridgefoot.

The trail divides a couple of minutes after passing the Red Heather Shelter. Take the east (right) trail if you are cycling up. The west (left) trail is for hikers and it goes through lush alpine meadows. As you continue up the trail above Red Heather Meadow, the forest gives way to groves of cypress trees that are at least 300 years old. Despite their age, the trees remain small due to the short growing season. The view from this part of the trail is superb

Red Heather

This small, mat-forming shrub is found in the high mountains. When it blooms in June and July, it is topped with hundreds of bell-shaped, rose-coloured flowers. Its evergreen leaves are needle-like, short and grow in an alternating pattern. This plant usually grows to 30 cm.

and you can see the Diamond Head area, the Opal Cone, Columnar Peak, The Gargoyles, Atwell Peak and the ranger hut.

The route starts to level out as it reaches the high point, and from here you can see the trail winding northeast along the ridge in front of you. Follow it downward to the tiny, idyllic Elfin Lakes and the old Diamond Head Lodge.

The lodge was built in the 1940s by Joan Matthews and brothers Ottar and Emil Brandvold. Matthews, who later married Ottar, met the two men at a ski meet in Wells Gray Park. The two Norwegian brothers were world-class ski jumpers, and Matthews was a champion slalom ski racer. They opened the lodge, which offered overnight accommodation and guided trips, in 1946. The lodge was operated until the late 1960s, when it was sold to the province for the park. It was closed in 1972.

Swimming is allowed in Upper Elfin Lake while the lower lake is used for drinking water only. A ranger station and shelter are also located near the lakes. The shelter was built next to the lodge in 1975 by the Ministry of Parks. The shelter is very large and well-maintained. Bicycle racks are located outside the shelter while inside there are a propane and wood burning stove, sink, tables and bunk beds for 34 people. The shelter is a favorite overnight spot among skiers.

From the signed intersection at Elfin Lakes, you can continue hiking to the Saddle, Opal Cone or to Mamquam Lake. The Elfin Lakes campsite is located one km away to the west (left) of the intersection. If you are continuing on, bring water as the next water source is just before Opal Cone at Ring Creek.

There are more panoramic views as you head downhill from the Elfin Lakes toward Ring Creek. To the north starting at the left, you see Columnar Peak, Atwell Peak and the Gargoyles. In winter, the Saddle between Columnar and the Gargoyles is a popular spot for telemark skiing. More ambitious skiers often continue on down to Ring Creek and onto the Garibaldi Neve to do the popular "Neve Ski Traverse." The term "neve" refers to high-density snow that survives at least one melt season on a glacier.

The trail follows the tracks of an old wagon road and it is very wide open, level and well-groomed. There is a junction about half a

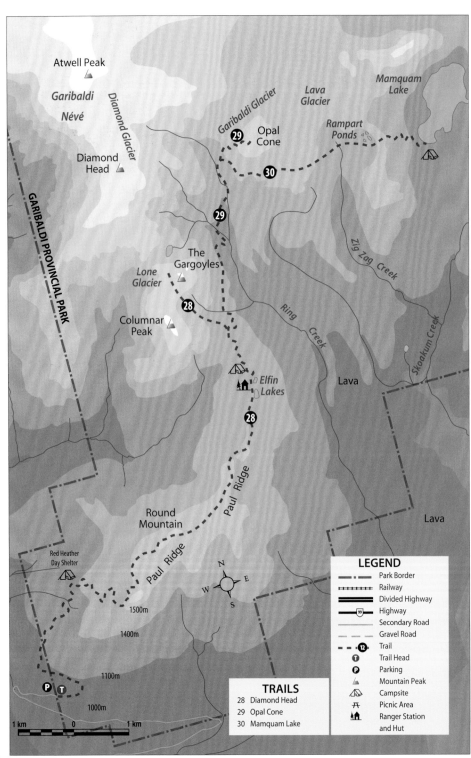

Atwell Peak

Garibaldi
Névé

Diamond Glacier

Diamond
Head

GARIBALDI PROVINCIAL PARK

Garibaldi Glacier

Lava
Glacier

Mamquam
Lake

Rampart
Ponds

29 Opal
Cone

30

29

The
Gargoyles

Lone
Glacier

28

Columnar
Peak

Zig Zag Creek

Ring Creek

Skookum Creek

Elfin
Lakes

Lava

28

Paul Ridge

Round
Mountain

Lava

Paul Ridge

Red Heather
Day Shelter

1500m

1400m

1100m

1000m

N
W   E
S

P **T**

1 km   0   1 km

LEGEND

—··—··—	Park Border
┼┼┼┼┼┼	Railway
═══════	Divided Highway
══99══	Highway
───────	Secondary Road
─ ─ ─ ─	Gravel Road
● ● **12** ●	Trail
T	Trail Head
P	Parking
▲	Mountain Peak
⛺	Campsite
🎪	Picnic Area
🏠	Ranger Station and Hut

TRAILS

28 Diamond Head
29 Opal Cone
30 Mamquam Lake

Diamond Head Gargoyles

~ 29 ~
Opal Cone

29. Route (map, page 96)

Distance: 6.5 km one way from Elfin Lakes, 5 hours, day hike or overnight
Rating: ** Intermediate
Route: Elfin Lakes: 1,460 m
Opal Cone: 17.5 km one way, 5-7 hours
Topographical maps: 92G/14, 92G/15

29. Trailhead

The trail begins at Elfin Lakes. From the town of Squamish, follow Highway 99 north for four km. Turn east onto Mamquam Road and drive for 16 km along a rough gravel road to the parking lot.

29. Camping, Cycling, Dogs (see pg 94)

kilometre down the hill. The Elfin Lakes Campsite is located in the meadow to the west (left) and the main trail continues straight ahead north. No mountain biking is permitted past this intersection and it is recommended that you leave your bikes in the racks at the Elfin Lakes Shelter.

The trail starts to ascend and soon meets another junction. If you wish to go to the Saddle and on to Little Diamond Head, take the path which leads straight ahead and northwest. To continue to Opal Cone, go north and northeast (right).

The Saddle Trail leads to a pass that is located between the strange-looking Gargoyles and Columnar Peak. It also provides access to Little Diamond Head, a sloping shoulder located in front of Atwell Peak. The Saddle Trail is a short 1.5 km steep hike. Once you are there, you can climb up to Columnar Peak to the west (left) or you can hike up to the Gargoyles to the east (right). Both of these summits are unusually shaped lava formations that were created during past volcanic activity.

From the Saddle you can continue on a fairly strenuous hike for another five km to 2,100-m Little Diamond Head.

If you are looking for a journey through a stunning landscape of glaciers, mountains, ancient volcanoes and an otherworldly terrain, then this is a hike for you. This trail, which begins at Elfin Lakes, takes you through valleys filled with wildflowers, over and along terminal moraines, alongside the Garibaldi Glacier and up the disintegrating volcanic face of Opal Cone. In the summer months, the area boasts a great variety of wildflowers such as Indian paintbrush, lupin, arnica and heather.

This is an excellent day hike to do from Elfin Lakes. If you combine it with the hike to Elfin Lakes, you are in for a very long day of approximately 13-16 hours. You may want to ride your bike up to Elfin Lakes, leave it at the shelter, hike Opal Cone and then ride out. By doing this, you can save about one to two hours on the descent from Elfin Lakes, and the ride down is fast and fun.

To reach Opal Cone, head north from the Elfin Lakes Shelter along a meandering trail as it traverses the west side of a valley, through which Ring Creek flows. The trail goes slightly uphill to where it meets another fork. For the Opal Cone Trail, go north and northeast (right) at the intersection. The other trail, which goes straight ahead and northwest, leads up the Saddle and onto Little Diamond Head.

As you continue along, the trail makes its way down into the flower-filled creek valley, sometimes going through talus and lightly treed areas. From here, you can see Mount Garibaldi and the Sharkfin, and to the east is the massive Mamquam Icefield.

The trail rounds the edge of a narrow, disintegrating dirt ridge; Ring Creek flows by below and to the east. It then runs downhill to where the creek branches to the east (right) of the trail. The west (left) branch of the creek flows out of Lava Lake and the north (right) branch flows from Garibaldi Glacier. The trail crosses the west branch of the creek and goes uphill. In the summer months, beautiful magenta monkey flowers and fireweed bloom around the creek area.

The terrain around the creek is barren except for occasional plants or flowers. Red and brown rock debris, recently deposited by the retreating glacier, covers the area and above you to the right are the disintegrating rocky slopes of the Opal Cone. The gleaming white Diamond and Garibaldi glaciers loom to the north, providing a striking contrast to this desert-like landscape.

The trail runs upward between the creek branches until it reaches the north creek branch. Here, it crosses a small bridge to the east bank and continues ascending at a steeper grade. There is rubble and rock scattered about, and the trail becomes easy to lose. Look for cairns to guide you as you continue climbing the switchback trail.

The trail reaches a fork just before the mud moraine. Turn north (left) to continue to Opal Cone or take the east (right) fork if you wish to hike to Mamquam Lake.

The route for Opal Cone skirts the west side of the ancient crater. The area looks like a lunar landscape, as huge lava boulders protrude from the slope to the east (right). The route through may become confusing here. Continue scrambling through the rock and follow the cairns along the left side of the creek.

The trail becomes sketchy at this point, but it is easy to pick your way up the rocky, steep slope. Just follow the cairn markers for about 15 minutes and you will reach the top. Once

you are there, you can explore the crater of the defunct volcano and take in the fabulous panoramic view. There are superb vistas of Mamquam Lake to the east, Sky Pilot to the south and Columnar Peak and the Gargoyles to the southwest. To the north, you can see the Garibaldi Neve toward Garidbaldi Lake with Diamond Head, Atwell Peak and Mount Garibaldi to the west.

~ 30 ~

Mamquam Lake

30. Route (map, page 96)

Distance: 11 km one way from Elfin Lakes, 9 hours, overnight.
Rating: ** Intermediate
Elfin Lakes: 1, 460 m
Opal Cone Junction: 1,525 m, 6.5 km
Mamquam Lake: 1,280 m, 11 km

30. Trailhead

From the town of Squamish, follow Highway 99 north for four km. Turn east onto Mamquam Road and drive for 16 km along a rough gravel road to the parking lot.
Trailhead: Junction on Opal Cone Trail. See the trailhead for Elfin Lakes.

30. Camping, Cycling, Dogs (see pg 94)

Mamquam Lake is another optional destination that can be reached from the Elfin Lakes area. You may wish to camp overnight at Mamquam Lake, as it features a truly unique, rugged setting that feels very remote. The hike takes you to Ring Creek, past Opal Cone and on to Mamquam Lake, which sits just below Pyramid Mountain. Along the trail, you will see a variety of dramatic landscapes. The volcanic rock, glaciers, mountain valleys, creeks, mountain peaks and placid lakes will keep you fascinated for the entire hike.

Indian paintbrush

To go to Mamquam Lake, follow the Opal Cone Trail all the way to Ring Creek and over the bridge that crosses to the northeast side of the north fork of the creek. Using the cairns to guide you, continue following the trail as it zigzags upward to just before the mud moraine. Here the trail forks, with the north (left) trail leading to Opal Cone. Take the east (right) fork for Mamquam Lake.

The trail heads eastward from Opal Cone and winds across a stark moonscape of volcanic rock, huge boulders and granite that was created by the glaciers that once scoured this area. It continues over a large moraine and then goes downward into a valley to the banks of Zig Zag Creek. Once you have crossed the creek, begin climbing to the next moraine, where you can rest and take in some fabulous views of Mt. Garibaldi to the northwest and Pyramid Mountain and Mamquam Lake to the east. Small glacial lakes called Rampart Ponds are located just to the north of this moraine.

From the moraine, the trail switches back down 250 m to the Mamquam Lake. This is a peaceful spot from which you can explore the lakeshore or fish for rainbow trout. A campsite is located at the south end of the lake, but there is no overnight shelter. There are countless mosquitoes and horseflies swarming around the lake, so come prepared.

Garibaldi Neve Traverse

This popular two-day alpine traverse follows magnificent glacial terrain from the Diamond Head area to Garibaldi Lake. It is considered one of the classic ski tours in the B.C. coast range. The Neve was first crossed by a party on skis in the 1940s.

Travel on the Garibaldi Neve is extremely difficult in poor weather and should only be attempted by experienced hikers and skiers. The best times to do this trip are in midwinter, when the ice is covered with a thick layer of snow, or in late summer, when the snow has melted so that the ice and crevasses can be seen. Lake Garibaldi can normally be crossed on skis only between January and mid-May. Note that there is crevasse danger at the icefall northeast of The Sharkfin. Check with the Parks District Office for avalanche conditions.

Start the traverse at the Elfin Lakes Cabin and ski to Opal Cone. Note that there is serious avalanche danger around the west side of Ring Creek. From there, continue skiing directly onto the Neve, heading in a north by northwesterly direction. Continue along the ridge that runs northeast from The Tent. Then head north down to the elongated rock outcrop known as the Sharkfin. From there, continue to the head of Warren Glacier and through the pass west of Glacier Pikes. From there, head down the steep slopes of Sentinel Glacier and onto Garibaldi Lake. Shelters are located at Garibaldi Lake in Sentinel and Sphinx bays. You can exit from the Rubble Creek, Black Tusk or Helm Creek trails.

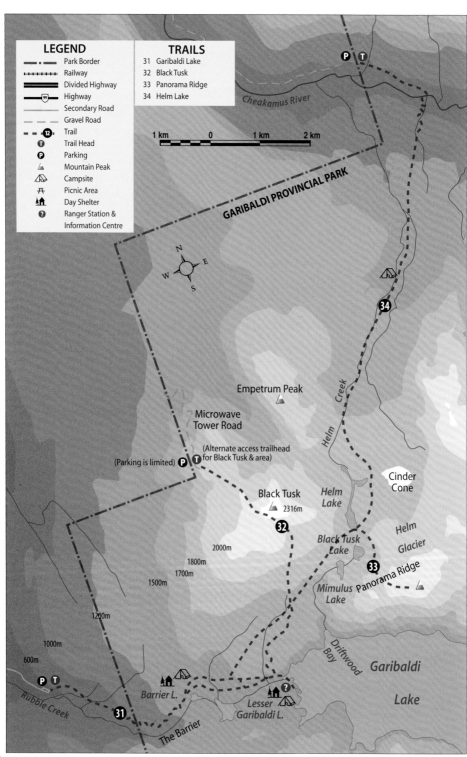

LEGEND

—·—·—	Park Border
┅┅┅┅	Railway
▬▬▬	Divided Highway
▬🕙▬	Highway
———	Secondary Road
— — —	Gravel Road
━ ⓐ ━	Trail
ⓣ	Trail Head
ⓟ	Parking
⛰	Mountain Peak
⛺	Campsite
⛱	Picnic Area
🏠	Day Shelter
❓	Ranger Station & Information Centre

TRAILS

31 Garibaldi Lake
32 Black Tusk
33 Panorama Ridge
34 Helm Lake

Cheakamus River

GARIBALDI PROVINCIAL PARK

1 km   0   1 km   2 km

N E W S

Empetrum Peak ⛰

Microwave Tower Road

(Parking is limited) ⓟ ⓣ (Alternate access trailhead for Black Tusk & area)

Black Tusk ⛰ 2316m
32

Helm Creek

⛺
34

Cinder Cone

Helm Lake

2000m
1800m
1700m
1500m

Black Tusk Lake

Helm Glacier

33

Mimulus Lake

Panorama Ridge ⛰

1200m

1000m
600m

ⓟ ⓣ

Rubble Creek

⛱ ⛺
Barrier L.

31

The Barrier

Driftwood Bay

❓ ⛱ ⛺
Lesser Garibaldi L.

Garibaldi Lake

~ 31 ~

Garibaldi Lake

31. Route (map, page 100)

Distance: 9 km one way, day hike or overnight, 6 hrs
Rating: *** Intermediate
Rubble Creek Parking Lot: 609 m
Taylor Meadows Junction: 1,500 m, 6 km
Taylor Meadows: 1,600 m, 8 km
Garibaldi Lake: 1,500 m, 9 km
Topographical maps: 92G/14, 92G/15, 92J/2

31. Trailhead

The park is located 97 km north of Vancouver, on the east side of Highway 99. Turn right off Highway 99 onto a road that leads to the Black Tusk Recreation Area. Continue for 2.5 km to the Rubble Creek Parking Lot.

Garibaldi Provincial Park provides the hiker with a wide range of trails and activities. This hike is one of the best in southwestern B.C. and it should not be missed. The scenery is a strange mixture of alpine and volcanic landscapes. Among the park's intriguing features are extinct volcanoes, glaciers, snowfields, Garibaldi Lake, alpine meadows, the weird Black Tusk Mountain and a lava dam called The Barrier.

The Garibaldi area was explored in the early 1900s by members of the British Columbia Mountaineering Club (BCMC) and the Alpine Club. They established summer climbing camps at Garibaldi Lake and in 1912, the BCMC began a campaign to preserve the Garibaldi area as a park. It officially became a park in 1920.

This area is very accessible and the trails throughout the park are extremely well maintained and well signed. Thus, it is almost impossible to lose your way. The smooth Rubble Creek trail is comprised of dirt and pine needles and there are no steep sections on the way to Mimulus and Black Tusk Lakes.

The one drawback of hiking in Garibaldi is that it can be very crowded, mostly on summer weekends. If possible, plan to hike on a week day if you want to try to avoid the crowds. Be sure to carry plenty of water as the route from the meadows onward can be very dry.

Garibaldi Lake is the main access trail that leads into the heart of Garibaldi Park. As the trail leaves the Rubble Creek Parking Lot, it begins to switchback southeast through a forest of western red cedar, western hemlock and giant Douglas fir. The trail grade remains easy as you walk through the open forest. Ground

How The Barrier Was Formed

The Barrier is a lava plug that was formed when Mount Price erupted approximately 12,000 years ago. Two craters opened up when the mountain erupted. Lava poured from the western crater and flowed down. The Barrier was formed when the mass of lava from the mountain met the face of an old ice sheet. The lava solidified when it hit the ice sheet and formed a wall. When the ice sheet melted, it left behind the sheer lava face of The Barrier.

Much later, after the ice sheets and volcanoes subsided, the lava plug was left behind. It barred the western end of what is now Garibaldi Lake and soon, the lake began the natural process of filling up with water.

Debris on the face of The Barrier was formed in 1855 when a massive landslide occurred as a result of an earth tremor. An area of rock 365 m thick and 547 m wide broke free from the Barrier and crashed into the valley below. Approximately 50 million tons of rock was carried along in the slide and debris spread all the way to the Cheakamus Valley.

The Barrier is still considered unstable. In the 1980s, the B.C. government relocated residents living beneath The Barrier in order to avoid any future catastrophes. The areas beneath and adjacent to The Barrier are regulated and you are not allowed to camp or remain overnight in the Rubble Creek Parking Lot. Stopping or lingering in the zone is also discouraged.

Garibaldi Lake

cover is sparse and is dominated by fern, devil's club, salmonberry and huckleberry.

The trail continues to ascend until it forks at six km. The north (left) fork leads two km north to the Taylor Campground and three km to Black Tusk Meadows. The east (right) fork goes to Garibaldi Lake and the campgrounds at the west end of the lake. This trail is the more scenic of the two.

As you continue on the east fork, a side trail leads to the south (right) and onto slabs of rock. From this spot, you get superb views of the great Barrier lava dam. The Barrier acts like a plug and holds back the waters of the 246-m-deep Garibaldi Lake, Lesser Garibaldi and Barrier lakes. Surrounding The Barrier are a jumble of massive boulders and rocks that have been deposited around it as a result of erosion. The upper 90 m of The Barrier are intensely fractured, and sometimes you can see rocks tumbling down. On the south bluff of The Barrier, the soft volcanic rock is striated and worn by water draining from above. Higher up you can see the flow lines that form a great "U" in the rock face, marking where the liquid lava

cooled as it filled the valley.

As you continue on the main trail to Garibaldi Lake, the trail stops switching back and forth and levels out. The route continues through the forest and skirts above the north side of the Barrier. As the trail gains elevation, mountain hemlock starts to dominate the forest and lichen hangs from the trees. Some good views of the Barrier continue to the right.

Soon, you reach the lovely, dark green Barrier Lake. The trail goes

A pika suns itself on a rock

around the north side of the lake to the turquoise Lesser Garibaldi Lake. It then passes over a bridge where Taylor Creek cascades down underneath it and into the lake.

The trail reaches another signed fork at 8 km. Straight ahead (east) is the Garibaldi Campground and one km away to the north (left) is Taylor Campground. As the trail moves eastward, away from Lesser Garibaldi Lake, it continues through the forest along the slope. Below, you can hear the rushing waters emptying from Garibaldi Lake.

The trail reaches a bridge at the west end of Garibaldi Lake where the scenery is breathtaking. There are views to the north of Polemonium Ridge and the Sphinx Glacier. The trail

Phyllis Munday

Phyllis Munday was a remarkable woman who became one of the most accomplished mountaineers in B.C. In 1924, she became the first Canadian woman to climb Mount Robson, the second highest peak in B.C. She also made 33 first ascents of other peaks including Blanshard Peak in Golden Ears and Foley Peak in the Chilliwack Valley.

Munday was born in 1894 in Ceylon and moved to Canada when she was seven. Her climbing career began with day hikes on Grouse and Seymour mountains. She went on to make many first ascents in the Coast Range with her husband Don, who was also an accomplished mountaineer.

The couple was a dynamic duo and they dominated exploration of the big ranges in the Coast Mountains north of Bridge River. They were responsible for much of the early exploration of Mount Waddington and the surrounding area. Mount Munday, located in the Cascade Range, is named after the couple. They were among the first ski mountaineers in southwest B.C. and they made ski ascents of a number of peaks around Garibaldi Park.

The following story illustrates Munday's determined character. In 1926, she and her husband went on an exploratory trip up the Mt. Waddington glacier. Munday became snowblind during the trip. For days, she put teabags on her eyes to ease the pain. The party continued to move camp, however, and she had to be led by hand as they advanced. Despite her pain and handicap, Munday continued to carry her share of the load.

Munday was active with the Girl Guides and was awarded the Bronze Cross, their highest decoration, for rescuing a boy who was injured in a fall on Grouse Mountain. She was admitted to the Order of Canada in 1973 and awarded an honorary Doctorate of Law from the University of Victoria. She was made Honorary President of the Alpine Club of Canada from 1971-90. Munday continued to hike well into her eighties and passed away in 1990.

History of Garibaldi Park

In 1860, British Royal Navy surveyor Captain George Richards was carrying out a survey of Howe Sound on board the Royal Navy survey ship, H.M.S. *Plumper*. Captain Richards saw Mt. Garibaldi (2,678 m) and named it after the 19th-century Italian hero Guiseppe Garibaldi.

Mt. Garibaldi was first climbed in 1907 by a party of six climbers led by A.T. Dalton. It was their third attempt to climb the peak and their success in doing so was quite a feat. In those days, there were no highways or park trails leading into the area. The group had to bushwhack through dense forest for more than 40 km just to get to the base of the peak. They also had the extra burden of carrying heavy and unreliable climbing gear.

Soon, summer climbing camps were being held at Garibaldi Lake. In 1912, the British Columbia Mountaineering Club initiated a campaign to save Garibaldi from being logged and mined. A trail was created by N.J. Gray in 1912 from Rubble Creek and the Cheakamus River Junction to the Black Tusk Meadows. In 1920, the provincial government set aside Garibaldi as a parkland reserve. The area to the north, which included Singing Pass and Wedge Mountain, was included in the park in 1928. Construction on Highway 99 was completed in 1965 and this opened up the area from Vancouver to Pemberton. Suddenly, the park became accessible to the average person and visitors have flocked here ever since.

Black Tusk

crosses over the bridge to the south shore, where you start to see clumps of white, pink and red heather growing on the slopes alongside. Just ahead to the east is the lovely Garibaldi Lake. The lake is surrounded by Mt. Price (2,049 m), Guard Mountain (2,185 m), Sentinal and Sphinx glaciers, Polemonium and Panorama ridges.

Garibaldi Lake was formed by the eruption of Mt. Price 12,000 years ago. It was created when a wall of lava formed in the area now known as The Barrier. The wall blocked the only outlet for water and this caused the valley above it to fill with water until the lake was formed. Look for a reddish volcanic ridge to the south where the trail follows the shore of the lake. This ridge is part of the lava flow from Price Mountain. Animals to look for around the lake include pika, squirrels and chipmunks. Fishing for rainbow trout in all three lakes is said to be good.

The Garibaldi Campground and ranger station are located 400 m straight ahead to the southeast. This campground is the more popular one, and it usually fills up first because of its location beside the lake. Sphinx

Glacier, Castle Towers (2,675 m) and Guard Mountain (2,185 m) can all be seen from the campground.

31. Camping, Cycling, Dogs

Camping: Camping is allowed at Taylor Meadows and the west end of Garibaldi Lake. Day shelters are also located at the campsites. A $7 per party per night camping fee is charged at the Taylor Meadows and Garibaldi Lake campgrounds. No fires are allowed and day shelters are located at both campgrounds.

Mountain biking: Cycling is not permitted.

Dogs: Dogs are not allowed.

Why is the Snow Red?

Often, pools of water will form on top of ice in warm weather. This allows snow algae to bloom and give off a red colour. Snow algae has adapted to grow at the freezing point and it begins to develop in May or June. Orange and green algae may occur at lower elevations.

Daisies

~ **32** ~

Black Tusk

32. Route (map, page 100)

Distance: 5 km one way, 5 hours, overnight or day hike from Garibaldi Lake
Rating:*** Intermediate
Route: Garibaldi Lake: 1,500 m
Black Tusk: 2,350 m, 5 km
Topographical maps: 92G/14, 92G/15, 92J/2

32. Trailhead

The park is located 97 km north of Vancouver, on the east side of Highway 99. Turn right off Highway 99 onto a road that leads to the Black Tusk Recreation Area. Continue for 2.5 km to the Rubble Creek Parking Lot.

32. Camping, Cycling, Dogs (see pg 104)

Black Tusk is a distinctive volcanic peak that stands out from all the other mountain peaks in the area due to its isolation and unique appearance. The Tusk is a popular landmark in the area and a perennial favorite among hikers. The trail to Black Tusk can be done easily as a day hike from Garibaldi Lake or Taylor Meadows. If you want to do the trail as a day hike from the Rubble Creek Parking Lot, plan on hiking a 28 km round trip, which takes about 10 hours.

To get to Black Tusk Peak, take the north (left) fork at Garibaldi Lake and continue over the bridge that crosses over the outlet creek. The trail switches back upward on the north side of the lake as it heads into the forest. As you climb higher, you can see alpine fir, white bark pine and yellow cedar. In the subalpine area, the trees become sparse, twisted and fewer in number. Ground cover is replaced by mountain ash, copper bush and mountain alder.

The trail soon comes out at the meadows, where it levels off. The meadows offer fabulous views of Black Tusk Peak to the north and wide expanses of flower-covered fields. Idyllic little ponds of water and streams are set among the flowers and white, red and pink heather line the trail. Some of the flowers that bloom in these meadows are white Sitka valerian, lupine, Indian paintbrush and glacier lilies, columbine, mountain daisy, phlox, pussytoes and western anemone. The best time for viewing the flowers is in late summer.

The meadows were a popular spot for summer climbing camps that were held from the 1920s to the 1940s. The camps were serviced by packhorses, which hauled in all the equipment and supplies. Today, restoration work is being undertaken to repair the meadows, which were worn with deep ruts by the packhorses.

Keep going through the meadows until the trail reaches a junction where there is an interpretive sign and outhouse. From the junction, take the northeast (right) trail for the Black Tusk Junction, Panorama Ridge and Helm Lake. The southwest (left) trail goes back down to the Taylor Campground, which is two km away.

After half a kilometre, the trail reaches the intersection for Black Tusk (2,315 m). This is

Indian Hellebore along the trail

where you take the north (left) fork and continue heading northeast up the steep trail. This trail is an alternate route into the Black Tusk area and it is also the quickest way to reach the Black Tusk. In summer, the lush meadows that surround the trail bloom with yellow cinquefoil, blue lupine, red heather and Indian paintbrush.

As you continue up the trail, lush meadow is replaced with rocky talus, disintegrating granite and little streams that cross the trail at intervals. The trail angles to the left and heads onto a narrow ridge high above the Cinder Flats and Helm Lake. This is a good rest spot as there is a fantastic view of Mount Garibaldi, Price, Table and Castle mountains, Mimulus and Black Tusk lakes, Panorama Ridge and the Fitzsimmons Range. The appropriately named Black Tusk Mountain is over 26 million years old and is the oldest feature in Garibaldi Park.

The Tusk is the basalt rock core that solidified in the pipe of a volcano that used to exist at this spot. The loose, deteriorating material that comprised the volcano has fallen away, leaving the towering peak. The landscape at the base of the Tusk is dominated by talus, and the bluffs that support the south sides of the Tusk are made of masses of lava.

Many people choose to end their hike on the ridge, but you may want to keep going and attempt to climb to the top of the Tusk. To climb the Tusk, simply follow the obvious rough path that heads up the southwest shoulder to the peak. The climb is very popular and fairly easy, so expect to see many people on the route. Over the years, this intensive use has caused the chimney to disintegrate rapidly, so exercise caution as the rock is unstable. The proper summit of the Tusk is actually the north peak, which is located across a gap and up a metre. Bring proper climbing gear if you want to attempt it and watch out for falling rock. The peak on the northeast ridge of the Tusk is known as "The Bishop's Mitre," and it has never been climbed.

From the top of the Tusk, there are superb views of Garibaldi Lake to the south, the Tantalus Range to the southwest, Helm Lake and Cinder Flats to the east.

A trail continues two km northwest from the Tusk to a microwave relay tower. This is an alternate way of accessing the Black Tusk area. Thre trail in from the microwave relay tower is shorter than the one from Garibaldi Lake; it heads to the base of Black Tusk. A steep, rough road leads down from the tower to Highway 99. To reach the tower from the highway, turn east onto a logging road 51 km north of Squamish. Take the right (south) fork and cross over the Cheakamus River. Continue for six km and then take the right (south) fork following the road south to the tower.

~ 33 ~

Panorama Ridge Trail

33. Route (map, page 100)

Distance: 6.5 km one way from Garibaldi Lake, 5 hours overnight or day hike from Lake Garibaldi
Rating:* Easy
Garibaldi Lake: 1,500 m
Panorama Ridge Junction: 1,706 m, 3.5 km
Panorama Ridge: 2,130 m, 6.5 km
Topographical maps: 92G/14, 92G/15, 92J/2

33. Trailhead

The park is located 97 km north of Vancouver, on the east side of Highway 99. Turn right off Highway 99 onto a road that leads to the Black Tusk Recreation Area. Continue for 2.5 km to the Rubble Creek Parking Lot. The trail begins at Garibaldi Lake.

33. Camping, Cycling, Dogs (see pg 104)

Panorama Ridge is a plateau that treats you to dazzling views of the Helm Glacier, Garibaldi Lake, Cinder Flats, Castle Towers Mountain, Phyllis Engine and Black Tusk. It lets you get close-up views of areas of the park that are normally only visible from higher elevations. At the top, you can spend hours contemplating the stately scenery that spreads out before you. This hike can be done as an overnight hike or as a long 31 km (round trip), 10 hour day hike from the Rubble Creek Parking Lot.

To go to Panorama Ridge, turn north (left) at the fork at Garibaldi Lake and cross over the bridge. The trail switches back up on the north side of the lake, heading into the forest. It soon pops out at the meadows, where it levels off. The meadows offer fabulous views of Black Tusk Peak to the north and wide expanses of flower-covered fields. Continue through the meadows along the heather-lined trail until it reaches an intersection. At the intersection,

take the northeast (right) trail for the Black Tusk Junction, Panorama Ridge and Helm Lake. The southwest (left) trail goes back down to the Taylor Campground.

The trail continues eastward and passes by the Black Tusk fork. As you walk along this section of trail, you get outstanding views of Garibaldi Lake, Panorama Ridge and flat-topped Table Mountain (2,020 m). The Table was created when volcanic action caused it to form inside a hole that was burned through the ice sheet. The mountain was climbed by Tom Fyles in 1917. He climbed it by himself as his two partners would not follow him because of the hazardous loose rock. In fact, the climb has seldom been attempted since for this very reason. After conquering the peak, Fyles climbed back down onto a ledge where his partners were waiting for him. They all had tea and then began their long trip out.

The trail skirts the hillside, going through very lush and wet meadows. The meadows are covered with wildflowers such as columbine, pink phlox, Indian paintbrush and Indian Hellebore. The large, green leaves of the poisonous Hellebore plant and the many cascading streams in the area make it look tropical.

As the trail continues, it passes the lovely waters of Black Tusk and Mimulus lakes, located

Pink Monkey Flower

The brilliant magenta-coloured flowers of this plant make it one of the prettiest to be found in southwestern B.C. The large, 30-55-mm-long flowers form a trumpet shape and have bright orange to yellow, hairy ridges on the bottom lobe. Insects follow these ridges when looking for nectar, thus pollinating the flowers. A monkey flower will close if you touch its two-lobed stigma.

The plant is found along streams and other wet areas and it grows to 30-32 cm tall. Pink monkey flower is also called Lewis' monkey flower and is named for Captain Meriweather Lewis of the Lewis and Clark Expedition of 1806.

below to the southeast. Many of the place names around Black Tusk, like Mimulus Lake, Parnassus Creek and Empetrum Ridge, were named by botanist John Davidson when he visited the area in 1912. The names came from floral species that he found in the area. Interestingly, he was accompanied on the trip by the BC Mountaineering Club, which was making its first trip into the Black Tusk area. The view from this part of the trail to Panorama Ridge junction is superb.

Soon, the trail reaches an intersection with the Panorama Ridge Trail, where you take the southeast (right) fork. The top of the ridge is an easy three km from here. The trail heads downward along heather meadows and the odd patch of snow as it passes around the east side of Black Tusk Lake. It then begins to climb up the ridge, passing through patches of trees and more heather until you are on open, rocky terrain. Continue upward along the bare windswept ridge, following cairns until the trail reaches the top of the first ridge. The trail to the second ridge goes over loose, slabby rock and is only a short distance away.

The sweeping views from the ridge are some of the finest in Garibaldi Park. You can see glaciers, meadows, lakes, volcanic debris and the surrounding mountain peaks. To the north are Black Tusk, with the Helm Glacier, Castle Towers Mountain, the Sphinx Glacier and Gentian Peak to the east. To the south are Garibaldi Lake and the Table. As you walk

along the ridge, if you can peel your eyes away from the scenery, look for the marmot and ptarmigan that live among the rocks.

~ 34 ~
Helm Lake

34. Route (map, page 100)

Distance: 10 km one way from Panorama Ridge Junction to Cheakamus Lake Trailhead, 7-8 hours, day hike or overnight
Rating: *** Easy
Route: Panorama Ridge Junction: 1,706 m
Cheakamus Lake Trailhead: 914 m, 10 km
Topographical maps: 92J/2, 92J/3, 92G/14

34. Trailheads

See the trailhead for Garibaldi Lake or Cheakamus Lake. You can either start from the Garibaldi Lake trailhead and hike until you reach Panorama Ridge Junction, or you can hike up from the Cheakamus Lake Trailhead (see hike #35). Add an hour or two in hiking time if you are beginning at Cheakamus Lake.

34. Camping, Cycling, Dogs (see pg 104)

Volcanoes in Garibaldi Park

British Columbia's geography has been influenced by volcanic activity and many of its mountains are former volcanic cones. The last volcanic eruption in B.C. ended in approximately 1750 at Nisga'a Memorial Lava Bed Provincial Park, near Terrace, B.C. The Garibaldi area is part of a larger area called the Pacific Ring of Fire. This area of volcanic activity stretches from the tip of South America to Alaska and along the coast of Asia.

Price Mountain, Black Tusk, The Table and Cinder Cone are all volcanic in origin. It is thought that the mountains formed into unusual shapes, like The Table, is a result of the interaction between hot volcanic rock and icy glaciers.

Mt. Price and Mt. Garibaldi are volcanoes that are recently extinct. Mount Price is a cluster of

cones in which four separate vents have been identified. The oldest cone is located at about 610 m east of the summit.

Mt. Garibaldi last erupted 11,000 years ago and the original core of the volcano is visible on the south slope of the mountain. Much of the volcanic cone was built on a glacial ice sheet and when the ice retreated, the side of the mountain collapsed into the valley. When you look at Mt. Garibaldi, you are looking at the core of a volcano that is usually hidden from view.

The Cinder Cone was created when a volcano erupted underneath the glacial ice. The ice shaped and moulded the molten rock when it began to rise. Some estimate that Cinder Cone erupted only a few centuries ago.

Helm Lake, Cinder Flats and Cinder Cone

Helm Lake is located immediately north of the Panorama Ridge Junction. A trail leads to the lake from the Panorama Ridge Junction, and from there you can continue on to the Helm Creek Trail, which is another access trail to Garibaldi Park. The Helm Creek Trail heads north along Helm Creek to the Cheakamus River and then northwest along the Cheakamus River to the Cheakamus Lake Trailhead.

From Panorama Ridge Junction, the trail meanders down to the south side of the Helm Lake, where you can see more volcanic features of the park. The sides of the hills are covered with black and red lava rock, white snowfields sit to the east, green vegetation grows on the western slopes and blue lakes rest in the middle.

The lake is surrounded by the black Cinder Flats and at the far end is the strange-looking Cinder Cone. Cinder Flats is comprised of lava flow that came out from beneath the Cinder Cone, and now it forms the floor of the Helm Creek Valley. The flow spreads northeast and ends on the slopes of the Cheakamus Valley.

Cinder Cone was once covered in glaciers, but they did not change its shape much. The tan, orange, black and red crater is wonderfully preserved and it is a fascinating place to explore. To reach it, cross the creek on the east side of Helm Lake and continue along the trail

for a few hundred metres. Then turn east (right) and climb the steep slope ahead. The hike takes about one hour from Helm Lake.

Another trail leads east from Helm Lake and goes through the cinder-walled valley between Cinder Cone to the Helm Glacier. The creek that runs through this valley is fed by the Helm Glacier. The trail goes right up to the base of the glacier, where you spend more time exploring it.

When mountaineers first came to this area in 1912, the Helm Glacier spilled down through the gap at the west end of Cinder Cone. The glaciers in Garibaldi grew to their greatest sizes in 1725 and 1860. However, records show that from 1910 to 1940, the glaciers were shrinking. This is due to the almost 2°C rise in mean annual temperatures during this time period. Today, the Helm Glacier is much smaller than it was in 1912. The area of the Helm Glacier is currently 3 km².

The main trail on the east side of Helm Lake continues north for 10 km down to the Cheakamus River. This trail goes past Helm Lake, where it crosses through the many braided tributaries that drain down from the Helm Glacier. Expect to get your feet wet in this section, especially in the spring when there is an excess of meltwater. You can either take your boots off and wade through icy water to

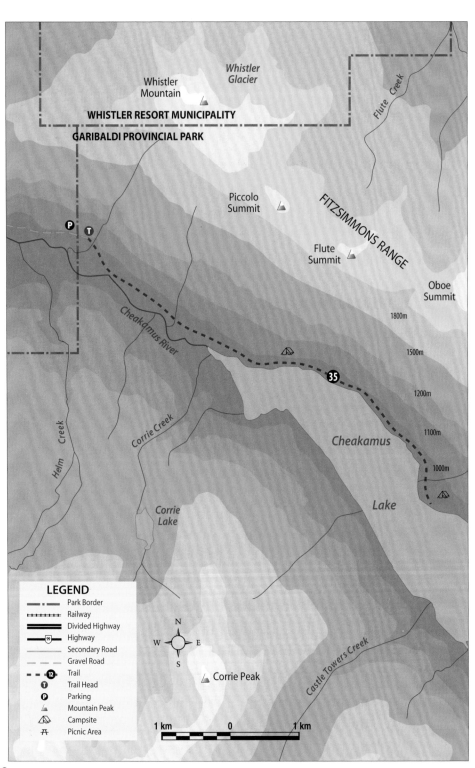

Whistler Glacier

Whistler Mountain

WHISTLER RESORT MUNICIPALITY

GARIBALDI PROVINCIAL PARK

Flute Creek

Piccolo Summit

FITZSIMMONS RANGE

Flute Summit

Oboe Summit

1800m

Cheakamus River

1500m

35

1200m

Corrie Creek

1100m

Helm Creek

Cheakamus

1000m

Corrie Lake

Lake

LEGEND

—··—··—	Park Border
┼┼┼┼┼	Railway
▬▬▬	Divided Highway
▬99▬	Highway
——	Secondary Road
— —	Gravel Road
– ·12· –	Trail
T	Trail Head
P	Parking
◬	Mountain Peak
⌂	Campsite
⊼	Picnic Area

N
W · E
S

Corrie Peak

Castle Towers Creek

1 km   0   1 km

Cheakamus Lake

cross the streams or you can try hopping across the sandbars and boulders.

As you continue north, there is a great view of the solitary Black Tusk Peak, which sits to the west. As you keep hiking down the trail, you will reach a wilderness campground that is located at the halfway point (1,555 m). This small wilderness campground is located in a lovely sub-alpine meadow alongside Helm Creek. Empetrum Ridge and Empetrum Peak (1,950 m) are located just to the west of the campground. The scramble to the top of the peak is easy and from there, you get a unique view of the north wall of Black Tusk.

From the campground, the trail goes down-hill through the forest, staying on the east (right) side of Helm Creek. Eventually, the trail drops down to the Cheakamus River, where you cross a newly built bridge that leads to the north side. After crossing the river, follow the trail that goes up the bank and into the forest. In a couple of minutes, you will come to a junction. Take the northwest (left) fork at the junction, as the right fork leads to Cheakamus Lake. From here it is an easy, level walk through a forest of massive trees to the Cheakamus Lake Parking Lot and the trailhead.

~ 35 ~

Cheakamus Lake

35. Route (map, page 110)

Distance: 6 km one way, 5 hours, day hike
Rating: ** Easy, early season hike
Trailhead: 914 m
Cheakamus Lake: 853 m, 3 km
Cheakamus Lake to Singing Creek: 853 m, 6 km
Topographical maps: 92J/2, 92G/15

35. Trailhead

Turn east off Highway 99, 56 km north of Squamish or 2.5 km south of Whistler onto a gravel road. Drive 0.5 km beyond the B.C. Railway crossing called Function Junction. Turn left at the first signed fork and drive for 3.2 km to the next fork. Turn left again and continue to the parking lot. The trail starts at the east end of the parking lot.

Cheakamus River bridge

This hike is located inside the western boundary of Garibaldi Provincial Park. It takes you through a very accessible, towering, old-growth forest to the glacier-fed Cheakamus Lake, where you can enjoy a variety of activities from fishing to kayaking. This short hike is a great one to bring small children on as there is virtually no elevation change and the trail is wide, smooth and well-maintained.

A pleasant, shaded forest of small trees greets the hiker at the trailhead. Head southeast into the forest and soon the Cheakamus River, Helm (2,134 m) and Corrie (2,073 m) mountains come into view. The trail passes over some small creek areas that are surrounded by skunk cabbage. Blackberries and falsebox are also common plants along the trail. Falsebox is a low, dense evergreen shrub that grows 20-80 cm tall and has fragrant, three to four mm-wide maroon flowers. The plant has oval, shiny leaves that are one to three cm long. Its branches provide winter food for deer and are often used as decorative greenery in floral arrangements.

The trail soon reaches a magnificent grove of giant red cedar, western hemlock and Douglas fir. These giant trees are amazing and seeing them is becoming a rare treat. The shaded, light undergrowth beneath the huge trees is very open and green with a resplendent moss cover.

The route continues straight ahead, passing intermittent patches of cow parsnip and several small streams on the banks of which the green, spiked stalks and leaves of devil's club dominate. In the swampy areas of the trail, the Douglas fir trees are replaced by huge red cedar and hemlock.

Soon the trail reaches a junction. Cheakamus Lake is approximately one km straight ahead from this point. If you want to hike 14.5 km to the Garibaldi Lake Campground, take the southwest (right) fork up the Helm Creek Trail. This leads up Desolation Pass to Taylor Meadows. The trail starts with a five-minute trek down to a bridge that goes over the Cheakamus River.

As the Cheakamus Lake Trail continues southeast, it passes by some small brooks with

35. Camping, Cycling, Dogs

Camping: Camping is allowed at the west end of Cheakamus Lake and at Singing Creek. Fires are prohibited.

Mountain biking: Cycling is permitted on the trail as far as Singing Creek. Bikes may not be taken across the Cheakamus River bridge on to the Helm Creek Trail.

Dogs: Dogs are not allowed.

Hoary marmots

glimpses of the blue-green Cheakamus River appearing to the right. Growing in the forest and along the river are twisted stalk, fungi, wild ginger and starflower.

As you reach the lake, you will come upon a large sign. This is this first campsite area and it is a great spot to have a picnic or to fish. The lake is stocked with rainbow trout and Dolly Varden char. In fact, the name Cheakamus means "those who fish with cedar rope nets." The fishing is said to be quite good in the early season and the lakeshore is a good place to watch for birds. These include common loon, barred owl, rufous hummingbird, northern flicker and varied thrush.

From this point on, you can keep hiking along the trail to Singing Creek, which is about an hour away. The trail continues straight ahead, skirting along the north edge of the lake. It passes by alternating areas of treed slopes and open avalanche paths. There are several small, cleared areas along the shore where you can camp or fish.

At about four km, the trail passes a wooden helicopter pad at the side of the lake. Then the route goes over a series of wooden foot bridges. Devil's club and cow parsnip grow thick and jungle-like in these swampy areas. Blackberry shrubs and alder trees grow around the small creek areas.

Soon, the trail skirts a rocky ridge that goes above the lake. Small clumps of orange Indian paintbrush and blue tansy grow in these semi-arid embankments.

The trail then returns to the lakeside and continues on. Soon, you get a view of the surrounding area. To the southeast is the McBride Range and to the northwest are Whistler and the Fitzsimmons Range.

Eventually, the trail passes through another old-growth area. Then it reaches Singing Creek where it ends at a large camping area. If you want to go down to the beach area, turn west (right) at the creek. A storm with hurricane-force winds blew through this area in 1987, resulting in many blown down trees. A small, secluded campsite on the shore is located about five minutes down a rough trail across Singing Creek.

~ 36 ~

Singing Pass and Russet Lake

36. Route (map, page 114)

Distance: 11.5 km one way; 4 hours one way, dayhike or overnight.
**Rating: ** Intermediate
Trailhead: 700 m
Singing Pass: 1,675 m, 7.5 km
Russet Lake: 1,875 m, 9.5 km
Topographical map: 92J/2

36. Trailhead

Head north on Highway 99 to Whistler Village. Turn east on Village Gate Boulevard and south (right) on Blackcomb Way. Look for the bus loop. The trailhead is the gravel road adjacent to the bus loop. Park in any day lot. If staying overnight in Singing Pass, stay in Lot 4.

Located in the northwest section of Garibaldi Provincial Park, this hike takes you along a forested trail to the alpine splendor of Singing Pass. The wildflowers in the meadows at the pass add splashes of colour to a landscape of glaciers, snowfields and mountain ranges. The panoramic views of the sparkling glaciers and green valleys beyond are unforgettable.

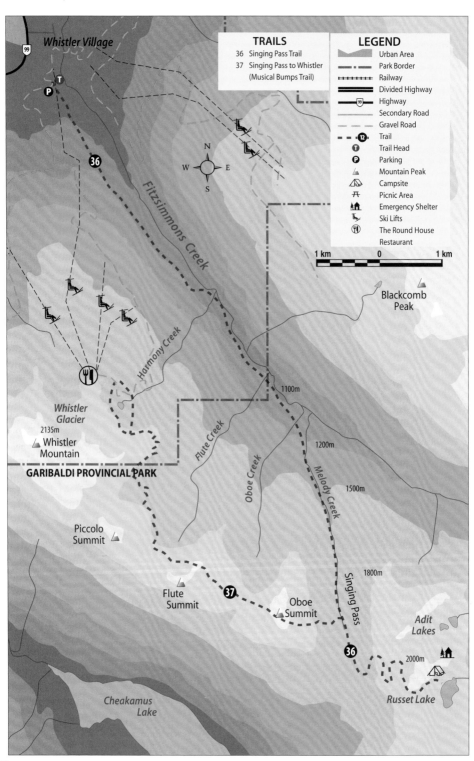

TRAILS

36 Singing Pass Trail
37 Singing Pass to Whistler
(Musical Bumps Trail)

LEGEND

	Urban Area
— · — · —	Park Border
+++++	Railway
━━━	Divided Highway
99	Highway
——	Secondary Road
– – –	Gravel Road
■ ■ 12	Trail
T	Trail Head
P	Parking
⛰	Mountain Peak
⛺	Campsite
🎋	Picnic Area
🏠	Emergency Shelter
🎿	Ski Lifts
🍴	The Round House Restaurant

1 km   0   1 km

Whistler Village

Whistler Glacier
2135m
Whistler Mountain

GARIBALDI PROVINCIAL PARK

Piccolo Summit

Flute Summit

Oboe Summit

Fitzsimmons Creek

Harmony Creek

Flute Creek

Oboe Creek

Melody Creek

Singing Pass

1100m
1200m
1500m
1800m
2000m

Blackcomb Peak

Adit Lakes

Russet Lake

Cheakamus Lake

This moderately graded trail is well maintained and smooth.

To start the hike take the gravel road and keep left as you pass by a water tower. The Whistler Control Road is the road that goes

White-Tailed Ptarmigan

Look for these members of the grouse family above the timberline and in alpine meadows. You may have to look carefully to spot one, as their feathers provide excellent camouflage. Ptarmigan plumage changes with the seasons and they turn pure white in winter. In summer, their feathers turn a mottled brown and black colour. Their belly and wings remain white year round. The male Ptarmigan is distinguished by a red comb over his eye in spring.

These ground-dwelling birds prefer running to flying. However, they will resort to flying in short bursts in times of danger. Ptarmigans grow to 30 cm and feed mostly on insects and seeds.

right. You will reach a parking lot where the old trailhead used to be. Take the trail at the south end of the parking lot and head into the forest. The trail steepens and heads southeast, following Fitzsimmons Creek, which flows in the valley to the left. This part of the trail was originally a gold mining and logging road. The route remains in a shaded forest and occasionally gives glimpses of Blackcomb Peak and Decker Mountain. This is not the most exciting part of the hike, but the easy grade makes it enjoyable nonetheless.

The trail continues past stands of thin, tall lodgepole pine that are covered with large, hanging lichen. The forest floor is fairly open and covered with moss, ferns, huckleberries and red raspberries. Birds you may see in the forest include hummingbirds, woodpeckers, blue jays, northern pintail, American wigeon and jays.

The route soon passes an old, wood-framed entrance to a mine. Beside it along the ridge are rusty train tracks. You can walk a short distance into the mine, but it has been blocked off. Just past the mine is a washed-out area where a creek cascades down a cliff.

At 1.5 km, you reach the end of the old road where there is a signed fork. This is the Garibaldi Park boundary, and mountain biking is not allowed from this point on. Take the east (left) fork for Singing Pass. The grade of the trail levels off here and becomes easier. As you hike, keep an eye out for the squirrels, weasels and deer that live in the forest. Also, look for wild strawberries, columbine and dwarf dogwood along the trail.

Devil's Club

Devil's club has a terrible reputation among hikers in southwestern B.C. The reason becomes obvious if you look under the shrub's large leaves, which grow to 20-25 cm across. The leaves look like a maple on top but are riddled with sharp, stiff spines underneath. These spines extend all the way down the thick stems of the shrub. You won't soon forget the experience if you ever come into contact with these spines. The spines cause terrible pain and inflammation of the skin.

Devil's club is found in the undergrowth of damp forests at low elevations on western

slopes. It grows to three m and produces greenish flowers that grow upward from the sides of its stems. These flowers produce shiny, red berries that are quite pretty.

As you walk over the bridge at Flute Creek, you can feel the refreshing spray of the creek as it cascades down the hillside. Blackcomb Peak is still visible to the left, and as you move on, more views of the valley start to open up.

After Flute Creek, the trail moves away from Fitzsimmons Creek. Forest now surrounds the trail on both sides as it heads southward up past Oboe Creek and then up along Melody Creek. Soon, Melody Creek appears and you start to see open slopes to the east. The vegetation starts to change from sparse and dry to lush and wet. Suddenly, streams, ponds and brooks appear everywhere with slide alder, blue lupines and sunflowers growing in profusion.

As the forest is left behind and meadows open up, clumps of red, pink and white heather start to appear. Finally, you can see wide open areas of green meadow, snowfields and the surrounding mountains. The sight of these meadows is a delightful change from the forest.

A trail branches off the main one to the west (right) soon after you enter the meadows.

This trail is an alternate route to and from Singing Pass that heads west over Oboe, Flute and Piccolo summits, ending back at Whistler. The main trail continues heading eastward and down to the Pass. Though they are rarely seen, coyotes, bobcats and black bears live in this area. Mountain goats can often be seen high on the mountain slopes.

The information board at Singing Pass describes the flowers that can be seen in this area. The alpine meadows are filled with a wide array of wildflowers that include orchids, lupines, hellebores, mimulus, Indian paintbrush and mountain daisies. Although these flowers are

36. and 37. Camping, Cycling, Dogs

Camping: Camping is permitted at the northwest end of Russet Lake, and a shelter is located there.

Mountain biking: Mountain bikes are not allowed.

Dogs: Dogs are not allowed.

Big Trees

Certain areas of B.C.'s coastal rainforest are known for the monumental size of their trees. The trees in mature Pacific rain forests grow to an average 60 m high with giant trees often growing as high as 90 m. In contrast, trees that reach 30 m are considered tall in most forests. Douglas fir can live for 10-12 centuries, while Western red cedar can live up to 15 centuries.

The Coastal Western Hemlock Zone, as this area is called, is the

best tree-growing region in Canada. Trees here grow to amazing size because of the long growing season, the abundance of water and the fact that conifers are a long-living group. Fire also rarely burns the wet forests. These factors combine with the trees' competition for sunlight to produce amazingly huge trees.

These are some of the biggest trees in southwestern B.C.:

- B.C.'s tallest Douglas fir is 92 m and is located near the Puntledge River in the southeastern corner of Vancouver Island's Strathcona Park.

- The greatest diameter on record for a Douglas fir is 6.4 m. This tree grew near Westholme, Southern Vancouver Island. When it fell over as a result of butt rot in 1913, it was estimated to be 1,500 years old.

- The tallest known tree in Canada and the tallest known Sitka spruce in the world is the 95-m-tall "Carmanah Giant." This tree was discovered in 1988 and is located in Carmanah Pacific Provincial Park, on the south side of Vancouver Island.

- The single largest Western red cedar on record was found on Meares Island near Tofino. It has a circumference of 20 m.

- Canada's oldest known tree was a yellow cedar found in the Caren Range of the Sechelt Peninsula, 80 km northwest of Vancouver. The stump revealed 1,835 annual growth rings. The tree was destroyed by logging.

tough enough to grow in such a harsh environment, they are very delicate. Please stay on the paths to avoid damaging them.

The panoramic view at Singing Pass is spectacular; mountain peaks, glaciers and snowfields take over the scenery where the flowers leave off. To the north is the Spearhead Range and to the south is the Fitzsimmons Range, with the massive Cheakamus Glacier dominating the view.

The trail continues to Russet Lake from the northeast side of the meadows. This part of the trail offers the most spectacular view, and it should not be missed. The panoramic view becomes more magnificent with every step you take up the gentle switchbacking trail. There are more valleys, snowfields and peaks to gaze at, and you can now see Castle Towers, Mount Davidson, Black Tusk, Gentian Pass and Corrie Ridge. The turquoise waters of Cheakamus Lake look like a little puddle sitting in the valley to the right.

Continue following the trail along the ridge as it winds northward on its final switchback. Clumps of pink phlox and heather line the trail here, and at the top, there is a view of

Fissile Peak—a volcanic-looking mountain covered in black, loose rock. If you have time, you may want to tackle the fun and easy scramble up Fissile Peak. At this point, you can also see the tiny Russet Lake and the hut.

To continue to the hut, follow the trail that goes down the slope to the north side of Russet Lake. Look for pikas, marmots and ptarmigan as you walk along the lakeshore. The red Himmelsbach Hut sits at the northwest end of the lake, to the west of Overlord Glacier. This A-frame hut was erected in the summer of 1968 by the British Columbia Mountaineering Club. The wooden hut has sleeping room for approximately 10-15 people. This is a great area to spend some time exploring. The hut is very popular with backcountry skiers in the winter.

~ 37 ~

Singing Pass to Whistler Mountain

37. Route (map, page 114)

Distance: 9.5 km one way, 7 hours one way or overnight
Rating: *** Intermediate
Route: Singing Pass: 1,675 m
Roundhouse Lookout: 1,837 m, 9.5 km
Topographical maps: 92J/2

37. Trailhead

See trailhead for Singing Pass (hike #36). The trail begins at the eastern base of Oboe Summit in Singing Pass. For the Whistler trailhead, head east off Highway 99 onto Village Gate Boulevard and continue for 0.4 km to a T intersection. Go left on Blackcomb Way, then right into the parking lot. The gondola is across Blackcomb Way. Take the gondola up to the Roundhouse Lookout.

Arctic Lupine

One of the more memorable sights you may come across when hiking is an alpine meadow filled with purple lupines. Lupines are perennial plants that grow to 60 cm tall. These flowers can be found in open areas at all elevations, but they appear mostly at middle to subalpine elevations. Lupines have sweet-smelling, pea-like flowers that bloom from June to August. The flowers grow in clusters or long spikes on the plant stem. When the flowers have finished blooming, they become hairy seed pods.

The leaves of the plant are thin and radiate out from the stem. During the day, the heads of the leaflets rotate to follow the movement of the sun. At night, the leaflets fold down.

Singing Pass

If you want to hike out of the Singing Pass area by a different route, this is the trail to take. Alternatively, you can begin this hike at Whistler Mountain and continue all the way to Singing Pass. Either way, you will go cross sweeping alpine terrain that is surrounded by stunning scenery. From Singing Pass, the trail passes by Obee, Flute and Piccolo mountains as it makes its way toward the world-famous terrain of Whistler Mountain.

At the end of the hike, you can treat yourself to a gondola ride down Whistler Mountain or continue hiking down the 1,157-m descent along the ski runs. Bring plenty of water as there are no water sources along the dry ridge top. If you decide to take the this trail, which is also called the Musical Bumps Trail, out from Singing Pass, you will have to arrange for transport back from the Whistler trailhead.

This trail goes northwest from Singing Pass to Whistler Mountain via Oboe, Flute and Piccolo summits. The trail begins on the west side of Singing Pass at the base of Oboe Summit. The trail is hard to make out, but if you know it is there, you will have no problem finding it. To hike it from Singing Pass, follow the trail up the steep climb as it winds its way up the east side of Oboe Summit. The trail passes through lovely colourful flowers and lush vegetation as it heads upward. From the summit, the trail

becomes even harder to see, so follow the rock cairns as you cross the rocky and grassy landscape downward into the pass between Oboe and Flute Summit. The trail then goes up Flute Summit, from which there are great views of Cheakamus Lake to the southwest and the Spearhead Range to the northeast.

Whistler Resort

The Singing Pass Trail lies on the outskirts of the world-famous Whistler Resort. Whistler Village is located 100 km north of Vancouver, just off Highway 99. The Whistler area includes Whistler and Blackcomb mountains, which have been developed with lifts, gondolas and ski runs. Over 5,000 people work and live in Whistler year round. The area began as a summer resort, but it soon became popular for its winter activities. Today, it attracts summer and winter visitors in equal numbers.

The village offers a wide range of activities and amenities that include retail shops, a golf course, residential areas (condominiums, estates, hotels), restaurants and a dynamic nightlife.

Whistler has a stellar reputation as a world-class ski resort. It offers downhill skiing, heli-skiing, snowboarding and cross-country skiing. Ice climbers tackle pitches on Blackcomb mountain. In summer, mountain biking, glacier skiing, mountaineering, fishing and hiking are popular activities.

Continue down Flute Summit and then up again along the east slope of Piccolo Summit. From there, the trail goes down again, passing Piccolo Summit and continuing down to the small idyllic pond called Burnt Stew Lake. This beautiful sub-alpine spot, which is surrounded by groves of Englemann spruce and subalpine fir, is a good place to take a break before continuing on. Keep an eye out for hoary marmots, which are hard at work collecting grass to store in their in their winter shelters. When you are ready to continue, hike over a rockslide and up the east side of Whistler Mountain. Continue along the well-marked rocky path through open, alpine meadow and head downward to a signed junction.

At the junction, you can take either fork, as they both lead to the Harmony Lake Trail. As you walk along the trail, you can see the Fitzsimmons Valley below Blackcomb Peak and the peaks that make up the Spearhead Range. Walk down the trail until you reach the

Taylor Campground Option

The Taylor Campground and meadows can be reached by taking the north (left) fork at the six-km mark on the Rubble Creek Trail. However, this is not the only access trail to the area. Farther on, there are other branches in the trails that also lead to the meadow and campground.

The trail climbs up through the forest and pops out at the open expanse of meadows. The meadows surround the campsite to the north and east. This is a good spot to look at the alpine flowers like white rein orchids, lupines, grass of Parnassus, fireweed and mimulus. The meadows are also rich with fungi that include boletuses, coral mushrooms, puff-balls, Russulas and Amanitas.

Shrews live in these meadows, too. They look like mice but have sharp little noses. Amazingly, they must eat more than their weight in food every day and can starve to death in a few hours. Other animals that live in the park include snowshoe hare, mountain goat, brown bat, pine marten and northwestern chipmunk. Grizzlies, black bears and mountain goats also live here but they are rarely seen. We were lucky to see a large marmot sunning itself underneath the maintenance cabin at the ranger station in the Taylor Campground.

Whistler Mountain Express Gondola. From here, you can either continue walking down on the ski trails or take the gondola to the bottom. If you want to take the lift, make sure it is operating by calling Whistler Mountain Ski Corporation at 664-5614 from Vancouver or (604) 932-3434 before you begin your hike.

~ 38 ~
Rainbow Lake

38. Route

Distance: 8 km one way, day hike, 6 hours
Rating: * Intermediate
Trailhead: 620 m
Rainbow Lake: 1,470 m, 8 km
Topographical map: 92J/2, 92J/3

38. Trailhead

Drive south on Highway 99. Just before Whistler, turn left onto Alta Lake Road and drive for 7 km. Parking is just past Twenty-one Mile Creek beside the road.

This hike lets you explore more alpine terrain in the Whistler area. The trail begins on the west side of the Alta Lake road and follows the south bank of the Twenty-one Mile Creek until it meets a new, improved trail. It continues past a gated watershed building and a slide area to another gate. Continue through an old forest, along bridges and boardwalks to sub-alpine meadows. There, the trail crosses the creek and reaches the lake. Camping is not recommended at the lake as this is the watershed supply for Whistler.

From the lake, you have the option to make some side trips. Rainbow Mountain is an easy climb. Just follow the lake to the end, where you go up the ridge south of the peak. To reach Gin and Tonic Lakes, turn left off the main trail before it crosses Twenty-one Mile Creek and continue up the valley to the west.

Pemberton

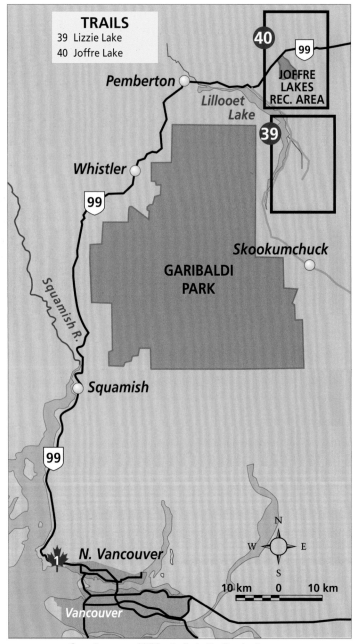

TRAILS
39 Lizzie Lake
40 Joffre Lake

Overview map of hiking trails in the Pemberton area

Lizzie Lake

L ocated 35 km north of Whistler on Highway 99, the fertile Pemberton Valley is a rural community set in a pastoral valley surrounded by rugged mountain peaks. The valley is used as a starting point for hikers destined for the Joffre Lakes/Peak area, one of the finest sub-alpine

settings in the Coastal Mountains. It also provides access to the Stein Valley.

This area is reached by heading north on Highway 99 and then east on Duffy Lake Road. The Duffy Lake Road has only recently been paved, thus opening up an area to which access was previously limited. Whistler Village is the major centre in this region and all accommodation, services and supplies are available. Basic supplies are also available at the villages of Pemberton and Mount Currie.

An information kiosk is located at the Joffre Lakes Trailhead. Wilderness camping and forest access sites are located in the area. A private overnight shelter is open for public use on the Lizzie Lake Trail at the alpine area, and a hostel is located at Whistler.

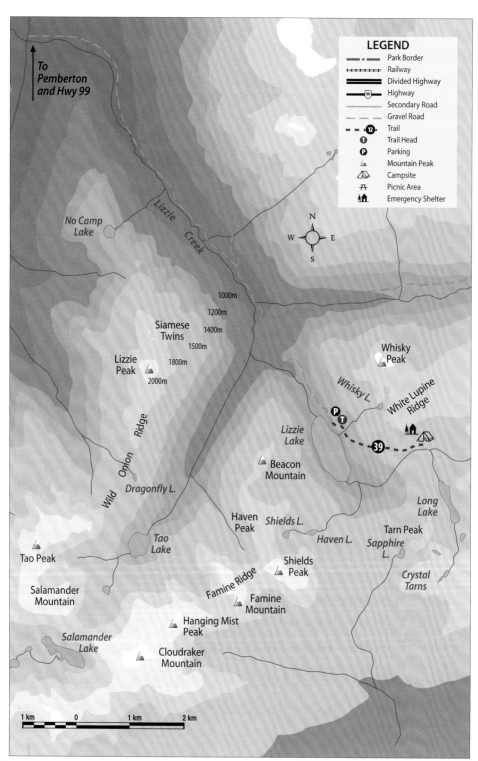

To Pemberton and Hwy 99

LEGEND

- — ·· — Park Border
- ┼┼┼┼┼ Railway
- ━━━━ Divided Highway
- ━━(95)━ Highway
- —— Secondary Road
- – – – Gravel Road
- ● ● ●(12) Trail
- T Trail Head
- P Parking
- ◭ Mountain Peak
- ⌂ Campsite
- 🛪 Picnic Area
- ⌂ Emergency Shelter

No Camp Lake

Lizzie Creek

N
W E
S

1000m
1200m
Siamese Twins
1400m
1500m
Lizzie Peak
1800m
2000m

Whisky Peak

Whisky L.

White Lupine Ridge

P T

39

Lizzie Lake

Beacon Mountain

Onion Ridge

Wild

Dragonfly L.

Tao Lake

Haven Peak

Shields L.

Haven L.

Long Lake

Tarn Peak

Sapphire L.

Tao Peak

Salamander Mountain

Shields Peak

Famine Ridge

Famine Mountain

Crystal Tarns

Hanging Mist Peak

Salamander Lake

Cloudraker Mountain

1 km   0   1 km   2 km

~ 39 ~

Lizzie Lake

39. Route (map, page 112)

Distance: 2.5 km to the cabin (one way); 3 hours, day hike
Rating: ** Easy
Trailhead: 1,305 m
Boulder field: 1,590 m, 1.6 km
Cabin: 1,650 m, 2.5 km
Topographical map: 92J/1

39. Trailhead

From Pemberton, turn right at the T junction and drive to the town of Mount Currie. Turn right at the Lillooet Lake Road turnoff. Drive to the Lillooet Lake Lodge and turn right on the In-SHUCK-ch Forest Service Road. The road turns to gravel at this point. Follow the road for 16 km along the lakeshore. Turn left 600 m past the Lizzie Bay Recreation Site. Drive 10.9 km up the road, follow the signs for Lizzie Lake Recreation Site and stay right at all road forks. The parking lot is lined by logs and is signed. The trail is marked with orange markers.

This short hike provides quick access to a pristine alpine setting located between Lizzie Lake and Stein Lake. The trail leads to a rustic cabin and camping site which can serve as a base point if you wish to explore further the Stein Divide and Upper Stein Valley. The hike leads from the lake to a beautiful rockslide area that is surrounded by mountains and glaciers. It ends at an open alpine meadow.

The trail starts at Lizzie Lake, where the fishing for small rainbow trout is said to be good. The route goes into the woods and comes to a fork after 100 m. The right fork leads south to the lakeshore and the left fork leads southeast up to the cabin. Continuing on the left fork, the trail remains flat as it winds its way along the side of the lake. It passes through blown-down trees, logs and roots, which makes it confusing to follow. Once you are past the windfall area, the route passes through a number of small streams and muddy areas as it ascends parallel to the lake.

Soon, the lake is left behind as the trail passes by a small waterfall and a rocky slope. Here, it becomes steeper as it continues upward. The trail then leaves the forest and passes a rockslide area where you can see the Lillooet and Pacific mountain ranges. At this point, the view of a dramatic landscape of

39. Camping, Cycling, Dogs

Camping: Campsites are located at Lizzie Lake and around the cabin area.
Mountain biking: Cycling is not appropriate but there is some great, dusty cycling on the forest roads on the approach to the trailhead. Look out for logging trucks.
Dogs: Dogs are allowed.

Pika

A Pika is a cute, round and tiny (less than 20 cm long) mammal that is a close relative of the rabbit. It has a gray coat and a tiny tail. Pikas inhabit alpine areas between grassy meadows and rockslides where their colour allows them to blend in easily. They also live near sea level on the coast of B.C.

Pikas' shrill "peeep" warns others of the presence of people and predators. The cry is also a territorial warning to other pikas. They eat grass, leaves, lichens and wildflowers. They do not hibernate, so they must stash food away for the winter.

A pika gathers vegetation in the summer and then dries it, like hay, in the sun before storing it. The construction of the haystack is an individual project that each pika undertakes. Pikas are hard workers, as they may make more than a hundred foraging trips each day in order to ensure that they have enough vegetation. Hawks, eagles, owls and members of the weasel family are the pika's principal predators.

ponds, a waterfall and a massive rockslide area is revealed.

The trail skirts along the north side of the rockslide and winds in and out among boulders. This part of the trail is known as the "Gates of Shangri-la." Two rock-strewn cliffs hover high above on the north and south sides of the trail, while before you is a gushing creek and the Arrowhead and Tynemouth Mountains.

The trail becomes a scramble through and then down the rockslide. Look for some obscure red dots painted on the boulders to guide you through the rocks. Pretty clumps of purple phlox are scattered among the rocks, lending colour to this barren area. Lichen and heather grow in the surrounding meadows.

Once you are through the rockslide, the trail continues to follow the creek where it levels off and re-enters the open forest along the creek's north side. Soon, it passes another very short boulder section close to the creek. To the south are Tarn Peak and Intern Ridge, where more rockslide areas begin halfway down the ridge.

As you follow the creek, the cabin will appear where the creek divides into two different branches. At this point, the rockslide area is still to the south; to the north there are forested mountain slopes down which a small waterfall cascades. Engelmann spruce, also known as

krummholtz, can be seen growing on the surrounding slopes. This tree is found at elevations above 1,100 m. It is often dwarfed so that it can remain insulated within the snowpack, thus protected from the wind during winter. This alpine area makes for easy travelling if you wish to explore it further.

Gray Jay

The Gray jay, also known as the whiskey-jack or Canada jay, has fluffy gray feathers, a dark neck patch and a white face. It is common in coniferous forests where it feeds largely on conifer seeds. This bird is very curious and bold. It will frequently visit hikers and campsites looking for food scraps. If you start to feed the bird, you may be surprised to find yourself suddenly surrounded by others. It is best to let the birds find their own food.

Cosy Cabin

The cabin at the end of the Lizzie Lake Trail was built in 1968 by Tom Anderson, M. Juri, D. Nickerson and G. Richardson. Although the cabin was built with their own funds, it is open to the public.

This impressive log cabin has a stove, a wooden table and chairs, makeshift sink, bunk beds and a loft that can sleep about eight people. Someone with a sense of humour provided additional furnishings: a phone and thermostat (not

working, of course). The wood on the side of the building is for cabin use only. Use other wood and debris for campfires outside. A spiffy "A" frame latrine is located on the side of the cabin.

Log books that make great bedside reading can be found in the cabin. The books are filled with interesting stories and the drawings of people who have used the cabin over the years.

~ 40 ~

Joffre Lakes

This trail winds past avalanche slopes and three beautiful, turquoise glacial lakes to spectacular views of the Matier Glacier and surrounding mountain peaks. The trail offers

40. Route (map, page 126)

Distance: 6 km one way; 4-5 hours, day hike
Rating: ** Easy
Trailhead: 1,245 m
First Lake: 1,240 m, 1 km
Second Lake: 1,535 m, 4 km
Third Lake: 1,600 m, 5.5 km
Rock pile: 1,675 m, 6.5 km
Topographical maps: 92J/7, 92J/8

40. Trailhead

Drive north on Highway 99 for 160 km past the villages of Whistler and Pemberton. Turn right at the Pemberton T intersection and continue to the town of Mount Currie. At the town, turn east at the Duffey Lake Road and continue for 23 km to the BC Parks Joffre Lakes Recreation Area Trail parking lot. The trail is marked with pink markers.

40. Camping, Cycling, Dogs

Camping: Wilderness walk-in camping is located at Upper Joffre Lake.
Mountain biking: No cycling.
Dogs: Dogs are allowed and must be on a leash.

quick access to the bottom of Matier Glacier and to the snowfields that surround it. At the end of the trail, you can wander up the talus slope to snowfields at the foot of the glacier, or you can sit back and admire the scenery as you watch mountaineers pick their way up the side of the mountain.

The first part of the trail is well maintained with a smooth surface of small pebbles. From the parking lot, the trail heads southeast into the forest, where it forks after approximately five minutes. Take the southwest (right) fork onto the Upper Joffre Lakes Trail. The trail leading south (straight ahead) continues for another five minutes to a viewpoint of Lower Joffre Lake.

The route winds briefly through a swampy area, where you get your first view of the Matier Glacier towering above the beautiful blue-green lake. Surrounding the trail are moisture-loving lodgepole pine, Labrador tea and cranberry shrubs.

The trail goes over a series of small creeks and wooden bridges along the south end of Lower Lake. Douglas fir, cedar, small spruce and a sparse underbrush dominate the forest. The damper areas are lush with a profuse growth of devil's club and ferns. The trail starts to head upward at the far end of the first lake and keeps ascending as it moves away from the lake. The view is limited and the trail becomes rougher at this point as it winds through stretches filled with boulders and tree roots.

Head downward toward Joffre Creek, which is to the east. Continue through a marshy environment filled with spiked devil's club and then upward over boulders through a rockfall area. At this point, the forest finally opens up and you get a view to the left of Mount Chief Pascall and an avalanche slope. If you look back, you can see the Lillooet Cayoosh Range.

The trail continues southeast past a series of rockslide and forested areas. It runs parallel to the creek and follows it upward. This is a good spot to fill your water bottles. The route then steepens and begins to move away from the creek, once again passing through a boulder-filled rockslide area. Keep an eye out for wildlife like mule and Columbia blacktail deer, black bears and mountain goats that frequent the area.

The trail then turns left and crosses over a log bridge where the mountains and glacier can be seen on the right. This valley is U-shaped, which means that it was once intensely glaciered. The surface of the valley is overlain with colluvial deposits that were formed when glaciers scoured the mountains. There are also enormous deposits of glacial silt and large, lateral moraines at the base of the mountains.

Soon, you will come to the small, beautifully

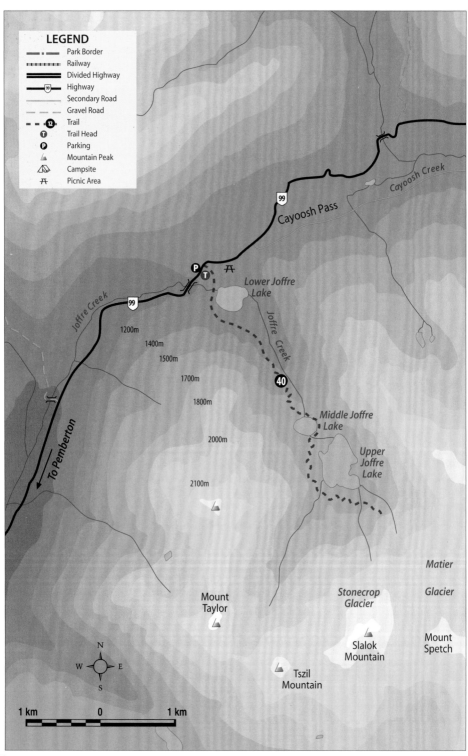

LEGEND

— · — · —	Park Border
▪▪▪▪▪▪▪	Railway
═══════	Divided Highway
══**99**══	Highway
————	Secondary Road
– – – –	Gravel Road
– ■**12**–	Trail
T	Trail Head
P	Parking
◣	Mountain Peak
◭	Campsite
⛬	Picnic Area

Cayoosh Creek

99 Cayoosh Pass

P **T** ⛬

Lower Joffre Lake

Joffre Creek

99 Joffre Creek

1200m

1400m

1500m

1700m

1800m

40 Middle Joffre Lake

2000m

Upper Joffre Lake

2100m

To Pemberton

Matier Glacier

Mount Taylor

Stonecrop Glacier

Slalok Mountain

Mount Spetch

Tszil Mountain

N
W ✦ E
S

1 km   0   1 km

Joffre Lake

The Colour of Glacial Lakes

Glacial lakes owe their exquisite colouring to the hard work of the glaciers that created them. Glaciers grind rock into rubble and sediment of various sizes. They then dump this rock at the lower end of the glacier where the ice melts. The melting water transports the sediment to the lake. When it empties into the lake, the larger sediment drops out of the flow to form a delta. The rest of the sediment is distributed throughout the lake water, where it eventually settles at the bottom.

The smallest of these particles, however, remain suspended in the water. These particles are called glacial silt. Glacial silt reflects the green and blue spectra of light, giving the water its enchanting colour. As the glacier-melt season progresses, the density of glacial silt in the water increases. This makes the lake colours even more saturated and rich.

Ice Worms

Glaciers are the most unlikely places in which you would expect to find any kind of life form. This is why it is so amazing to find that ice worms live there. Next time you are on a glacier, stop and try to spot some. Look closely at the surface of the glacier for what looks like fine, dark hairs that are moving.

In the summer, ice worms move near the glacier surface. Look for them on cloudy days or after the sun has left the area. They often gather around patches of red algae. It is believed that red algae is a food source for the worms. If you are gathering snow for water, look for areas where there are no ice worms.

Ice worms are the only animals known to live in snow and glaciers. There are several species, and they range in colour from yellow to reddish brown. They are less than one mm in diameter and three mm long.

coloured Middle Joffre Lake where there are some campsites. The trail winds along the east side of the lake to the south end, where several channels of water drain from the third lake, which is located 65 m above. Cross over the log bridges to the west side and continue through some large boulders. It is easy to lose the trail at this point, so look for the pink trail markers to the right of Joffre Creek.

Continue switching back up the hillside, following the creek. The trail winds away from the creek and skirts along a bouldered gully located to the west (right) where shrub alder, salmonberry, stink current, moss heather and alpine fireweed grow. As the trail leaves the gully, spectacular views unfold of the Upper Joffre Lake, glaciers and the Joffre Group mountains.

The trail continues along the west side of Upper Lake, where there are spots for camping. It then heads over talus to just below the glacier, where you may see hoary marmots and rocky mountain pika. This alpine area is very fragile, as the shallow soil is only held in place by the root systems of small

plants like lichen, liverwort and heather.

A fantastic view of the hanging Matier Glacier unfolds from this spot. You can see crevasses, couloirs and blue chunks of ice that have broken off the glacier and fallen below.

Waterfalls can be seen cascading down the rocky cliffs of Mount Spetch. On the south side of Matier Glacier is Stonecrop Glacier with Slalok Mountain (2,650 m) towering over it. Mount Spetch (2,590 m) sits to the east of Slalok Mountain overlooking Matier Glacier. Mount Matier (2,770 m) is the highest peak between Lillooet and Duffey lakes and it is located behind the glacier. Joffre Peak (2,710 m) sits to the north side of Matier Glacier. Often, climbers can be seen moving up on the moraine or glaciers, as this is a popular spot for mountain-eering.

Mountain goat

Golden Ears Provincial Park

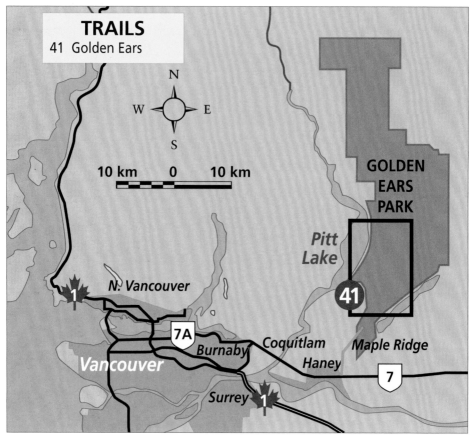

TRAILS
41 Golden Ears

N
W —⊕— E
S

10 km   0   10 km

GOLDEN
EARS
PARK

Pitt Lake

41

N. Vancouver

1

7A

Coquitlam   *Maple Ridge*

Burnaby

Vancouver   *Haney*

7

Surrey 1

Overview of hiking trails in Golden Ears Provincial Park

View of Alouette Valley from Golden Ears Trail

L ocated 48 km east of Vancouver, Golden Ears Provincial Park makes up the southern boundary of Garibaldi Provincial Park. This park extends 55 km north from its southern boundary near Maple Ridge, through mountain wilderness to the southern boundary of Garibaldi Provincial

Park. At one time, this 55,594 ha park was joined with Garibaldi Park. Travel between the two parks is made almost impossible by a wall of rugged, almost impenetrable mountain peaks and steep valleys.

The park is named after the Golden Ears peaks, which glisten like gold when the sunlight falls on their snowy summits. The twin peaks are located on Mount Blanshard near the park's western border. This park has lakes, mountains, rainforest, waterfalls and 80 km of hiking trails.

Highway 7 on the north side of the Fraser River will take you to this area. Passenger bus service is available to Maple Ridge. Maple Ridge (30 km east of Vancouver) is the closest major centre and supplies, accommodation and services are available here.

Two very large campgrounds are located in the park near Alouette Lake. Wilderness campsites are scattered throughout the park. A mountain shelter is located on Golden Ears Trail just before the peak. A ranger station/information centre is located soon after you enter the park, near Mike Lake. There are no hostels in the area.

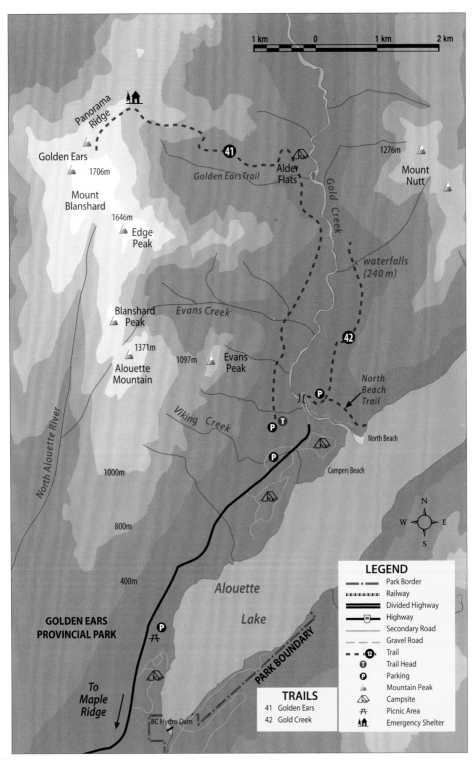

1 km 0 1 km 2 km

Panorama Ridge

Golden Ears
1706m

Mount Blanshard

1646m
Edge Peak

Blanshard Peak

1371m
Alouette Mountain

1097m
Evans Peak

41

Golden Ears Trail

Alder Flats

1276m

Mount Nutt

Gold Creek

waterfalls (240 m)

Evans Creek

42

North Beach Trail

Viking Creek

P **T**

P

North Beach

Campers Beach

North Alouette River

1000m

800m

400m

GOLDEN EARS PROVINCIAL PARK

Alouette Lake

P

To Maple Ridge

BC Hydro Dam

PARK BOUNDARY

LEGEND

–··–··–	Park Border
+++++++	Railway
▬▬▬	Divided Highway
▬🛡▬	Highway
▬▬	Secondary Road
– – –	Gravel Road
- - **12**	Trail
T	Trail Head
P	Parking
▲	Mountain Peak
⌂	Campsite
🛆	Picnic Area
🏠	Emergency Shelter

TRAILS

41 Golden Ears
42 Gold Creek

N
W E
S

~ 41 ~

Golden Ears

41. Route (map, page 132)

Distance: 24 km (round trip), 12-14 hours, day hike or overnight.
Rating: * Difficult
Trailhead: 160 m
Panorama Ridge: 1,000 m,10 km
North Ear Summit: 1,706 m, 12 km
Topographical maps: 92G/7, 92G/8

41. Trailhead

Take Highway 7 east from Vancouver for 41 km to Maple Ridge. Follow the signs northeast into the park from Haney or Albion. Park at the West Canyon Parking Lot. Follow the West Canyon Trail from the parking lot. An overnight campground is located at Alder Flats and Panorama Ridge. Yellow markers and pink or orange tapes on trees mark the route, and it is well signed.

41. Camping, Cycling, Dogs

Camping: Three large campgrounds are located at Alouette Lake, North Beach and Gold Creek. Various walk-in wilderness campsites are also available. A shelter is located on Panorama Ridge.
Mountain biking: Cycling is permitted only on East Canyon Trail, Alouette Mountain Fire Access Road and park roads.
Dogs: Dogs are allowed except at the beach areas, and must be kept on a leash.

Golden Ears is home to a variety of hiking trails of which the most challenging is the Golden Ears Trail. This long hike takes you through a variety of terrain that includes forest, streams, river beds and snowfields. Most of the hike goes through lush rainforest and there are few open viewpoints along the way until the trail nears Panorama Ridge. The trail ends at the top of the north Ear peak. You may want to take an ice axe to cross the snowfield located just below the peak. Sturdy waterproof boots are recommended as you will be walking over boulders, roots, rock and through streams. Water is scarce between Alder Flats and the snowfield in dry weather.

From the parking lot, take the West Canyon Trail north (right) into the forest. The beginning of the trail is level, rocky and well maintained with little elevation change. Though the forest undergrowth is sparse, it is green and lush with ferns, moss and old man's beard.

Soon, you reach a signed intersection where the east (right) fork goes to the Lower Falls while the north (left) fork continues to Golden Ears. As you keep hiking, you can see the stumps of huge old trees that were once logged in the 1920s when the valley was the site of B.C.'s greatest railroad logging operations. By the 1930s, prime lumber was becoming hard to find and all logging ceased in 1931 when a disastrous fire burned through the valley. Today, you can still see abandoned steam donkey sleds, steel cables and railroad rails scattered throughout the trails. A second-growth forest of Douglas fir, western red cedar and western hemlock now dominates the valley.

At this point, the trail narrows and becomes more rugged, as it is scattered with roots and rocks. A thick coating of green moss covers the forest floor. Birds such as owls, swallows, wren, osprey and black swifts all make their homes in the forest.

Eventually, you reach a clearing that provides a view of Gold Creek and the valley. About 4.5 km from the start, the trail goes along a ridge, meandering up and down over roots, rocks and some muddy sections.

The trail soon reaches a creek, where ropes guide you to a short wooden ladder that leads down to a bridge. Continue over the bridge through some wet, boardwalked sections and along the side of the creek, over wet roots, logs and swampy, muddy sections. After about two hours, you will reach a large bridge that crosses over to the Alder Flats camping area. This is a good lunch spot if you are day hiking. Thimble and blueberries grow in this area, and Douglas squirrels can be seen dashing from tree to tree.

The trail leaves Alder Flats and continues through the forest, where it heads up a rocky creek bed at a steeper grade toward Panorama

133

Rainforests: A Rare Habitat

Rainforests are mainly evergreen, where western red cedar, Douglas fir, Sitka spruce and western hemlock trees grow. They are extremely humid and receive at least 1,000 mm of rain per year over a minimum of 100 days. They can receive up to four m of rain per year. Rainforests have a long growing season and a gentle maritime climate. Growth in the forest is lush and sometimes dense, featuring moss, lichens and ferns. The soil is deep and well drained.

Some of the largest and oldest trees in Canada live in rainforests. Most of the trees have an average lifespan of 300-800 years, however some trees live for over 1,000 years. Temperate old-growth rainforests have approximately 4,000 plant and animal species, many of which are unique to this ecosystem.

About two thirds of the world's temperate rainforests are located in western North America. Almost all of the temperate rainforests in B.C. are located on the mainland coast, along the west coast of Vancouver Island and the Queen Charlotte Islands.

Unfortunately, these forests are among the last of a rapidly disappearing habitat. After the last ice age, only 0.2 % of the earth's land area was coastal temperate rainforest. Today, 10 % of these forests are left, and B.C. is home to about one quarter of them. Much of B.C.'s rainforest has been destroyed and continues to be threatened by logging. Nearly 25 % of the 8.8 million ha of temperate rainforest that once covered B.C.'s coast has disappeared, mostly in the last 20 years.

Rainforests are among the richest ecological areas in Canada. They support fascinating processes of renewal and regrowth. An example of this can be seen when a tree falls in a rainforest. As the tree lies on the ground, hundreds of tiny seedlings take advantage of the rich nutrients found in the log. The seedlings use the log as a nursery and send roots around it and into the soil. In about thirty years, the seedlings that have survived become sturdy young trees.

The old log takes 100 to 300 years to decompose. When this happens, the trees that grew on top of the log are left standing on their exposed roots like stilts. Over time, the roots of the tree grow together. This fills the space that the nursing log once occupied and completes the process of renewal.

Ridge. You emerge on a ridge where the gothic-looking Alouette, Blanshard and Edge Mountains loom to the left. Waterfalls and streams can be seen flowing down the steep slopes of the mountains, and pink fireweed grows along the ridge.

From here, the trail reenters dense forest and continues up the creek bed. The route becomes very narrow and is overgrown with shrubs and alder trees. If it were not for the creek bed, it would be almost impossible to see the trail in this jungle-like environment. Keep your eyes open for a piece of logging cable on this part of the trail. Soon, the trail passes a massive, dead tree that has been gouged out at the base to create a roomy shelter or camping area.

Eventually, the trail leaves the overgrown area where it becomes much steeper. You will gain most of your elevation on this section. Continue up the side of a slope, scrambling over logs, gnarled tree roots, rocks and boulders. The tree roots make perfect handholds to pull yourself up as you climb, and the higher up you get, the more impressive is the view.

The trail reaches Panorama Ridge after about four hours. Walk along the bump on the left-hand side of the ridge heading west.

The trail passes a little cabin that sits atop a short rise on the right-hand side of the ridge. The cabin can accommodate up to eight people. Unfortunately, the shelter has seen much abuse over the years. However, it still looks reasonably weather-proof and has a loft. You can camp around the cabin as well, though there is no obvious water supply.

From the cabin, continue southwest to the summit of the north Ear. There are good views of Pitt Lake and mountains to the west. The trail climbs over a number of bumps as it gains height. Sometimes mountain goats, with their long, shaggy, white coats and pointed black horns, can be seen on the rocky slopes above the treeline.

The ascent of the north Ear is made from the east (left) side across a permanent snowfield. Proper equipment and care are recommended when crossing the snowfield. Once you get to the peak, you will be rewarded with a fantastic view of the surrounding area.

~ 42 ~

Gold Creek

42. Route (map, page 132)

Distance: 2.7 km one way, 1 hour, day hike
Rating: * Easy, early season hike
Route: Trailhead: 160 m
Second Waterfall: 200 m, 2.7 km
Topographical maps: 92G/7, 92G/8

42. Trailhead

On Lougheed Highway, turn left (north) at 228 St., then right (east) on Dewdeny Trunk. At 232 St. turn left (north) and continue straight ahead, following the signs to Maple Ridge Park. At the park, a sign will tell you to turn right and keep going straight to Golden Ears Park. Park at the Gold Creek Day Use Parking Area, which is located at the north end of the park. The trail begins at the south end of the parking lot.

42. Camping, Cycling, Dogs

Camping: Three large campgrounds are located at Alouette Lake, North Beach and Gold Creek. Various walk-in wilderness campsites are also available. A shelter is located on Panorama Ridge.
Mountain biking: Cycling is permitted only on East Canyon Trail, Alouette Mountain Fire Access Road and park roads.
Dogs: Dogs are allowed except at the beach areas, and must be kept on a leash.

Located in Golden Ears Provincial Park, this pleasant hike winds along Gold Creek, through the lush, cool rainforest and ends at a picturesque waterfall. As you hike along the trail, you will pass a small beach area located alongside Gold Creek where you can enjoy fine views of Alouette Mountain (1,371 m), Blanshard Needle (1,558 m) and Edge Peak (1,646 m). This is a good hike to do on a hot day as the

A gnarled root along the trail to Golden Ears

walk is shaded by the forest and you also get a refreshing, cool spray of water once you are at the waterfall viewpoint. This is also a good hike to do if you are pressed for time, as it gives you a good introduction to the park over a relatively short distance. Expect to see crowds on summer weekends, as this is one of the most popular trails in the park.

At the trailhead, follow the smooth, wide trail down into the forest where ferns, skunk cabbage, salmonberry and moss seem to cover everything. When you look into the forest you can see the great, sometimes hollow stumps of the trees that were logged here during the 1920s and 30s when this valley was the site of B.C.'s greatest railroad logging operations. Some of the trees that were logged measured up to four m in diameter. After they were cut down, the trees were carried away on flat cars to the Fraser River, where they were dumped. By the 1930s, prime timber was becoming hard to find in the area. A fire swept through the valley in 1931 and after that, logging was permanently stopped. Some of these massive stumps have now become nurse logs for new trees to grow on. The red cedar, Douglas fir, vine maple and western hemlock trees that were once

Salal

Salal is common along the coast of B.C. and is one of the most abundant shrubs of the Pacific rainforest. Salal grows in many forms that can range from a single vine to an impenetrable wall that reaches two m or more in height. It produces bell-shaped white or pink flowers that hang like little lanterns from the twigs. The flowers, which bloom from May 15 to July 1, mature into mealy reddish blue to dark purple berries that ripen by the middle of August.

The salal plant has leathery evergreen leaves that are shiny and thick. Commercial flower businesses often use the attractive leaves in flower arrangements. If you ever find yourself in the woods and need a drinking cup, find a salal leaf and shape it into a cone.

Salal is a Coastal Indian word that means "plentiful shrub." The plant was used extensively by aboriginal peoples. The fruit was eaten fresh, made into syrup or dried into cakes that looked like fruit leather. The berries were also used to sweeten other foods. Today, they are still used to make jam or preserves.

logged have begun to grow back, although they are nowhere near the massive size they once were.

As the trail continues, you will soon be able to hear the gushing noise of Gold Creek and then see it as the trail moves alongside it. Boulders appear intermittently above the surface of the lovely green water. At about one km you will catch the first glimpses of Mount Blanshard, Alouette Mountain and Edge Peak and as you continue, the view becomes gradually less obscured. The mixed sand and beach area is the best place along the trail for enjoying the view of the surrounding peaks. Here, there are good views of Edge Peak, Blanshard Needle and the two peaks of Golden Ears, with Gold Creek in the foreground. The beach is also a good place to try your luck fishing for Dolly Varden, kokanee, rainbow trout and coastal cutthroat.

From the beach area, the trail re-enters the forest and then crosses over a small wooden bridge. It continues to cross over more tiny creeks and wooden bridges as it takes you toward the waterfalls.

At 2.45 km, the trail reaches the first viewpoint of the Lower Falls. As you stand there, you can feel the cool, misty spray of the water as it plunges about 25 m over the falls. Gold Creek begins in the northern part of Golden Ears Park and runs through a wide valley. As it

nears Alouette Lake, the valley is narrowed by a huge rock face, of which half has fallen away. Tons of water plunges down the canyon, continues over a series of rock slabs and gushes down into the boulder-filled bed below. To the west, Mount Blanshard and Evans Peak tower above.

After you have taken a good look, continue up the steep and rough path that heads into the trees. You will soon reach the more dramatic second and final viewpoint. A wire fence has been erected here as a safety precaution. The water flows down the smooth rock from the waterfall into deep pools, where it boils and churns before finally flowing over the side of the cliff. From here, you can also see the top part of the turbulent Gold Creek, which feeds into the waterfall.

Once you are back at the trailhead, you may want to extend this walk by going east on the North Beach Trail. This trail is about a 15 minute walk through the forest along Gold Creek. It leads to the shore of Alouette Lake and the North Beach walk-in campsite. At the beach, there are campsites and good swimming spots. There are also fantastic views of the lake and mountains, and you get a particularly good view of Golden Ears Peak (1,706 m) to the northwest.

Slimy Banana Slugs

You may think that you are in a horror movie the first time that you see a banana slug. Banana slugs are huge and can grow to a length of 20 cm.

They are the second largest slug in the world and the largest in western North America.

Banana slugs are snails without shells. They come in a variety of colours, but most species are greenish-yellow with dark blotches. They have green blood, more teeth than sharks and they eat mainly plants and decaying matter.

The mucous that slugs produce is essential to their survival. Slug mucus absorbs water, which

helps to protect it from dehydration. It is used for traction and navigation when the slug travels. Banana Slugs can ooze along the edge of a razor blade without getting cut. Mucous also fends off predators. It stopped you from picking it up, didn't it?

Here's a tip. If you ever get slug slime on your hands, don't try to get it off by washing your hands with water, as the mucous will absorb it. Instead, rub the mucous off with a dry towel or rub your dry hands together, rolling the mucous into a ball. It can then be thrown away.

Fraser Valley

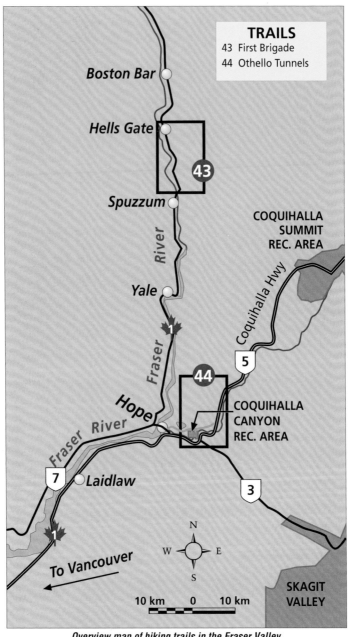

Overview map of hiking trails in the Fraser Valley

View of the Fraser Valley from the First Brigade Trail

This triangle-shaped valley is located between the Coast Mountains to the northwest and the Cascade Mountains to the southeast. The area is dominated by the mighty Fraser River and Fraser Canyon, which cut into the fertile, rolling valley. From Hope, the river continues to flow across the delta, eventually spilling out into the ocean. This region is steeped in history. Gold was discovered here in 1858 and the area still retains a pioneer flavour. A number of hiking trails run through the region, many of which are old pioneer and pack trails used by early explorers.

Hope is the major centre in this area and supplies, accommodation and services are available here. It is located 147 km east of Vancouver and is accessed by Highway 1. Camping is available at Emory Creek Provincial Park, 15 km north of Hope on Highway 1 and at Nicolum River Provincial Park, seven km southeast of Hope on Highway 3. There are no hostels in the area. Park wardens are can be contacted at BC Parks, Fraser Valley District.

Gold Rush

In 1858-59, a small gold rush occurred in the lower Fraser River, especially around the town of Yale. Yale was founded in 1848 as a Hudson's Bay Company fur post. In 1858, Yale's biggest gold strike occurred from June to September, when about three tons of gold were taken from the area—worth $20 million at today's rates. The gold rush turned Yale into the largest town in North America west of Chicago and north of San Francisco. Saloons and dance halls were a common sight. At least 3,000 miners were working gravel bars in the 24 km between Yale and Hope at the height of the gold rush.

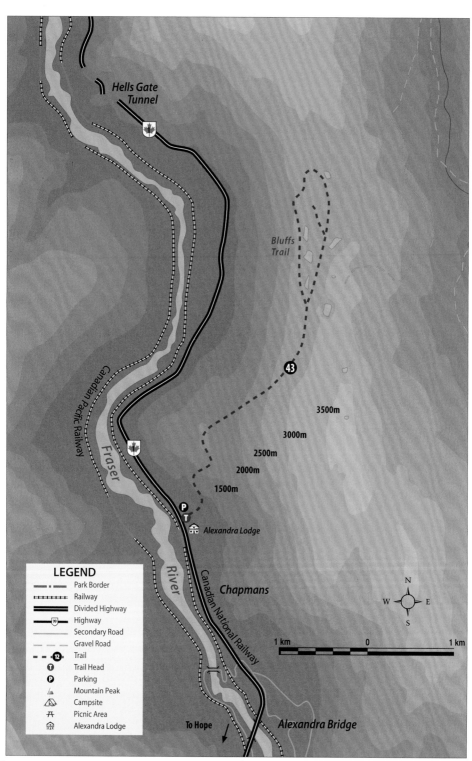

Hells Gate
Tunnel

Bluffs
Trail

Canadian Pacific Railway

Fraser

43

3500m

3000m

2500m

2000m

1500m

P
T
Alexandra Lodge

River

Canadian National Railway

Chapmans

LEGEND

––•–	Park Border
+++++	Railway
━━━	Divided Highway
━99━	Highway
–––	Secondary Road
–––	Gravel Road
––•12•–	Trail
T	Trail Head
P	Parking
▲	Mountain Peak
⌂	Campsite
🛆	Picnic Area
🏠	Alexandra Lodge

N
W ✦ E
S

1 km   0   1 km

To Hope   *Alexandra Bridge*

~ 43 ~

First Brigade and Bluffs Trails

43. Route (map, page 140)

Distance: 13km, day hike or overnight, 5.5 hours
Rating: * Intermediate, early season hike
Trailhead: 137 m
Lookout: 580 m, 1.75 km
Branch: 700 m, 3.75 km
Summit Junction: 870 m, 5.5 km
Bluffs Trail: 760 m, 7.5 km
Alexandra Lodge Parking Lot: 137 m, 13 km
Topographical maps: 92H/11, 92H/14

43. Trailhead

From Hope, take Highway 1 past Yale towards Boston Bar. Cross over the Alexandra Bridge. A few hundred meters north to your right is the historic Alexandra Lodge. Park right after the Lodge in the open area beside the highway. The trail starts 150 m south of the parking area at a tiny stream, and is marked by an orange marker on the tree. Pink and orange markers mark the trail. Camping is available at Emory Creek Park located on Highway 1, halfway between Hope and Yale.

43. Camping, Cycling, Dogs

Camping: No designated campsites exist, however there are some spots on the ridge that are adequate for camping. Obtaining water could be a problem. Camping is available at Emory Creek Provincial Park, 15 km north of Hope on Highway 1.
Mountain biking: Cycling is allowed.
Dogs: Dogs are allowed on the trail.

This trail lets the hiker explore many aspects of the Fraser Canyon area. The trail is one of the earliest pioneer routes to the interior of B.C.,

and it is steeped in fascinating history from the exciting days of the gold rush. The hike also offers exceptional views of the mighty Fraser River with a ridge walk that passes by a series of lovely, peaceful little lakes.

The fur trade and later, the gold rush, relied on several pack trails in the Fraser Canyon area as a way of shipping goods. This trail is one of the longest sections surviving from any of these pack trails. In 1848, A.C. Anderson of the Hudson's Bay Company established this route to move horses from Fort Yale to Kamloops. This trail was built to bypass the Black Canyon and Hell's Gate section of the Fraser and the mountain sections where the Alexandra and other tunnels now exist. The section that this trail avoided now has sixteen railway tunnels, four highway tunnels, three fish ladders, innumerable bridges and retaining walls.

The hike begins with a five minute climb to a fork in the trail. Turn left at this fork. The right trail is the original route and is a five minute hike down to the historic Alexandra Lodge. The trail climbs up an open forest heading northeast. The path is covered by a soft carpet of pine needles and moss, and is very well maintained. You may hear ruffed grouse drumming as you pass by. Male ruffed grouse make a distinctive sound by flapping their wings rapidly in order to attract females.

About half a kilometre up the trail is a large aluminum plate on a tree that reads "Part of the 1847 HBC Brigade Trail from Fort Yale over Lake Mountain to the Cold Water, Kamloops and the North. Built A.C. Anderson 1847-48."

There is a relentless climb as the trail continues up through a forest of small Douglas fir and mountain ash. Soon after passing a small creek, the trail nears a moss-covered rockslide. The route steepens as it passes along a ridge, where the first of a series of viewpoints begins. Facing west are views of the Lillooet Mountain range, Fraser River and Spuzzum Mountain(1,909 m), with the Alexandra Tunnel at its base.

The trail moves off the ridge and back into the forest. There are plenty of tree lichens, known as "old man's beard" hanging from trees in the forest. Lichens are a type of vegetation in which an algae and a fungus coexist. The algae provides food for both and the fungus provides shelter for the algae. If you are hiking this trail in May, look for colonies of purple calypso orchids growing along this part of the trail. The trail veers around the ridge again, with more views to the left.

As the trail leaves the last viewpoint, it passes through a series of forest groves and more steep terrain. If you think you are working hard, picture men walking up this trail with horses and supplies. Consider that 27 horses and about 22, 90-pound packs, bales or kegs of goods were lost on this route.

The trail comes to a fork where a metal plaque attached to a tree reads "Straight ahead. HBC Trail to Lakes and Anderson Road. Left Bluffs Trail used by miners to Boston Bar and Lytton 1858 foot traffic." Stay right and the trail will level off as it gains the ridge of Lake Mountain.

The ridge walk along the mountain is surprisingly closed in by trees. It passes another creek that is suitable for a water supply, although a water filter is recommended. There are six lakes along the top of the mountain. Four of these lakes fit into a strong north-south groove in the mountain. Note that the grain of the rock runs north-south in the Fraser Canyon.

Soon, you will pass by a small lake to the right. Here, you will find a fork with a trail to the left marked with yellow flags. This side trail goes up to a bluff that has a great view of the Fraser river. This is a good place to eat lunch or camp. In gold rush days, there were two large cabins called "Lake House" situated among the series of lakes on the ridge.

The main trail continues past a second lake

Calypso Orchid

This exquisite orchid is one of Southwestern B.C.'s most beautiful native flowers. It is found throughout much of northern and western North America and also in Asia and northern Europe.

The purple-pink flower is slipper-shaped and sits atop a short, 15 cm stalk that has a round leaf at its base. The inner surface of the flower is streaked and spotted with golden yellow hairs. The flower blooms in May, after which the flower and leaf wither and wilt. In the fall, a new leaf appears from the base of the stem. This leaf persists throughout the summer months.

The plant derives its name from the Greek word meaning "hidden" or "covered from view." Its name is fitting, as the plant thrives in deep, moist woodlands where its small size makes it easy to overlook. Do not pick this flower. The corms are attached by delicate roots that are easily broken, so when a flower is picked, the plant usually dies.

Fraser River

This hike leads to spots where you can view the mighty Fraser River. The explorer Simon Fraser journeyed down this river in 1808 to search for a route to supply Interior fur trade posts. The trip was full of disappointment and hardship. At the head of the Stein River, 50 km downstream from Lillooet, he was greeted by 1,200 natives.

The Fraser River delivers 121 billion m^3 of fresh water to the ocean each year. It is the fifth largest river system in Canada. It is also the fifth longest river in Canada. It flows 1,370 km from its headwaters to the Pacific Ocean.

The river begins about 35 km southwest of Jasper, Alberta and is joined by many streams and creeks along its way to the Strait of Georgia. More than 1.8 million people live along the banks of the Fraser River and its tributaries. The river remains the world's largest salmon-producing system, with annual returns of 12 million fish in recent years. All five Pacific salmon species spawn in the Fraser watershed, along with 48 other fish species.

The banks of the Fraser are said to contain more than 600 varieties of rock. Many of these are semiprecious. People have discovered black and green nephrite, rhodonite, dumortierite of the rare viole colour and famous B.C. jade.

Othello Tunnel

Common Wild Rose

This shrub is found in a variety of open habitats at low to middle elevations. It grows to three m tall. The stems and branches of the shrub are covered with soft prickles. The gorgeous, pinkish red flowers grow to nine cm and flower from May to June. The fruit that is produced are capsule-like "hips" that stay on the plant throughout winter.

The hips of several rose species were eaten by many northwest coastal natives. The hips were considered a famine food. A concoction of the branches or strips of bark was also used as an eyewash for sore eyes.

and moves through thickets of yew and several patches of slough grass. Just past the third lake is a pink marker tape on a tree to the right. This side trail leads to a logging road. The area to the right was logged in the 1960s.

At this point, the main trail loops back and comes to a junction where the Brigade Trail intersects with the Bluffs Trail. There are some nice camping spots here. Continue heading south on the Bluffs Trail. The trail will pass three small lakes to the left.

This part of the trail is more of a bushwhack than the one on the other side of the lakes, but it is still well marked and easy to follow. Soon, the route will go up a narrow bluff, where there is a breathtaking view. Spread out to the west are the Fraser River, Black Canyon, Lillooet and Coast Range mountains. The Black Canyon is rarely seen from the road. Ahead is more bushwhacking until the Bluffs Trail intersects with the Brigade Trail. From this point it is a fun hike down. Ticks are common, so check yourself carefully for ticks after you hike this trail.

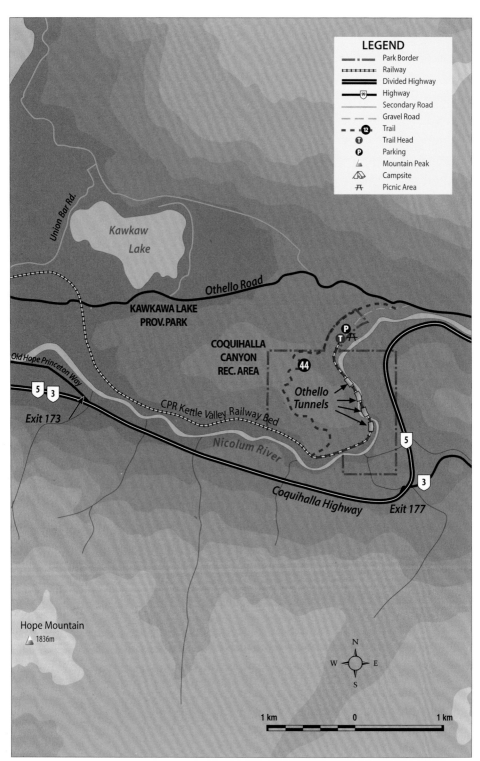

LEGEND

— ·· — ·· —	Park Border
┠┼┼┼┼┼┨	Railway
══════	Divided Highway
━━99━━	Highway
────────	Secondary Road
─ ─ ─ ─	Gravel Road
▪ ▪ ▪ 🔵12 ▪	Trail
🅣	Trail Head
🅟	Parking
⛰	Mountain Peak
⛺	Campsite
⛩	Picnic Area

Union Bar Rd.

Kawkaw Lake

Othello Road

KAWKAWA LAKE PROV. PARK

COQUIHALLA CANYON REC. AREA

🅟 🅣 ⛩

44

Othello Tunnels

Old Hope Princeton Way

CPR Kettle Valley Railway Bed

Nicolum River

5 3

Exit 173

5

3

Coquihalla Highway

Exit 177

Hope Mountain
⛰ 1836m

N
W — E
S

1 km   0   1 km

~ 44 ~
Othello Tunnels

44. Route (map, page 144)

Distance: 5.5 km round trip; 2 hours, day hike
Rating: * Easy, early season hike
Trailhead: 150 m
High point and sign: 363 m, 4 km
Parking lot: 150 m, 5.5 km
Topographical map: 92H/6

44. Trailhead

Drive 6 km northeast of Hope on the Coquihalla Highway. Take the turnoff for the town of Hope, then take Othello Road east for 8 km to the Coquihalla Canyon Recreation Area. The trail begins at the parking lot. This trail is also known as the Hope Nicola Valley Trail.

Coquihalla Canyon Provincial Park is a picturesque area of mountain peaks and lush forested valleys that are cut through by the dramatic Coquihalla river and canyon. The first part of the hike takes you through the Othello Tunnels, which lead over the Coquihalla Canyon. These four tunnels are linked together by two bridges and are infused with the history of the Kettle Valley Railway. The hike then proceeds along the old Kettle Valley Railway bed, where it enters the forest and goes along a ridge.

From the parking lot, hike on the road that parallels the Coquihalla River running south toward the four tunnels. Fishing for trout, steelhead and char is allowed on the river during certain times of the year. Contact BC Parks, for fishing regulations

44. Camping, Cycling, Dogs

Camping: No camping facilities exist. This is a day-use area with picnic sites. Camping is available at Nicolum River Provincial Park, 7 km east of Hope on the north side of Highway 3.
Mountain biking: Bikes are allowed. They are not permitted in the tunnels.
Dogs: Dogs must be on a leash.

Construction of the Othello Tunnels

The Kettle Valley Railway was built to connect the Kootenay region with the B.C. coast. Construction began in 1910, when 61 km of track was laid from the Coquihalla Summit across the Fraser River from Hope. The railway crossed three major mountain ranges. However, the greatest challenge in creating the railway arose at the Coquihalla Gorge, where the Coquihalla River cut a 91-m-deep channel through solid granite.

The construction of these tunnels was an amazing feat. Chief engineer Andrew McCulloch hung above the gorge in a wicker basket so that he could survey the canyon. From here, he developed a plan to build a series of tunnels through the granite by excavating directly through the gorge. A series of short tunnels had

to be blasted through five different rock faces.

The men whose job was to blast the rock faces displayed amazing courage. Risking their lives, they climbed down into the canyon on ladders where they would light the charges. They would have to scramble up these ladders to get out of the canyon before the charges exploded.

The Kettle Valley Railway opened in 1916 and provided freight and passenger service from the Kootenays to the coast for 48 years. The demise of the railway began when better roads and air travel offered alternative ways to travel. In 1959, heavy rains caused sections of the Coquihalla line to be washed away. These sections were never repaired, and the railway closed in 1961.

Othello Tunnel

and licensing.

The road soon reaches the first tunnel, which is the longest and darkest. As you enter the tunnel, the cool darkness descends on you and a pinprick of light at the other end is your only guide through. It is surprising how wide and lofty the tunnels are, rising to over 91 m. This height, combined with a level roadbed to walk on, makes the hike through the tunnels easy and safe.

As you continue to the second tunnel, rock climbers will be interested to note that there is a bolt to the left at the beginning of the second tunnel face. The climbing route appears to be a 5.9-m crack that goes to the top. Once you walk through the second tunnel, you come to a bridge with the raging Coquihalla gorge running underneath it. In July, you may see steelhead trout jumping into the air as they struggle to spawn upstream.

Hollywood Scenery

The dramatic scenery around the Othello Tunnels has made the area a favorite spot among movie producers. Look for these famous areas along the tunnels where movie scenes have been filmed:

• At tunnel #2, the cliff above the stump was used in the canyon jump in Sylvester Stallone's film *Cliffhanger*. The sandbar you see just before you enter the tunnels was also used for scenes in this movie.

• The mountain peaks in the Fraser Canyon were used in many of the scenes in Stallone's blockbuster climbing film *K2*.

• The cliff at tunnel #2 was also used in filming *Shoot to Kill*, a film featuring Sidney Poitier. The same cliff was also used in a romantic-adventure movie called *Fire With Fire*.

• All four tunnels were filmed in scenes of *National Dream*.

• A huge log placed across the canyon in front of tunnel #2 was used for the rescue scene in *Far From Home: The Adventures of Yellow Dog*, a Disney remake of the classic *Old Yeller* film.

The bridge leads to the third and fourth tunnels. Once you are past the fourth tunnel, continue along the wide, open, forested trail. This section of the trail is the old railway bed and runs for approximately three km west to the town of Hope.

When you reach the kiosk at the yellow gate, turn north (right) off the old railway bed and head into the forest. The trail leads into a lovely moss-covered cedar and fir grove along the hillside, and there a wonderful view of Cheam Peak and the Coquihalla River unfolds. Some of the giant Douglas fir trees in the grove may be 150 to 200 years old. Continue up the moderately graded trail along the ridge where devil's club and ferns can be seen growing on the forest floor.

The trail leads gently uphill and moves slowly away from the ridge. It then turns right and begins to head northeastward. As it reaches its high point, the grade levels out and the trail starts to descend. Soon after, you will see a sign nailed to a tree that says "Engineers mule road to Similkameen built fall 1860 by E. Dewdney from mile four on the HBC Trail between the two conical hills to the Coquihalla River and then up the north side of the Nicolum River to the Skagit. "

Edgar Dewdney was commissioned by the colonial government to build a trail from Fort Hope to Rock Creek, east of Osoyoos. The Dewdney Trail was used as a transportation route by packtrains of the Hudson's Bay Company, miners, fur traders and pioneer settlers for 20 years. Only a few sections of the trail remain today.

From here, the route continues downward and around a large gravel pit. It then heads eastward, switching back slightly down a steep slope. Then, the trail turns onto an old logging road, where it widens and continues northeastward. Keep following it to where it intersects with a larger gravel road. Then turn right at this intersection and follow the road until you meet Tunnel Road. At Tunnel Road, turn right and walk 0.8 km back to the parking lot.

Cheam Peak

45. Route

Distance: 5 km one way, 4.5 hours, day hike
Rating: ** Intermediate
Trailhead: 1,482 m
Cheam Peak: 2,112 m, 5 km
Topographical map: 92H/4

45. Trailhead

Turn left off Chilliwack Lake Road 27 km east of Vedder Crossing on the north side of Chilliwack River. Drive for 2 km, then cross Foley Creek. Turn left at the T junction. Drive for 2.2 km west to a logging road just past Chipmunk Creek. Turn right and stay on the main logging road for about 7 km. Turn right onto a steep, rough road for 4 km to a parking area.

Note: You need a 4-wheel drive to access the trailhead.

45. Camping, Cycling, Dogs

Camping: There are sites available at Cultus Lake
Mountain biking: Bikes are allowed on the logging road.
Dogs: Dogs are allowed.

The trail takes you up Cheam Peak to a superb view of the Fraser Valley and mountain ranges to the south. The route ascends to Spoon Lake, where it begins to switch back upward past Lady Peak to the saddle between the two mountains. You pass through meadows to rocky terrain. The trail reaches an intersection as it nears the peak. Turn right and continue on to the peak.

Manning Provincial Park

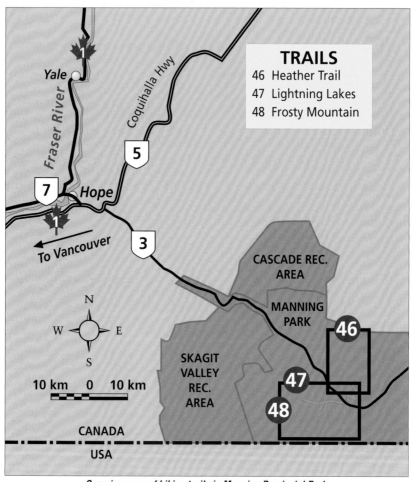

TRAILS
46 Heather Trail
47 Lightning Lakes
48 Frosty Mountain

Overview map of hiking trails in Manning Provincial Park

Sub-alpine meadows and panoramic views along the Heather Trail

Manning Provincial Park is located 224 km east of Vancouver on Highway 3. The Cascade Mountains and the Similkameen and Skagit Rivers make up the heart of this 71,400 ha park. The park was established in 1941 and is named for E.C. Manning, Chief

Forester of British Columbia from 1935 to 1949. The park lies between the west coast and the interior, thus providing the hiker with an opportunity to explore a transitional landscape where the lush coastal growth gives way to drier terrain. There are forested mountains, alpine meadows, lakes, valleys and abundant wildlife.

The park has an extensive system of excellent trails that total 276 km. It is also a popular ski destination in the winter, with over 100 km of ungroomed trails. The Gibson Pass Ski Area is located nearby. Winter camping is allowed at designated campsites.

The park has four campgrounds, and wilderness camping is permitted in designated areas. Accommodation is also available at Manning Park Lodge, a 73-unit complex that features cabins and chalets.

Highway 3 bisects the park and access is gained by car and passenger bus service. The town of Hope is the closest major centre. Supplies, accommodation and services are available here. Basic amenities are also available at the Lodge. A ranger/visitor centre is located one km past Manning Park Resort. There are no hostels in the area.

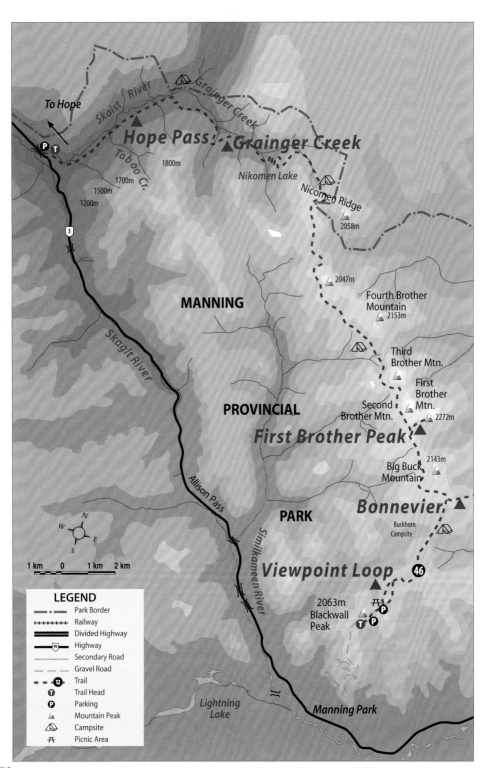

To Hope

Skaist River

Grainger Creek

Hope Pass   Grainger Creek

Taboo Cr.

1800m

Nikomen Lake

1700m

Nicomen Ridge

1500m

1200m

2058m

3

2047m

MANNING

Fourth Brother
Mountain
2153m

Skagit River

Third
Brother Mtn.

First
Brother
Mtn.

Second
Brother Mtn.

2272m

PROVINCIAL

First Brother Peak

2143m

Big Buck
Mountain

Allison Pass

Bonnevier

PARK

Buckhorn
Campsite

N

W   E

S

1 km   0   1 km   2 km

Viewpoint Loop

46

2063m
Blackwall
Peak

Similkameen River

LEGEND

–·–·–	Park Border
┼┼┼┼	Railway
━━━	Divided Highway
━99━	Highway
───	Secondary Road
─ ─ ─	Gravel Road
▪▪▪ 12	Trail
T	Trail Head
P	Parking
▲	Mountain Peak
⌂	Campsite
🏕	Picnic Area

Lightning
Lake

Manning Park

~ 46 ~

Heather Trail

46. Route (map, page 150)

Distance: 23 km to Nicomen Ridge, 2 days
Rating:* Easy
Blackwall Peak Parking Lot: 2,133 m, 0 km
Buckhorn Campsite: 1,860 m, 5 km
Bonnevier Trail Jct: 2,000 m, 6.5 km
First Brother Junction: 2,134 m, 10 km
Kicking Horse Campground: 1,950 m, 13.5 km
Nicomen Lake Campground: 1,798 m, 23 km
Topographical maps: 92H/2, 92H/7

This is the most popular hiking route in the park and one of the best trails in southwestern B.C. Starting at the sub-alpine level, the trail winds through outstanding mountain terrain where colourful meadows are filled with masses of wildflowers. Sweeping views and meadows surround you all the way up to the Three Brothers alpine area. Try to hike this trail from late July to mid-August, when the flowers are in full bloom. The blooms are so colourful, profuse and varied that it would be a shame to miss this spectacular display.

This area was a favorite for guided pack-horse trips from 1919 to 1930. However, the area was threatened by the overgrazing of domestic sheep. The public became concerned about this issue, and this led to the creation of the Three Brothers Mountain Reserve in 1936 and the establishment of Manning Provincial Park in 1941. It is not difficult to see why

46. Trailhead

At Hope, there is a junction of Highways 1 and 3. Take Highway 3 east of Hope off the Trans Canada. Drive 70 km to Manning Park Lodge. To the north, across from the lodge, drive 15 km up the lookout road to Blackwell Peak Parking Lot. The trail starts at the parking lot.

46. Camping, Cycling, Dogs

Camping: There are four campgrounds: Lightning Lake, Hampton, Mule Deer and Coldspring. Lightning Lakes is the closest. Wilderness walk-in camping is located at Kicking Horse, Nicomen Lake and Buckhorn.
Mountain biking: Bikes are permitted on some trails.
Dogs: Dogs are allowed, but must be on a leash.

Blooming Flowers

The Heather Trail encompasses an area that stretches for 24 km northwest of Blackwall Peak. It is known for its spectacular blooming wildflowers. The flowers start to bloom when the snow melts and lasts until about sixty days before the frost of early September.

There are two distinct bloom periods during the summer season. The first occurs just as the snow leaves. The blooms during this period contain mostly cream-coloured western anemone, white spring beauty and yellow snow lily. The second and more colourful bloom period is dominated by purple/blue lupine, red Indian paintbrush and yellow arnica. These flowers bloom

Wildflowers

from mid to late July.

Other flowers to look for in this area include fireweed, pussy-toes, arnica, showy aster, stonecrop, western columbine, shooting star, globe flower, moss campion and fan-leaf cinquefoil. You will also see Indian hellebore among the flowers. This moisture-loving lily with broad leaves blooms in July. It resembles skunk cabbage, but beware: it is poisonous.

These alpine meadows are very fragile and only exist as a result of a tenuous, long-standing relationship with the elements. Stay on the trails so that the flowers are not destroyed.

Lightning Lakes

people thought that this area should be conserved. The expansive alpine meadows in this area are truly exquisite. Blue, yellow, white, orange and pink cover the hillsides in all directions.

The trail is extremely well maintained, smooth and wide, with minimal changes in elevation. This is an excellent trail to use as your first overnight trip if you are a beginner hiker. It can be very dry though, so be sure to bring plenty of drinking water. Please stay on the trail, as these meadows are very fragile. Do not pick the flowers, as some take up to 25 years to bloom.

From the Blackwell Peak Parking Lot, head downward along a fire access road. You can also start from the upper parking lot, where you follow a ridge down along the Viewpoint Loop Trail to where it joins the Heather Trail. Wildflowers such as yellow and purple mountain daisies, white western anemone and white mountain valerian line the trail.

The trail continues north and downward through wide open meadows with panoramic views. You can see the Three Brothers mountains to the northwest and the Cascade Range to the south. As you walk further down the valley, the meadows become more lush with cow

First Brother Peak

This trail (2,272 m, 1 km, 1/2 hour one way) is fairly rocky and steep but can be easily climbed. At the base of the mountain, you can see the trail snaking over dry terrain up to the peak. To climb this peak, take the northeast (right) fork at the First Brother Junction. After the first short, steep section, the trail levels out as you continue along the ridge. Plants like juniper and krummholtz grow here, as they are hardy enough to withstand the harsh elements. A final climb to a cairn with a cross on it indicates that you have reached the top.

The view at the top stretches of the park is one obtainable only on this hike. To the northwest are Second Brother Mountain (2,250 m) and Third Brother Mountain (2,245 m). It is very exposed at the top and can be windy, so bring extra clothing.

parsnip and poisonous Indian hellebore growing among the flowers. The meadows are filled with blue to purple lupines, yellow glacier lily and red Indian paintbrush. Indian paintbrush is coloured with red pigment called anthocyanin. This pigment helps the plant to survive summer frosts by absorbing high-intensity sunlight and converting it to heat.

The trail winds through patches of forest and reaches the Buckhorn wilderness campsite at five km. This campsite is a good place to aim for if you are travelling with small children or if you intend to do a short hike. There are platforms on which to camp at the site and there is a stream where you can get water.

After passing the campsite, the trail starts to climb up through a burn area where the forest was destroyed by a fire in 1945. Expansive meadows span the area in all directions. The trail reaches a signed fork where the Bonnevier Trail intersects the Heather Trail. The trail to the First Brother continues north, straight ahead.

Heading on from the Bonnavier intersection, you will pass some remaining snow patches and tiny seasonal ponds. The area is filled with the pink and red mountain heather that is the trail's namesake. The profusion of purple lupines perfumes the air in late July or early August.

As you near the First Brother, the terrain becomes very dry. The Three Brothers mark the transition zone from the wet coast to the drier, rolling mountains and hills to the north, northwest and east. The smaller flowers in the area indicate that the trail has reached alpine terrain. As you walk along the ridge, look to the right of the valley for a spectacular view. To the south are Frosty (2,408 m), Lone Goat (2,004 m) and Snow Camp (1,980 m) mountains, and to the southeast is Blackwall Peak (2,063 m).

When the trail reaches the First Brother Junction, take the northeast (right) fork if you want to hike up to the First Brother Peak. The Kicking Horse Campground is 3.5 km straight ahead to the northwest. The moderate trail to the Kicking Horse Campground runs alongside the Second and Third Brother peaks before switching back just before the campsite.

From the campsite, you can continue for 7.5 km to Nicomen Ridge, where you get a good view of Nicomen Lake. From here, the trail to the lake descends for two km along a series of switchbacks to the Nicomen Lake Wilderness Campsite.

Once you are at Nicomen Lake, there are two ways to return to the trailhead. You can either take the same route back on which you came or travel 19.5 km along the Grainger Creek Trail, which heads west (left). At the Grainger Creek Campsite, continue southwest along the Hope Pass Trail down to the Cayuse Flats Parking Lot. If you choose this option, you must arrange for transportation at the parking lot. It is approximately 40 km back to the Blackwell Parking Lot.

~ 47 ~
Lightning Lakes

47. Route (map, page 154-5)

Distance: 12 km to Thunder Lake (one way), day hike or overnight, 7-8 hours
Rating: ** Easy
Trailhead: 1,082 m
Flash Lake: 1,109 m, 4 km
Strike Lake: 1,082 m, 9 km
Thunder Lake: 1,027 m, 12 km
Topographical map: 92H/2

47. Trailhead

Manning Park is 224 km east of Vancouver. Turn off Highway 1 at Hope onto Highway 3 (Hope-Princeton Hwy). Drive for 70 km to Manning Park Lodge. Drive past the lodge and turn right onto Gibson Pass Road. After 3 km, turn left to the Lightning Lakes Day Use Parking Lot. The trail begins at the southwest end of the parking lot. Overnight parking is allowed in the parking lot even though it is called a "day use area."

This is a fine trail on which to begin exploring Manning Park. Set against an exquisite backdrop of the Cascade Mountains, this relaxing shoreline hike takes you past Lightning, Flash,

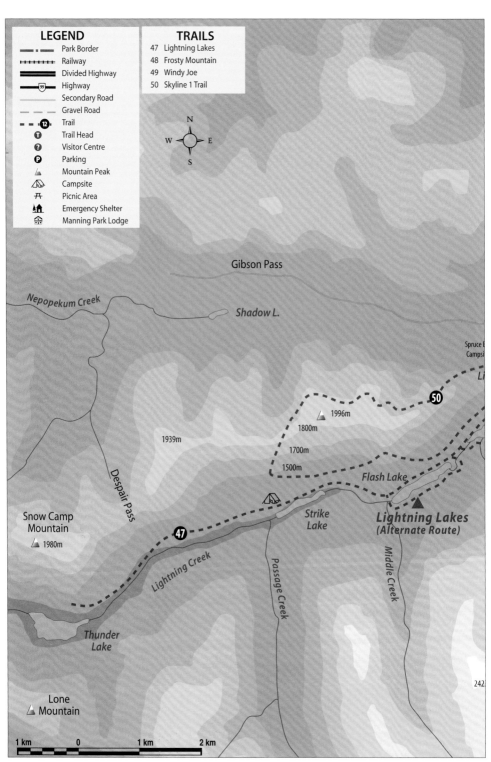

LEGEND
- ‒ · ‒ · Park Border
- ┼┼┼┼┼ Railway
- ▬▬▬ Divided Highway
- ▬ⓧ▬ Highway
- ── Secondary Road
- ‒ ‒ ‒ Gravel Road
- ‒ ‒ ⑫ Trail
- ⊤ Trail Head
- ❷ Visitor Centre
- ⓟ Parking
- ◭ Mountain Peak
- ◮ Campsite
- 〒 Picnic Area
- ⛺ Emergency Shelter
- ⌂ Manning Park Lodge

TRAILS
47 Lightning Lakes
48 Frosty Mountain
49 Windy Joe
50 Skyline 1 Trail

N W E S (compass)

Gibson Pass

Nepopekum Creek

Shadow L.

Spruce
Campsi

Li

50

◭ 1996m

1800m

1939m

1700m

1500m

Flash Lake

Despair Pass

Snow Camp
Mountain

◭ 1980m

◮

Strike
Lake

47

Lightning Lakes
(Alternate Route)

Lightning Creek

Passage Creek

Middle Creek

Thunder
Lake

Lone
◭ Mountain

242

1 km   0   1 km   2 km

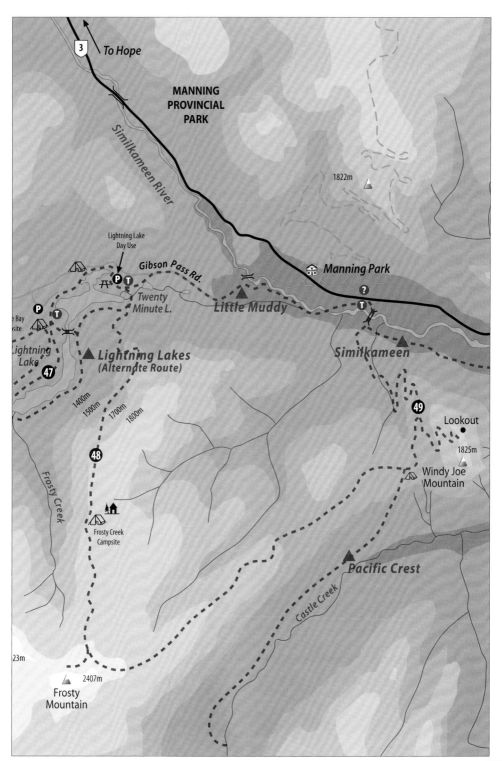

3 To Hope

MANNING
PROVINCIAL
PARK

Similkameen River

1822m

Lightning Lake
Day Use

Gibson Pass Rd.

P **T**

Twenty
Minute L.

Little Muddy

Manning Park

?

T

P

T

e Bay
site

Similkameen

Lightning
Lake

47

Lightning Lakes
(Alternate Route)

1400m
1500m
1700m
1800m

49

Lookout

1825m

48

Windy Joe
Mountain

Frosty Creek

Frosty Creek
Campsite

Pacific Crest

Castle Creek

23m

2407m
Frosty
Mountain

Strike and Thunder lakes. This area is teeming with wildlife and plants that are commonly found in marsh, stream, lake, forest and rockfall environments. Take along your binoculars and enjoy.

The hike starts at the north end of Lightning Lake, where there is a small dam. Before the dam was put in place, the area consisted of marsh and ponds, which the dam now connects. The ponds soon turned into the lakes you see today.

The start of the trail is level and covered with luxuriously soft pine needles. The route stays well groomed all the way to Strike Lake and there is little elevation change throughout. It is easy to meander along while still covering a fair amount of territory.

The trail curves around the north side of the lovely aquamarine Lightning Lake and heads southwest, following the "Main Trail" signs. As you walk along, you will see Frosty Mountain. Towering at 2,407 m, it is the highest mountain in the park.

At the midway point of Lightning Lakes is another sign with a trail map on it. The right trail goes up to the Spruce Bay Parking Lot, an alternative place from which to start the hike. To continue on the main trail, turn left and follow the trail along the lakeside. The shoreline is a good growing environment for alder trees. Don't be surprised if a tiny Rufous hummingbird zips by.

The trail passes over two small wooden bridges that lead into a pastoral lakeside landscape. The lake narrows at the second bridge. At this narrowing, the water flows from a small channel into the lower half of the lake as it slowly widens out again. Beavers are sometimes visible at the end of Lightning Lake in the afternoons and evening.

After about three km, you will reach the end of Lightning Lake. At the fork in the trail, take the right trail to continue to Flash and the other two lakes. To your left is Rainbow Bridge. This trail is an alternate route that goes around the south side of Flash Lake.

This park is a superb place to view songbirds such as red crossbills, clarke's nutcrackers or goldencrowned kinglets. Two hundred bird species have been recorded here, so the park is very popular among birdwatchers. You may see birdwatchers excitedly running back

Lightning Lakes Trail on the southeast side of Lightning Lakes

and forth on Rainbow Bridge, trying to get a closer look at a rarely seen species. If you do cross Rainbow Bridge, look for rainbow trout spawning in June.

The right trail continues on through a grassy area along Flash Lake. It soon moves higher up from the lakeshore and into a forest where lodgepole pine and kinnikinnick ground cover is common. You may see piles of flakes sitting atop fallen logs or stumps. These are

47. Camping, Cycling, Dogs

Camping: A walk-in wilderness campsite is located at Strike Lake. Campgrounds are located at Mule Deer, Coldspring, Hampton and Lightning Lake.

Mountain biking: Bikes are permitted on the following trails in the area: Corral to Lightning Lake campground via Lone Duck Bay, Beaver Pond Parking Lot to Corral, Windy Joe, Monument 78, Monument 83, north and south Gibson and Poland Lake.

Dogs: Dogs are allowed but must be on a leash.

Beaver

continue west, Flash Lake becomes thick with sedges and grasses. A bridge appears to the left of the trail as you leave Flash Lake. This bridge leads to the alternate trail around the south side of the lake.

Once the trail passes the bridge, it moves higher up on a ridge along the lake. This provides a good view of the area. Notice that a number of canals have been made by beavers. To maintain a constant water level in the canals, the beavers have also built a series of locks. A beaver dam is located at the western outflow of the lake.

The trees lining the trail are lodgepole pine, Engelmann spruce, and sub-alpine fir. Spruce is identified by its flaky bark and sharp needles. Three-toed woodpeckers chip off its flakes as they look for insects. A bit further along the trail, a chewed-up sign announces the avalanche area beyond. This trail is popular with cross-country skiers in the winter. The trail continues to meander in and out of the forest. Soon, Strike Lake comes into view. There are a few choice camping spots on the lakeshore to the left. Consider yourself lucky if you get one of these. A larger wilderness camping site is nestled in a grove of tall Engelmann spruce trees at the south end of the lake. While you are in this area, look for a small, gray bird called the dipper. A dipper uses its wings to propel itself under water, where it catches tiny fish and insects. Also, look for butterflies fluttering around. This park is known for a vast array of butterflies that include indra swallowtail,

created by red squirrels, whose winter supply of cones is stored in holes among the tree roots.

A series of rockslides will start to appear on the right-hand side of the trail.

At the second fork past the Rainbow Bridge is a sign for the Strike Lake Camp. Follow the trail straight ahead. The other trail to the right leads to the Skyline Trail. As you continue hiking, you may want to watch the forest floor intently for edible wild currant, blueberries and thimbleberry in the summer months. As you

47. Fishing

Consider taking along your fishing rod when you hike this trail. Lightning and Strike lakes are popular fishing areas, especially for fly fishing. Fishermen were the first white settlers to use this area when a party visited Lightning Lake in 1870. Fishermen also used an old Indian campsite that became known as Cambie Campground. It has since been closed and replaced by several larger campgrounds.

As you walk by the lakes, you can see many small rainbow trout swimming in the crystal clear water. This silvery fish is named for the distinctive "rainbow" band running down its side. This band is most prominent during spawning season from April to July. Dark spots are found along its back, upper fins and tail. The sea-run version of this species is

referred to as "steelhead." The lakes in this area are not stocked, so you are allowed to catch a maximum of four fish per day. Fishing licences can be purchased at the front desk of Manning Park Lodge.

You will also find good canoeing on Lightning Lake. A cartop boat-launching ramp is located at Lightning Lake day use. Boat rentals are available at the day use area. Canoes can be rented for $10.50 per hour or $40 per day. Rowboats can also be rented for $11.50 per hour and $45 for the full day. Power boats are prohibited in the park.

The nearby Similkameen and Sumallo rivers also have Dolly Varden, cutthroat and rainbow trout.

green-veined white, Compton's tortoise-shell, green hairstreak, silvery blue and blue copper.

The trail that leaves Strike Lake Campsite leads through shady forest and then a marsh area where the dreaded devil's club grows in profusion. Devil's club is hated by any hiker that comes into contact with it. The plant has a stem covered in sharp spines that cause inflammation of the skin. Its huge, maple-like leaves are also coated underneath with spines. Try not to touch it as you walk by.

Soon, a series of rockslides intersects the forest. Rockslides are home to a variety of flowers and animals. Pikas are among those that live here. Pikas look a lot like guinea pigs and are identifiable by their high-pitched warning cry.

The trail proceeds straight ahead through more forest filled with alder, skunk cabbage and cow parsnip. After about 10 minutes, you will reach dryer scree slopes. Flowers grow in clumps and mats on the scree in order to preserve moisture and to avoid wind on the rocky, dry slopes. Notice that the flowers are also smaller. They include Indian paintbrush, woolly sunflower, showy Jacob's ladder, saxifrage and fireweed.

As you approach the dark green Thunder Lake, the slopes begin to steepen dramatically. Just before the lake is a huge scree area where the rock has cascaded down from Snow Camp Mountain (1,980 m). Use caution here, as it is a slide hazard area.

The entire lake is enclosed in steep slopes of scree and exfoliating rock from above. Lone Mountain (1,828 m) sits to the left of the trail. The slopes of these mountains are so steep that the scree falls directly into the lake. If you lose your footing here, you could fall in.

The trail continues across the scree slopes about seven m above the water. It then moves up higher, to about 30 m, and becomes extremely steep. There are some very large poplar trees growing along the lakeshore, and some on the slopes.

Mule Deer

Both the mule deer and whitetail deer are found in western Canada. The Columbia blacktail deer inhabits only the Pacific Coast and its islands.

The Columbia blacktail deer is a smaller relative of the mule deer and is similar in appearance. A mule deer's tail distinguishes it from a whitetail deer. The tail of a mule deer is white and narrow with a black tip. The tail of a whitetail deer is broad, and white underneath.

The antlers of the mule deer and the Columbia blacktail deer differ from a whitetail deer's in that the blacktail's antlers grow in forked formation rather than as points from a main branch. The coats of the deer are reddish brown in summer, changing to gray in the winter.

Besides eating grass and wildflowers, the mule deer also browses on a variety of trees including willow and aspen. When food is scarce, it will even browse on fir trees or strip tree bark to get at the sugary cambium beneath. Besides hunters and predators, the main causes of death among deer are parasitic diseases and winter starvation.

This hike takes you through an amazing array of different environments that begins with lakeside forest and slowly leads to flowery sub-alpine meadows. From there, you pass through an ethereal grove of ancient larch trees to a dramatic alpine environment. The trail then leads you on a scramble up a 100-m talus slope to the first of Frosty Mountain's two peaks. Frosty Mountain (2,408 m) is the highest peak in Manning Park, and the views along the way and at the top are magnificent. Although the trail climbs quite high, it is well maintained and moderate until the last scramble to the top of Frosty Mountain.

Due to its north-facing slope, this is one of the last trails in Manning Park to become free of snow. It is accessible by late June, however an ice axe is recommended if you attempt to reach the peak when it is covered in snow. The best time to see blooming wildflowers on this hike is during the first two weeks of August. The larch trees turn golden from mid-September to early October.

The trail begins by heading south upward and into the forest from the shore of Lighting Lake. The trail is smooth and made up of dirt and pine needles. This is characteristic of the area; unlike trails closer to the coast, you do not find granite outcroppings here. The trail is lined with a forest of sub-alpine fir and Engelmann spruce.

The trail winds up three broad, nicely graded switchbacks that take you to a viewpoint where you can see the pretty Lightning Lake below. At the second switchback, there is

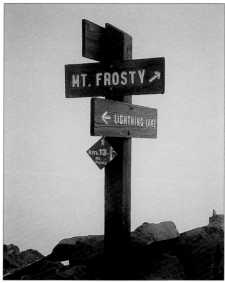

Frosty Mountain

~ 48 ~

Frosty Mountain

48. Route (map, page 154-5)

Distance: 11 km one way, 7-8 hours, day hike or overnight
Rating: ** Intermediate
Trailhead: 1,219 m, 0 km
Frosty Creek Campsite: 1,859 m, 7 km
Frosty Peak: 2,408 m, 11 km
Topographical map: 92H/2

48. Trailhead

From Hope, take Highway 3 (Hope-Princeton Highway) off the TransCanada Highway. Drive 70 km to the Manning Park Lodge. At the lodge, drive west for three km on Gibson Pass road. Turn south to the Lightning Lake Day Use Parking Lot. The trail starts at the eastern end of Lightning Lake. Cross the bridge over the dam. The trailhead is 100 m straight ahead.

48. Camping, Cycling, Dogs

Camping: There are four campgrounds: Lightning Lake, Hampton, Mule Deer and Coldspring. Wilderness walk-in camping is located at Frosty Creek and at the Windy Joe and Pacific Crest Trail intersection. A rustic shelter is located at Frosty Creek.
Mountain biking: Cycling is permitted on the following trails in the park: Corral to Lighting Lake Campground via Lone Duck Bay, Beaver Pond parking lot to Corral, Windy Joe, Monument 78, Monument 83, north and south Gibson and Poland Lake.
Dogs: Dogs are allowed except at beach and picnic areas, and must be on a leash.

Frosty Creek Shelter

a viewpoint where you can see Lightning and Flash lakes below, Silvertip Mountain and Gibson Pass Ski Area to the northwest and Washington's Hozameen Mountain to the southwest.

The trail meanders up the ridge after the third switchback. The undergrowth in the forest is quite sparse, giving it an open, airy feeling. This contrasts to the sometimes claustrophobic hikes through dense rainforest. The undergrowth is made up of wild rhododendrons, tall mountain huckleberry, blueberries and falsebox. Intermittently, the forest gives way to fields of wildflowers.

At six km, the trail opens up and levels out at a meadow where lupine, arnica and mountain valerian grow. A wilderness campsite and the Frosty Creek Shelter are reached one km later. Water is available at a creek near the campsite, however it is recommended that you treat the water before drinking it. This is a good lunch spot but a better one is located at the larch grove, just two km away.

The trail continues to meander upward and you soon break out over the ridge top. From here, you can see can see the Heather Trail to the northeast. After about 30 minutes more of walking, you reach a wondrous grove of larch

trees, and the grade of the trail levels off. The grove has a dreamy feel to it, especially if it is enclosed in fog or mist. The ancient larch trees are surrounded by open meadows where wood rush, partridgefoot, heather and pussy toes grow.

Some of these subalpine larch trees are believed to be more than 2,000 years old. Every autumn, the needles of these trees turn a brilliant gold, after which the they drop off. Once the tree sheds its needles, it becomes dormant as the buds for next year are already formed. As the trail continues through the grove, you are treated to panoramic views that include the west peak of Frosty Mountain.

The grove ends at about 10 km, when it suddenly turns into an alpine area of snowfields, talus slopes, gulleys and remarkable views. This area consists mainly of 45 to 200 million-year-old sedimentary and volcanic rocks. The rock is eroded and tends to form gentle scree ridges and debris-filled valleys. It can be very windy up here and the weather can change very quickly, so bring along some warm clothing.

As you continue, you will see a sign that says "Use Extreme Caution." Don't let this sign scare you away as the trail is easy to follow with orange arrows painted on the rocks. The trail

Larch Trees

The grove of larch trees on Frosty Mountain is remarkable for a number of reasons. Not only are these trees rarely found in southwestern B.C., but some believe that the grove may contain trees that are over 2,000 years old. John Worrall, a dendrologist with the Faculty of Forestry at U.B.C., believes that some of the sub-alpine larch trees in this grove may be the oldest trees in Canada. The cores of the older trees are rotten, so Worrall used the growth rates of the surviving outer rings of the trees to make age projections.

Larch trees are tall, slender trees that grow as tall as 12 m. They have sparsely foliaged branches that are both short and long. The branches may droop or be turned upward and they have short, stout, spur-like growths called dwarf branches. This gives the tree a ragged, unkempt look. The tree's soft, thin needles grow in clusters of 10-40. The pale, bluish-green needles turn gold every autumn and are shed. New ones grow back in the spring. Larch trees help to control erosion and runoff in the high mountains.

switches back up the talus slope for 1.5 km to the top of the ridge. Along the way, look for tiny pika, which live among the boulders and can be heard making warning cries to each other.

At the intersection at the top of the ridge, turn west (right) for Frosty Peak. The trail to the northeast (left) leads to the Windy Joe Trail and this is an optional route for going down.

Continue to the first summit of Frosty Mountain and follow the rocky ridge up steep switchbacks for about half a kilometre. Do not be daunted, as it is not a difficult climb and it takes about 15 minutes to reach the top.

The top of the first peak is marked by a cairn and on a clear day, the views are all-encompassing. You can see the peaks of the Three Brothers to the northeast and the North Cascade Mountains. It is recommended that hikers not attempt to climb the difficult 2,423 m Second Peak.

~ 49 ~

Windy Joe

49. Route (map, page 154-5)

Distance: 7 km one way, 4 hours, day hike or overnight
Rating: ** Easy
Trailhead : 1,219 m
Frosty Mountain Junction: 1,554 m, 4 km
Windy Joe Peak: 1,825 m, 7 km
Topographical map: 92H/2

49. Trailhead

From Hope, take Highway 3 (Hope-Princeton Highway) to Manning Provincial Park. At Manning Park Lodge, drive west for 3 km on Gibson Pass road. Turn south to the Lightning Lake Day Use parking lot. The trail starts at the eastern end of Lightning Lake. Cross the bridge over the dam. The trailhead is 100 m straight ahead.

49. Camping, Cycling, Dogs (see pg 159)

This hike begins at the Beaver Pond parking area, which is located 500 m east of the Visitors Centre, near Manning Park Lodge.

Most of this route goes along a wide fire-access road that ascends Windy Joe at an easy grade. The Windy Joe Trail is a great hike to do by itself, or you can combine it with the Frosty Mountain Trail. If you do decide to combine the trails, the hike will take nine to 11 hours. The 12.1 km descent of the Windy Joe route from Frosty Mountain is more moderate than the descent of the Frosty Mountain Trail. This alternate trail down begins at the signed inter-section on the ridge just before Frosty Peak. If you do this trail as a loop, you should arrange for transportation at the Beaver Pond Parking Lot or at Manning Park Lodge. If you choose to hike back to the Lightning Lakes Day Use Area along the Windy Joe Trail, take the west fork near the horse corral and continue head-ing west for another four km along Little Muddy Trail.

The hike up Windy Joe begins at the Beaver Pond Parking Lot. From there, hike west along the Beaver Pond Trail, which skirts the shore-line of Beaver Pond, going past a wide variety of flora and fauna. This trail leads through the best area in the park for bird watching. As many as 206 bird species have been seen in Manning Park and the best time for viewing them is in the early morning from May to June. Soon, you will come to a trail junction. The trail west goes to Little Muddy Trail, which leads westward to the Lightning Lake Day Parking Area. Take the left (south) turn and follow the signs for Windy Joe. Windy Joe Mountain takes its name from Joe Hilton, who worked in the park from 1946 to 1975. One of his old trapping partners named the peak for Hilton after hear-ing him comment over and over again about how the winds kept the peak clear of snow even in bad weather.

The trail continues over a bridge that crosses the Similkameen River to where you will meet up with another intersection. The trail going left (east) is the Similkameen Trail, and it eventually links up with the Castle Creek/Monument 78 Trail. Take the right (west) trail and continue up Windy Joe. This hike runs through dense forest and you have a good chance of seeing blue grouse, mule deer, whitetail deer and Douglas squirrels. As you

Blue grouse

continue upward, the trail will cross a moun-tain creek twice, and this is a good place to fill up on fresh drinking water if you need to. Fur-ther along, the road crosses the creek two more times before it reaches the four km mark. From here, there is a fine view of the Gibson Pass Road and the mountains behind it. The Gibson Pass Road leads to a downhill ski area where skiers of all levels can take advantage of the two

49. Indian Paintbrush

These striking flowers bloom from June to August and are commonly found in meadows and woodlands. The true flowers of this plant are the pointed green spikes that hide under crimson, leaf-like bracts. These brightly coloured bracts give the plant its brilliant colouring. Indian paintbrush are partially para-sitic on the roots of other plants.

chairlifts, T-bar, ski school, day lodge and rental facilities that operate in the winter.

At 4.2 km the trail splits, and the trail for Mount Frost and the Pacific Crest Trail continues up to the right (southwest). In about one km, the Pacific Crest Trail branches and goes south (right), while the trail for Mount Frost continues going southwest. A wilderness campsite is located 200 m from where the Pacific Crest Trail branches. Amazingly, the 4,200 km Pacific Crest Trail continues as far as Washington, Oregon and California, and it stops at the Mexican border. A stream is located at the Pacific Crest campsite, in case you need to fill up your water bottles.

For Windy Joe, keep going on the left trail (south). At about the five-km point, you will notice a change in the surrounding environment. The forest becomes more sparse and there are more grass-covered slopes that become filled with wildflowers during the summer season. Continue upward while taking in the views and soon you will reach the 1,825-m summit.

An old fire lookout that was built in 1950 sits on the summit. In those days, the location of a fire was determined by the use of a fire spotter. When a ranger saw smoke and fire in the distance, he would line up the sights of the finder with the smoke. Then he would send the information to the Park Headquarters in the valley below, and from there they would take action to contain and put out the fire. Before the lookout was constructed, rangers had to watch for fires from a tent. The tower was used for 13 years and then it was abandoned when fire-spotting duties were taken over by airplanes.

The treeless Windy Joe Peak offers a fine view of the surrounding scenery. To the north are mounts Outram, Ford and Dewdney, with Blackwell Peak and the Three Brothers Meadow Area to the northeast. In front of these mountains are the Similkameen River and valley. To the west are the rugged peak of Mount Frosty and Castle Peak, which sits in the United States. To the south are Monument 83, Ptarmigan Peak and Mount Winthrop, with the Cascade Range to the southeast.

~ 50 ~
Skyline 1 Trail

50. Route (map, page 154-5)

Distance: 20 km round trip, 7-9 hours, day hike or overnight
Rating: ** Easy-intermediate
Spruce Bay Trailhead: 1,219 m
Despair Pass: 1,969 m, 5.5 km
Spruce Bay: 1,219 m, 20 km
Topographical map: 92H/2

50. Trailhead

In Manning Park, pass the lodge and turn right onto Gibson Pass Road. Drive for 3 km and park at the Spruce Bay Parking Lot.

50. Camping, Cycling, Dogs (see pg 159)

This trail takes you up and over the ridge of mountains that sits behind the Lightning Lakes. Try to hike this trail from mid-July to mid-August, and you will be treated to an amazing display of wildflowers.

Start by hiking southwest along the South Gibson Trail to Strawberry Flats. Then head southwest onto the Skyline Trail. From here, it is an easy climb up to the Skyline Ridge.

At 5.5 km, you will reach a junction at Despair Pass. Continue eastward (right) and walk along the subalpine ridge. The trail traverses three knolls, offering a panoramic view. It is a quick descent from here to the shores of Lightning Lake, as the parking lot is located one km away. Camping is available at Lightning Lake.

General Information

Types of Boots

The type of boot you buy depends on how much money you want to spend, how much hiking you plan to do and the type of hiking you want to do. There are two basic types of boots; the leather boot and the lightweight boot.

Leather Hiking Boots

If you are looking for a long-lasting hiking boot, you should invest in leather boots, which provide excellent protection and support on rough or rocky terrain, can be waterproofed, and are durable. The drawbacks of leather boots are that they are heavy, more expensive and take longer to break in.

The traditional leather hiking boot features a semi-rigid shank, high uppers (12 to 18 cm) to protect and support the ankles, a Vibram-type sole for traction and midsoles for insulation. You should look for a boot that is stitched together by Norwegian welt stitching, as this is the longest-lasting type. Some other things to look for when buying boots include:

• Very few seams. This means that there are few openings for water to leak into the boot.
• A bellows or gusseted tongue will keep water from entering the boot easily .
• Areas of high wear, such as toes, should be re-inforced with double or triple-layered fabric or leather.

If you cannot afford leather boots, consider buying a second-hand pair. Not only will the boots already be broken in, but they will also be considerably less expensive. I hiked all of these trails in a great pair of leather boots that I bought at a second-hand store for a mere $30. The boots are still going strong.

Lightweight Hiking Boots

Medium and lightweight hiking boots are made of leather and nylon. Often, they weigh one-third to one-half as much as the traditional leather hiking boot. They are built to be sturdy enough for hiking on moderate terrain. Things to look for in a good lightweight boot include a high enough shaft for ankle protection, reinforcement in the high wear areas, and a toe and heel that are wrapped with a stiff counter. Usually, the uppers of these boots are glued to the sole.

The advantages of lightweight boots are that they are cheaper, their break-in time is shorter and they dry quickly. The disadvantages are that they cannot be made waterproof and they do not last as long as leather boots. Also, they do not support or protect your foot as well as leather boots do.

Proper Fit

Boots that fit properly are critical. If your boots do not fit, you may end up with a miserable, blister-ridden hiking experience. When you try on a pair of boots, bring along the socks you will be wearing and any insoles or orthopedic devices you plan to use. Wear the boots around the store and look for any creases, uncomfortable seams or discomfort. If possible, try walking up and down an incline with the boots on. No matter what the salesperson says, do not compromise on fit. Remember that any area of discomfort that you feel with the boot now will only be aggravated when you are out on the trail.

If the boots fit properly, your heel will feel firmly anchored in place and your toes will have plenty of room. You should be able to wiggle your toes and they should not jam against the toe box when you press forward. Consider trying on boots in the evening, as most people's feet swell during the course of the day.

Caring for Boots

If you want to make the most of your boots, you must care for them. Think of leather as being like your own skin in that it dries out, cracks and is subject to stresses from the environment.

Boots need to be washed often to keep mildew away. Dry them in a warm, ventilated area. Do not dry and store boots at high temperatures, as heat can damage the welt and adhesive on the boot soles. Resist drying them over a campfire as this can make them fall apart sooner. As a rule, boot soles wear out before the upper part of the boot. High-quality boots can often be resoled, although new soles may cause your boots to tighten slightly.

Waterproof your boots frequently if you expect your feet to stay dry. Apply a waterproofing product to your boots a day or two before you go on a trip, so that the product has time to penetrate the leather or fabric. Make sure your boots are clean and dry before you apply the waterproofing. Apply it directly to the threads and stitching holes. Let it dry and then apply waterproofing to the rest of the boot. The nylon in many lightweight boots often cannot be sealed completely but you can apply a silicone-based spray to make it more water resistant.

Socks

Socks play a big role in how well your feet will hold up after a long day of hiking. They reduce friction between the foot and the boot, insulate and cushion your foot, and absorb perspiration. Look for socks that are made out of wool or synthetic materials. Never buy cotton, as it absorbs too much water and as a result, it does not insulate your foot adequately. This will cause increased friction between your foot and the boot, which can only mean blisters and pain.

Try wearing two pairs of socks when you hike. Start with a smooth polypropylene or polyester sock. This sock will move perspiration from the foot to the outer sock. Then pull on a heavier wool or synthetic sock. Remember to keep your toes free enough to wiggle.

If you want extra cushioning or insulation in your boots, try adding insoles. Synthetic insoles are non-absorbent and have a loose structure that helps to ventilate your foot. Insoles made of leather, felt or lambskin absorb water so you will have to remove them when drying your boots.

Blister First Aid

Every hiker dreads getting blisters. They are painful, annoying and only get worse as the hike goes on. Prevention is the best way to tackle the blister problem.

The most common causes of blisters are new boots and boots that do not fit. If you want to avoid blisters, put protective bandages or tape on the blister-prone areas of your feet. This is especially important when you are breaking in new boots.

Try to keep your feet as dry as possible, as blisters often form in wet boots. Wear gaiters to help to keep water out of your boots and if possible, take your boots off when you cross streams and rivers.

If you notice a potential trouble spot on your foot, cover it with Moleskin or Second Skin (trade names). If a blister develops, remember that it is less likely to become infected if it is kept intact. If the blister breaks open or you have to drain it, try to keep the roof in place so that it can adhere to the base of the blister. This will protect the wound underneath the skin.

To drain a blister, clean the skin and then pierce the blister with a sterile needle. Cover it with a bandage or gauze. Then cut a hole in a piece of Moleskin and apply it, making sure that the hole goes over the blister. This will cushion your skin from whatever is irritating it. You can then put another piece of moleskin without a hole over the first one.

Clothing

Clothing protects and insulates us from the effects of weather. It helps to keep our body working well when we hike by regulating body temperature. Hypothermia occurs when the body experiences a dangerous lowering of its temperature due to the cold. If the situation is not remedied, hypothermia can eventually lead to death. At the other extreme, if our bodies get too hot, we can experience hyperthermia. Clothing can help the body stay cool in hot conditions.

The most basic principle to remember when dressing for hiking is to dress in layers. Layering allows you to adapt quickly to changing temperatures. Choose clothing made of pile, fleece, polypropylene or wool. Try to avoid cotton if possible; if you wear it, you may become a walking sponge. Cotton absorbs water and loses its insulating qualities when it becomes wet.

In the diverse climate of southwestern B.C., you will encounter many different types of weather. Most often though, it will be wet. When choosing clothing to wear in wet weather, look for a good, waterproof, breathable jacket that has a snug hood with a brim and adjustable cuffs. Choose one that is a size larger than normal so you can wear extra layers of clothing underneath it. A larger size will also allow for the pull caused by your backpack. Look for jackets with seams that have been sealed with tape, as sealed seams prevent moisture from entering along the stitching.

Another option is to buy a nylon rainsuit that can double as a windsuit. Ponchos do not work very well, as they flap about in the wind and will often catch on branches.

You will often need extra layers of clothing when travelling in cold weather or in the mountains. Carry a set of long underwear made of polypropylene, other synthetic material or wool. These are lightweight and when it gets cold, they are worth their weight in gold. Bring a warm hat such as a toque or balaclava. Also, bring some pile, synthetic or wool mitts. Mitts are warmer than gloves because they allow your fingers to stay together and share warmth. Bring a liner pair and a heavier pair of outer mitts. Pile mitts are great for wet weather because they can be wrung out while still maintaining most of their insulating loft. Wool is not quite as effective once it is wet. You can also don some waterproof overmitts.

On sunny days, put on a sun hat to protect yourself at higher elevations where the solar radiation is more intense. Cover yourself with sunscreen (SPF 30) to avoid burning. Choose a sunscreen that is waterproof, as it will last longer if you are sweating and it will not combine with the sweat on your face and drip into your eyes, which can be painful. Clothes are your best protection from the sun, so try to keep them on, even on a hot day. Finally, bring sunglasses that block UV radiation, and you will be ready to go.

Insects

The most effective thing that you can do to keep from being bitten by insects is to wear heavy clothing, head nets and gloves. But who wants to hike around like this, especially in hot weather? This is when insect repellent becomes your best friend.

Some new repellents on the market are made from natural substances like oil of citronella. These are good alternatives to the chemical-based repellents. You may have to apply them more often, but they are easier on your body.

Your other option is to use repellents that contain the chemical DEET. DEET is very effective for keeping mosquitos from landing and biting, but be aware that DEET can dissolve or discolour plastics, paint and synthetic fabrics. Think about this and consider what it is does to your body. Some people consider DEET to be a poison.

Your last and simplest alternative is to keep moving and slap bugs away. If the bug situation is not extreme, this can be just as effective as using a repellent.

Wood ticks are a serious concern, as they carry Lyme disease and Rocky Mountain spotted fever. Ticks are usually found in the montane ecoregion from April to June. They thrive in areas frequented by elk, deer and bighorn sheep. Going off the trail in high brush in spring is a good way to attract ticks. Ticks can be found in low shrubs and grasses, where they wait for their hosts to pass by. They pounce on them and start to seek out fleshy, warm areas to bite into so they can feed on blood.

Ticks resemble flattened, tiny spiders. When swollen with blood, they look like pinto beans. They have hard bodies, and it takes a surprising amount of effort to kill one.

If you are in tick country, check your hair and clothing frequently during the day. Check very carefully, as ticks are tiny and it is easy to overlook them. At night, give your body and clothes a thorough inspection. They will be found in clothing, hair or fur. Check scalp, armpits, under socks and any place where there are elastic or binding straps. It is important to locate ticks before they become embedded in your skin.

Don't panic if you do find a tick. It takes several hours for them to transmit disease. Dab the tick with kerosene or gasoline. The tick may fall off at once. If not, try to remove it gently with tweezers. Be careful, as you must try to remove all its body parts. Make sure its head is not left embedded in your skin. Keep the tick so that you can take it to your physician. If the tick is deeply embedded or if you have any concerns or doubts, see your physician as soon as possible.

Backpacks
Packing a Backpack
When packing a backpack, there are 10 essential items you should take. They are:
1. Map
2. Compass
3. Flashlight/headlamp, with spare bulbs and batteries
4. Pocket knife
5. Extra food
6. Extra clothing
7. First-aid supplies
8. Sunglasses
9. Matches in a waterproof container
10. Fire starter, e.g. a lighter

Try to keep the items you need during the day in an accessible spot. These items include a water bottle, food, map, toilet paper, knife, hat, sunglasses, extra clothing and first aid items. Nothing is so irritating as having constantly to pack and unpack your backpack looking for things.

Internal Frame Packs
Internal packs are currently the most popular type of pack. Internal frames help maintain the pack's shape and transfer weight to the hips. They do a good job of hugging the back and allow weight to be carried lower on your body. They are designed to move with you and are excellent for off-trail hiking. You will, however, get a sweaty back while wearing one.

When buying a pack, have a knowledgeable salesperson fit the pack to your body. Make sure you choose a pack that fits your body size and is comfortable. When a pack is loaded, most of the weight should be close to your body and over your hips.

When packing for trail hiking, distribute the weight evenly on both sides and make sure that your pack is balanced. Most people like to put heavy items near the middle or top of the pack, close to the back. Midweight items then go in between. Sleeping bags fit nicely at the bottom of the pack. It is better to have a lower centre of gravity if you are planning on hiking off the trail. In this case, you will want to carry the heavier items closer to your hips.

External Frame Packs
In these packs, the frame is held away from the back. The packs are designed to let the hips do most of the heavy work, providing excellent weight distribution. External frame packs are very good for trail hiking. These packs tend to shift suddenly, so it is easier to lose your balance when you are off trail. However, when hiking on the trail, your body does not twist around much so this should not be a problem. External frames also keep your back cooler.

Camping
Low-impact Camping
Most of the *Classic Hikes* have designated camping spots along the route. Designated camping spots are a good idea in popular areas, as they ensure that most of the impact from camping is concentrated in a small area. This way, the surrounding land is left alone. If you camp in an undesignated spot, remember to leave no trace. When you camp at any site, remember that you are taking on a responsibility to leave the area clean and untouched as possible.

When setting up your tent, remember that night air is often a few degrees cooler beside lakes and rivers than it is at higher elevations. It will also be colder in valleys and depressions, as cold air tends to settle there.

Campfires
It seems that the old romantic days of cooking over an open fire are just about over. Unfortunately, campfires leave scars on the environment and needlessly devour wood. Hikers now cook on lightweight stoves that they carry. These stoves are a great invention as they are efficient, fast, easy and dependable.

If you do want to build a fire, keep it small and do it only where it's safe and legal. Keep the fire within an existing fire ring. Stay with the fire until it is dead and burn only dead or fallen wood.

Sanitation
Be meticulous about packing out all of your garbage. Garbage is easy to carry out and the effects of pollution can be devastating to a fragile area. Never bury it or leave it in latrines. Minimize the amount of garbage you take into the backcountry by repackaging your food in plastic zip lock bags. The bags can be washed and reused. Larger plastic bags are ideal for carrying out your garbage, so bring one along.

The more popular campsites will usually have a pit toilet or an outhouse. It is important that you use it. Otherwise, drinking water sources and the environment will quickly succumb to the effects of pollution in these high-use areas.

If there is no outhouse, go at least 54 m away from open water and dig a hole about 20 cm wide and 20 cm deep. After use, burn your toilet paper or carry it out. Then fill the hole back up. Pack out all non-biodegradable personal hygiene items such as tampons in airtight containers.

Keeping Clean

You will be surprised to find that dishes can stay reasonably clean without being washed with soap. The trick is to clean dirty dishes as soon as you can after you use them. Clean them with water but wash them far away from water sources. It is handy to have a large water container along to save yourself from making multiple trips to get water.

You may want to bring along a scouring pad in case you have to do some scrubbing. However, sand or small pebbles can do as good a job as the scouring pad. If you do use soap, use a biodegradable product. If you have leftovers, carry them out with you.

Apply the same principles when washing your clothes or yourself. Stay at least 54 m away from water sources and go without soap or use a small amount of biodegradable soap.

Food and Animals

It is not unusual to find that an animal has made holes in your pack in its search for delicious-smelling food. To avoid this, use a food sack or pack to hang your food from a tree. A good rule of thumb is to hang food at least one m away from the tree trunk and two m up from the ground.

Keep your campsite clean. Never store food near where you sleep. Store it well away and conceal food smells by packaging it in plastic bags or sealed containers. If you are camping above the treeline, try building a cairn out of heavy rocks to cache your food in. Put the rocks back where they came from when you are finished with the cairn.

Tents

Buying a tent these days can be a mind-boggling experience. There is such a variety to choose from that it may almost seem impossible to make up your mind. Here are some questions to ask yourself before you set foot inside a store:

When and where will you be using the tent?
How many people will be sleeping in it?
How much weight are you willing to carry?
How much money do you want to spend?
These are some things to know about tents:
- Free standing tents are easy to set up, need no guy lines and can be picked up and moved as a unit. Tents shaped as tunnels and domes make maximum use of space and minimize the number of guy lines and stakes needed.
- Vestibules are great for providing more room for gear, dressing and cooking.
- Two-person tents offer the most flexibility in weight and choice of campsite.
- Remember that no tent is completely waterproof. It is the tent fly that keeps the water out, so seal all tent seams with a waterproof seam sealer as soon as you buy the tent.

It is a bad idea to cook inside a tent as most tent fabrics are flammable. Stove fumes and flare-ups can cause fires. If you have no choice and you must cook inside the tent, start the stove outside and bring it into the vestibule. Make sure the stove has an insulating pad underneath it when you bring it inside.

Sleeping Bags

A wide range of sleeping bags are made that can suit any need. When buying one, choose a sleeping bag that is comfortable, lightweight, warm and easily compressible. The bag should have a hood or another way to keep your head covered. Consider where you will be using the bag most often and what your sleeping body temperature usually is. Some people sleep warm, others sleep cold. In general, it is better to choose a warmer bag as you can open it up if you want to cool off. It is harder to stay warm in a cold bag.

Having an insulated mat underneath you when you sleep can make the difference between a sleepless night and a good night's rest. The mat will give you a warmer, softer bed. Inflatable mats weigh less and are the most comfortable, but they are expensive. Therm-a-Rest mats (trade name) are very popular and effective. Closed-cell foams are less effective, can absorb water and are bulky, but they are cheaper. A stuff sack can be used to carry your mat. If you are stuck without a mat, use your pack and clothing for insulation.

On the rainy West Coast, it is essential that you pack your sleeping bag inside a large plastic bag and then put it in a stuff sack. This will prevent it from becoming sodden, heavy and wet, a horrible thing to have to carry and sleep in.

Food

It is amazing what you can cook in the backcountry if you put your mind to it. You can make anything from jambalaya to cheesecake. The majority of backpackers, however, stick to the basics. Grains and pastas pack well and make great meals. Be creative and use different combinations of dried sauces and mixes to add to these staples. The possibilities of tasty meals using these basics are endless. Experiment and you will soon find what you like to eat best when you are out in the backcountry.

Put some thought and planning into what foods you are going to take on a trip and you should have no trouble meeting your body's daily requirements. The three major food components to consider when choosing what food to take on a trip are carbohydrates, protein and fat. Most of the calories in your diet should come from carbohydrates as they are easiest for your body to convert into energy. Good sources are rice, cereals, pasta, whole grains, bread and crackers.

Daily protein requirements are easily met by eating nuts, cheese, powdered milk and eggs, peanut butter and beef jerky. Once your body's requirement is met, excess protein is either stored as fat converted to energy.

Fats occur naturally in small amounts in grains, vegetables and beans. High-fat foods include peanut butter, nuts, butter eggs, cheese, oils, meat and seeds.

Consider buying food supplies in bulk and carrying them in zip lock bags. It is cheaper to buy in bulk and there is less wasteful packaging. Place a label or cooking instructions inside each bag or write it on the outside with a waterproof marker. The bags can be washed and reused.

Many foods can last longer than you may have thought possible without refrigeration. You will be surprised to find that cheese, salami, pepperoni, boiled eggs and yogurt last a long time without being refrigerated. Crackers or crispbread last forever and are easier to carry than bread.

Seasoning can transform a bland meal into a tasty one. Bring along some garlic, salt, pepper, dehydrated onion, herbs or Parmesan cheese. Dehydrated soups are delicious and can double as seasoning. Consider taking oil instead of butter as it keeps better and takes up less space in your pack.

On short trips, you can bring along fresh vegetables or fruits. If you are worried about a lack of fresh food, consider taking a daily vitamin/mineral supplement. Snack foods are essential for curbing low blood sugar and trail hunger. Chomping away at some corn nuts can do wonders to pep you up when it seems like the trail will never end. Some good choices for snack foods are fruit, candies, corn nuts, chocolate, raisins, fruit leather and nuts.

Try to avoid packing foods like meat, fish and peppermint tea, which attract animals. Any scented item such as toothpaste, scented soap or perfume will also attract animals.

Most importantly, take food that you enjoy eating. There is no point in lugging along bean and potato flakes if you get nauseous at the sight of it. If you prefer to snack on chocolate bars instead of trail mix, then do so. Just remember to include a variety of foods in your diet and you will be fine. Unfortunately, one cannot live on chocolate alone (although you can always try)!

Water

Hiking can make you sweat profusely, so it is imperative to your backcountry health that you get plenty to drink. Staying hydrated often helps prevent headaches, hypothermia, altitude sickness, frostbite and hyperthermia. Experienced hikers will tell you that the time to drink is before you become thirsty. Drink often and your body will appreciate it.

In general, you should drink about 2 to 3 litres of fluid per day. This amount will vary depending on the type of hike you are doing, weather conditions and individual body needs. For a longer or more demanding hike, plan on drinking from three to five litres or more. If you are unsure about whether you are drinking enough, check the colour and volume of your urine. Notice how often you urinate and how dark your urine is. If it is dark, then you need to drink more. If it is clear, you are drinking enough. If you urinate under three times in 24 hours, you need to drink more.

Water running in a clear mountain stream may seem safe to drink, but it may be contaminated with harmful bacteria. *Giardia* is a well known bacteria that can be dangerous, and other lesser-known parasites also inhabit backcountry water sources. It is best to purify all water.

Water can be purified by boiling it for three minutes at sea level with an additional minute for every 600 m of elevation gained. Iodine in a concentration of eight parts per million kills *Giardia* cysts and other bacteria within 10 minutes, or 20 minutes if the water is cold. Unfortunately, iodine also affects the taste of the water. Bring along some juice crystals to kill the taste of iodine. There are also some great water filters on the market that you may want to look into.

It is a good idea to keep a water bottle in the tent so that you can drink from it before you go to sleep. This way, you can make sure that your body is fully rehydrated before the next day of hiking begins.

Pots and Pans

Cooking utensils are very basic when you are camping. Use a spoon and a single large cup to eat out of. Large plastic measuring cups and insulated travel mugs work well. If you are concerned about carrying too much weight in your pack, you can get away with using only one pot although you may want an extra one for water.

Cooking sets should be durable, lightweight and easy to carry. You can get cooking sets in stainless steel, aluminum or coated cookware. Stainless steel pots tend to be more durable than aluminum. Pots should have handles or pot holders and tight-fitting lids to conserve heat. Lids can be used as a makeshift frying pan if necessary.

Each person should also carry a pocket knife. Pocket knives are essential for food preparation and function as a basic tool kit. The knife should have two folding blades, a can opener, scissors, a combination screwdriver and bottle opener and an awl. The inside of the knife casing and tools should be made of stainless steel.

Stoves

Stoves have become a necessity for backcountry travellers. Many camping areas either do not allow fires or no longer stock firewood. Stoves are easy to use, they work in bad weather and they are environmentally friendly.

Choosing a stove can be difficult as there are so many to choose from. Things to consider are weight, fuel availability, reputation and the circumstances in which you will be camping.

The most popular backpacking stoves are made by Coleman and MSR. These simple and dependable stoves use a variety of fuels including white gas, which burns hotter and boils water quicker than others. Unlike kerosene stoves, these stoves use white gas as their priming agent.

Cartridge stoves use prefilled, disposable gas cartridges containing propane or butane. The stove does not need to be pumped or primed as the pressure in the cartridge forces fuel out as soon as the valve is opened. Although these stoves are easy to use, they do not perform well at high altitudes or in cold weather.

Kerosene stoves have a high heat output and kerosene is safer to transport and store. However, these stoves must be pressurized and primed with alcohol, lighter fluid or white gas.

Fuel needs vary, but generally one to 1.5 litres of fuel is enough to last two people for one week. If you want to carry extra fuel, use metal bottles that have a screw top backed up by a rubber gasket. Your stove will run better if your fuel is of a good quality and is fresh.

Carry a repair kit and instructions for your stove. Practice starting a new stove at home before a trip to make sure it is operating well. Clean your stove often to avoid carbon and dirt build up.

Most stoves will generally boil one litre of water at sea level in four to eight minutes. However, wind can increase the time to as much as 25 minutes. Use windscreens, pot lids and heat reflectors to increase the stove's efficiency. Use the smallest pot that is practical when cooking, as these stoves are small and can be unstable.

Repair Kit

A repair kit often grows and changes over time as you add items that you wished you had along on a previous trip. Things to start out with include duct tape, thread or dental floss (which makes strong thread), needles, small pliers, safety pins, wire and patches.

First aid supplies

A first aid kit is one of the essentials that you should carry when you hike. This kit allows you to treat minor afflictions such as headaches or blisters. Although a first aid kit cannot do much to help a person who has a serious injury or illness, it can help stabilize the person before evacuation.

A first aid kit should be small and sturdy with the contents wrapped in waterproof packaging. Here are some things to carry at all times: Band-aids or small adhesive bandages, scissors, Moleskin, gauze, cleansers, adhesive tape and pain killer, triangular and butterfly bandage, closure strips and latex gloves.

Hiking with Children

Children and the outdoors are a perfect combination. Children love to explore, and their curious minds are open to everything. Hiking offers them a wonderful opportunity to access new terrain and elements of nature that they may otherwise never encounter.

If you have never hiked with children, you will find that it is a very different experience from hiking with an adult. The amount of distance that you cover decreases drastically when you hike with a child. They do not hesitate to complain when the going gets tough or when they are tired.

Hiking with children requires patience, planning and cooperation, but it can be great fun and provide rich, memorable experiences. Here are some tips to make your hiking experience with children a fun one:

1. Soft slings are great for carrying babies in. They can be used to hold the baby against your chest, back or side.
2. A sturdy backpack-style carrier can be used to carry children who can sit up (6 months or

so). The carrier should have padded hip and shoulder belts. Most people find it easier to carry the child facing forward. Dress the infant appropriately and watch out for low branches.

3. Be flexible and not too ambitious. Expect to stop early so that the child can settle down before bed. Try camping relatively close to your car on the first few outings. If anything goes wrong, you can return home.
4. Do some trial runs. Day hikes are a great way to get a feel for your child's interest, pace and endurance. You will also see how much you can handle and get a feel for the limitations of both you and your child. This will give you an idea of what to expect when you go on a longer trip.
5. Expect the pace to be slow. Children like to mosey along at an irregular pace and they like to stop often to examine things. Adults usually walk with a goal in mind. They want to get to a certain place within a certain time limit. Children don't live by the same rules as we do, so slow down and enjoy rediscovering the things your child finds so fascinating on the trail.
6. Take turns trading off with your hiking partner so that one of you can have a break. Spending all day with a dawdling, questioning child is enough to drive anyone crazy. Take turns letting one person go ahead to a pre-arranged spot while the other stays behind with the child.
7. Make sure there are plenty of snacks and water for the child. Dress children in bright colours so they are easier to spot. In bear or cougar country, keep them close by.

Fitness

Being physically fit can make a big difference in the type of backpacking experience you have. Not only will you have more endurance, but you will be able to cover more ground. Being fit also helps you to recover faster from your day's outing. Let's face it, hiking is much more enjoyable when you are not exhausted.

There are plenty of ways to get in shape for a hiking trip. Take any available opportunity to walk at a fast pace. Aerobic exercise such as jogging, cycling and swimming is also great. Climbing stairs and lifting weights will increase your strength. This will benefit you when you are climbing up a steep trail or carrying a heavy pack. You may want to carry your backpack around with you to get used to the weight. Put it on, fill it with heavy objects and go for a trail hike in your area.

Stretching is a good way to warm up and cool down when you are hiking. Muscles become stronger after each workout, shortening in the process. Stretching the muscle counteracts this tightening, thereby decreasing the risk of injury. It also prevents cramping and muscle soreness the next day. Stretch your calves, hamstrings and quadriceps. Remember to stretch your back, neck and arms. Stretch whatever muscle area feels stiff and sore.

If you do not have a regular exercise program, then start one. Getting fit for hiking is a great goal to work toward, and it will pay off when you hit the trail.

Bears

No other animal inspires so much elation, fear and awe in people than bears. B.C. residents should consider themselves lucky, as their province is home to both grizzly and black bears. The province has about one quarter of the black bears in Canada and half of the grizzly bears. There are few if any grizzly bears in the heavily populated Lower Mainland and the dry, southern areas of the province. There are also no grizzly bears on Vancouver Island.

It is estimated that the total population of black bears in B.C. is between 120,000 to 160,000. Vancouver Island has one of the province's highest density levels, with an approximate population of 10,000 black bears. It is believed that there are approximately 6,000 to 10,000 grizzlies in B.C.

It is easy to tell the two types of bears apart. Black bears are smaller than grizzlies. They reach a height of 90 cm at the shoulder and are about 1.5 m long. Male black bears weigh between 57 to 270 kg and female black bears are usually smaller than males. The colouring of black bears varies from black or brown to cinnamon or blond. They have a shoulder hump that is barely visible, short, curved claws and a straight face profile. They are good climbers.

Grizzlies are larger than black bears. They reach a height of just over one m at shoulder and are about two m long. Male grizzlies weigh between 250 and 500 kg; females are smaller than males. Their colour ranges from blond or brown to almost black. The fur on their back, shoulders and flanks is often coloured with flecks of white or grey on the tips. Sometimes they may have light-coloured patches around their shoulders, neck and rear flanks.

Grizzlies are distinguished by a prominent shoulder hump. They have long, curved claws and a dish-shaped profile. Young grizzlies are agile tree climbers but adult male grizzlies cannot climb as well because their claws are longer. They can, however, still climb up to four m.

All bears are strong, can run very fast, have good eyesight and hearing and are strong swimmers. Their diet consists primarily of plants, insects, fish, carrion and whatever mammals they can catch. Grizzlies will also dig for roots and worms.

Black bears prefer to live in forested areas that have an undergrowth of low-growing plants and berry-producing shrubs. They frequent small forest openings and lake and stream edges. Grizzly bears live in semi-open spaces. They like the high country in late summer and early fall and valley bottoms in spring.

A unique cream-coloured bear known as the Kermode lives along the central coast of B.C., especially near Terrace. Kermode bears are rare and are not found anywhere else in the world. These bears actually come in many hues of orange, yellow and gold, but the cream-coloured ones attract the most attention. The Kermode bear is a subspecies of the black bear.

Biologists believe that Kermode bears exist due to the presence of a gene variation that is a form of albinism. It is not known how many Kermode bears there are. The bear is known as "spirit bear" or "snow bear" in Indian legend.

Another pigmentation variant in black bears can be found in the glacier bear. The fur on this bear is a blue-black colour. The glacier bear is only found in the Tatshenshini-Alsek Wilderness Provincial Park and neighbouring glacial mountain regions.

Bears and their habitat are facing great risks from increasing human access and development. Before European settlement, 100,000 grizzly bears roamed the western half of North America. Today, grizzly bears are considered an endangered species. Grizzly bears need vast tracts of land in which to roam, so as the wilderness disappears, so do bears. It is essential that we recognize this and do all we can to protect bears and their home.

Safe Hiking in Bear County

Both species of bears try to avoid human contact, and most attacks are the result of ignorance and careless actions of people. Avoiding bears when you hike is a responsibility that you must undertake. Many black bear attacks occur when bears are trying to get at human food or garbage. Grizzly attacks, particularly by mother grizzlies with young, usually occur as a result of a sudden unexpected encounter. Such attacks remain rare; about one person in every two million visitors to Canada's national parks is injured by a grizzly. Be aware of dangerous situations such as bears that are surprised: mother bears with cubs, bears protecting a food source and bears that have lost their fear of humans.

When hiking in bear country, you should realize that you are entering the bear's home territory. Bears want to stay away from you as much as you want to stay away from them. The best way to avoid them is to let them know that you are in the area. Make noise as you hike to signal your presence. Yell out, clap your hands or bang two rocks together intermittently. Hike as a group and keep children near you.

Be aware of what is going on in your surroundings. Areas where noisy rivers or streams are gushing by may make it harder for bears to hear you. If you are downwind from the bear, it may not be able to smell you. Take special care when hiking through food sources like berry patches, when walking around blind corners, or if you see tracks and bear scat on the trail. If you are in these higher-risk areas, make as much noise as you can.

You should leave the area at once if you smell rotting meat or see circling crows or ravens. Grizzlies often stash food away, so if you smell something rotting, it's possible that you are close to a bear's larder. They will defend this food cache so you must leave the area immediately if you see an animal carcass. Report the location of the carcass to park staff.

Comfortable Camping

Here are some tips to make your camping experience more enjoyable:

• Carry a lightweight headlamp. These are great for reading in the tent, midnight trips to the outhouse and essential survival gear if you are caught hiking in the dark.

• Bring camp shoes. In summer, bring along some lightweight sport sandals, thongs or canvas shoes. In winter, pack along some toasty down booties. Your feet (and blisters) will love you.

• Pack a book in case you get stuck in the tent waiting out a storm.

• Use insulated mugs with snap-on lids. Hot drinks will stay hot longer, you will be able to sip away at your leisure without spilling your drink, and lids keep bugs from drowning in your beverage.

• Use small butane lighters.

• Plastic zip lock bags are great for carrying food, maps, toilet paper and books. This keeps everything dry and organized. You can reuse them, too.

• Sleep on a self-inflating mattress. These keep out the cold, are lightweight and comfortable.

Camping in Bear Country

A bear that comes into a camp is almost always after food. Often, the bear has lost some of its fear of humans and has learned to associate humans with food or garbage.

Always try to cook 50 m downwind from your campsite. Put all of your food in a bag and hang it at least four m above the ground. Include items that have an odour such as garbage, toothpaste, sunscreen and soap, and pack out all your garbage.

Encountering a Bear

If you see a bear in the distance, try to make a wide detour around it or leave the area. Do not turn and run if you see one at close range. Instead, move away slowly. Never walk toward the bear and avoid direct eye contact with it. Report your sighting to park staff.

If the bear stands up or sniffs the air, this means that it knows you are there and it is assessing the situation. Speak softly so that it can identify what you are. A bear is showing aggression if it starts to snap its jaws, makes growling noises, moves its head from side to side, lowers its head or flattens its ears. Leave quietly and slowly if the bear does this.

As much as you may want to, do not run unless you are very close to a safe place. Running triggers the predator/prey response, and the bear will chase you. You may want to drop your pack to distract the bear. If you are certain the bear is a grizzly, you may consider climbing a tree.

The situation becomes more complicated if you are attacked. The following are some guidelines which may be helpful. Each incident is unique and there are no set rules to go by, as bears can be unpredictable. Sometimes bears will bluff their way out of a confrontation by pretending to attack and then turning around at the last moment. If you fight back during an attack, this may cause the bear to be more ferocious, but it may also cause the bear to leave.

- You should play dead if you surprise a grizzly and it attacks. Curl up into a ball and clasp your hands behind your neck. Do not move until the bear leaves. Usually, these attacks do not last more than a few minutes.
- If a black bear attacks defensively (eg. because you surprised it), do not play dead. Try to get away.
- When both black and grizzly bears attack offensively (such as when you are sleeping), you should try to escape. Do not play dead.

Tips for Camping on the Rainy West Coast

The bad news is that it rains often on the West Coast. The good news is that it is often a "warm rain," unlike the bone-chilling showers of the Rockies. With experience, you will become used to hiking in the rain. Here are some tips on how to stay somewhat dry:

- Pack sleeping bags and clothes in large plastic bags, and reuse the bags.
- Carry a waterproof jacket with a peaked hat. The hat will prevent rain from pouring onto your face. Remember not to overdress. In the summer months, a waterproof jacket over a polypropylene shirt will be enough. Your legs will stay warm in lightweight pants of nylon or waterproof material.

- Waterproof your boots often.
- Wear polypropylene underwear. This will keep moisture from staying next to your skin.
- Use zip lock bags to carry items such as food, maps and toilet paper. You can reuse these bags.
- Wear gaiters. This will help keep the water out of your boots, thereby making your feet less susceptible to blisters.
- Cover your pack with a waterproof cover. Covers can be bought at sporting goods stores, or you can try making one yourself.
- Bring lighters in addition to waterproof matches.
- A tent with a waterproof fly is essential.

Handy Contacts

National Parks

For more information on national parks in southwestern B.C., contact the following:

National Parks—General information

Canadian Parks Service, Information Services,
Western Regional Office,
Room 520, 220-4th Ave. SE
Box 2989, Station M
Calgary, Alberta T2P 3H8
ph. (403) 292-4401

Pacific Rim National Park

Park Superintendent, 2185 Ocean Terrace Rd.,
Box 280, Ucluelet, BC, V0R 3A0,
ph. (250) 726-7721 or 726-4212,
www.parkscanada.gc.ca/pacificrim

National parks passes and information can be obtained by calling 1-800-748-7275 or homepage www.parkscanada.pch.gc.ca/parks/main_e.htm

Provincial Parks

For more information on provincial parks in southwestern B.C., contact the following district offices:

BC Provincial Parks—General information

BC Parks
800 Johnson St.
Victoria, BC V8V 1X4
ph. (250) 387-5002
wlapwww.gov.bc.ca/bcparks/index.htm

Vancouver Area

1610 Mt. Seymour Road
North Vancouver, BC, V7G 1L3
ph.(604) 929-4818

Vancouver District

Golden Ears Park, Maple Ridge, BC, V2X 7G3
ph.(604) 463-3513

Garibaldi District

Alice Lake Provincial Park
Box 220, Brakendale, BC V0N 1H0
ph.(604) 898-3678

Lower mainland District

1610 Mt. Seymour Rd.
North Vancouver, BC, V7G 2R9
(604)924-2200

Fraser Valley District

Box 10, Cultus Lake, BC, V0X 1H0
ph.(604) 858-7161

Manning Park

Box 3, Manning Park, BC, V0X 1R0
ph.(250) 840-8836

Regional parks

Contact the following for regional park information:

Greater Vancouver Regional District

Parks Department, 4330 Kingsway
Burnaby, BC, V5H 4G8
ph.(604) 224-5739
homepage
http://www.gvrd.bc.ca/go/aindex.html#parks

Forest Service Recreation Sites

For information on recreation sites, contact:

BC Forest Service, Recreation Section

4595 Canada Way
Burnaby, BC, V5G 4L9
ph.(604) 660-7500
www.for.gov.bc.ca

Tourism

Discover B.C.—Travel information, accommodation and reservations
1-800-663-6000

Discover Camping Reservation Service

Reservations can be made at some provincial campgrounds from March 1 to September 15 by telephoning:
Within Vancouver: 689-9025
Within North America: 1-800-689-9025
homepage http://www.discovercamping.ca

Tourism BC

Parliament Buildings,
Victoria, BC V8V 1X4

Transportation
BC Transit
ph. (604) 521-0400,
homepage
http://www.bctransit.com/main/main.htm
BC Ferry Corp
ph. (604) 277-0277,
homepage http://www.bcferries.bc.ca

Pacific Coach Lines
ph. 1-800-661-1725

Greyhound
ph. 1-800-661-8747
homepage http://www.greyhound.com/

VIA Rail
ph. 1-800-561-8630, homepage
http://www.viarail.ca

BC Rail
ph. 1-800-663-8238, homepage
http://www.bcrail.com

Vancouver International Airport
ph. (604) 207-7077

Weather
Environment Canada
www.weatheroffice.ec.gc.ca/canada_e.html

Maps
Geological Survey of Canada
605 Robson St.
Vancouver, BC, V6B 5J3
ph. (604) 666-0271

Environmental Organizations
Outdoor Recreation Foundation of B.C.
1367 W Broadway
Vancouver, BC V6H 4A9
ph. (604) 737-3058
homepage: www.orcbc.ca

Federation of Mountain Clubs of B.C.
47 W. Broadway
Vancouver, BC V5Y 1P1
ph. (604) 878-7007
homepage www.mountainclubs.bc.ca

Western Canadian Wilderness Committee
227 Abbott St.
Vancouver, BC V6B 2K7
ph. (604) 683-8220
homepage
http://www.wildernesscommittee.org

Sierra Club of Western Canada
314, 620 View St.
Victoria, BC V8W 1J6
ph. (250) 386-5255
homepage http://www.sierraclub.ca/bc

Greenpeace
1726 Commercial Drive
Vancouver, BC V5N 3A4
ph. (604) 253-7701
homepage
http://www.greenpeacecanada.org/

Recommended Reading

General Reference

Boga, Steve. *Camping and Backpacking With Children.* Mechanicsburg PA: Stackpole Books, 1995.

Fairley, Bruce. *A Guide to Climbing and Hiking in Southwestern British Columbia.* Vancouver, Gordon Soules, 1993.

Kals, W.S. *Land Navigation Handbook.* San Francisco: Sierra club Books, 1983.

Kavanagh, James. *Nature BC.* Edmonton: Lone Pine Publishing, 1993.

Leslie, Susan. *In the Western Mountains, Early Mountaineering in British Columbia.* Victoria: Provincial Archives of British Columbia, 1980.

Mathews, William H. *Garibaldi Geology.* Vancouver: Geological Association of Canada, Cordilleran Section, 1975.

The Mountaineers. *Mountaineering: The Freedom of the Hills.* Seattle, Washington.: The Mountaineers, i992.

McLane, Kevin. *The Rockclimbers' Guide to Squamish.* Squamish: Merlin Productions Inc., 1992.

Serl, Dan and Bruce Kay. *The Climber's Guide to West Coast Ice.* Squamish, BC: Merlin Productions, 1993.

Vogel, Aynsley. *Vancouver SuperGuide.* Banff: Altitude Publishing, 1993.

Whitney, Stephen R. *A Field Guide to the West Coast Mountains.* Vancouver: Douglas & McIntyre, Ltd., 1983.

Animals and Insects

Banfield, A.W. *The Mammals of Canada.* University of Toronto Press, Toronto, Ontario, 1987.

Gordon, David George. *Field Guide to the Slug.* Seattle, Washington: Sasquatch Books, 1994.

Herrero, Stephen. *Bear Attacks, Their Causes and Avoidance.* Piscataway, New Jersey, New Century, 1985.

Vegetation

Clark, Lewis J. *Fieldguide to Wild Flowers of Forest and Woodland in the Pacific Northwest.* Vancouver: Douglas & McIntyre, 1984.

Horn, Elizabeth L. *Coastal Wildflowers of British Columbia and the Pacific Northwest.* North Vancouver, BC: Whitecap Books, 1994.

Hosie, R.C. *The Native Trees of Canada.*

Toronto: Fitzhenry and Whiteside, 1979.

Kozloff, Eugene N. *Plants and Animals of the Pacific Northwest: an illustrated guide to the natural history of Western Oregon, Washington and British Columbia.* Seattle: University of Washington Press, 1976.

Pojar, Jim, MacKinnon, Andy et al. *Plants of the Pacific Northwest Coast.* Edmonton: Lone Pine Publishing, 1994.

Food and Cookery

Axcell, Claudia, Diana Cooke and Vikki Kinmont. *Simple Foods for the Pack.* San Francisco: Sierra Club Books, 1986.

Fleming, June. The Well-Fed Backpacker. New York: Vintage Books, 1986.

Fitness and Health

Logue, Frank. *Stretching and Massage for Hikers and Backpackers.* Birmingham, AL.: Menasha Ridge Press, 1994.

Wilkerson, James A. *Medicine for Mountaineering & Other Wilderness Activities.* Seattle, Wash.: The Mountaineers, 1992.

Ocean

Abbot, R.T. *Seashells of North America.* Golden Press, New York, N.Y., 1968.

Neitzel, Michael C. *The Valencia Tragedy.* Surrey, B.C.: Heritage House, 1995.

Rogers, Fred. *Shipwrecks of British Columbia.* Vancouver: J.J. Douglas, 1973.

Hewlett Paine, Stefani. *Beachwalker: Sea Life of the West Coast.* Vancouver: Douglas & McIntyre, 1992.

Harbo, Rick M. *Guide to the Western Seashore.* Surrey: Hancock House Publishers Ltd., 1988.

Zim, H. *Seashores, A Guide to Animals and Plants Along the Beaches.* Golden Press, New York, N.Y., 1964.

Index

Photography Credits

All photographs are taken by the author and Mike Sample except for the following:

Stephen Hutchings: OBC, 32, 33
Dennis & Esther Schmidt: 19, 23, 27, 29, 30, 35,36, 37, 50b, 61a, 93, 99a, 102b, 113, 121, 127, 155, 160a

Acknowledgments

I would like to acknowledge the contribution that my husband, Mike Sample, made to this book. Mike's help with photography, editing and his knowledge, experience and insightful suggestions were all invaluable in the creation of this book. Mike not only agreed to hike the West Coast Trail for our honeymoon, but he devoted his entire summer to hiking the trails with me. Thank you, Mike, you made it fun.

Others I would like to thank are: The Vancouver Public Library, BC Parks, Pacific Rim National Park, North Vancouver Museum and Archives, City of Vancouver Archives, BC Archives and Records Service, Jim Burton Photography, Markus Kellerhals, Nicola Stevens, Roberta Kuzyk Burton, Barry Brachman and Anna and John Cancian.

This book is dedicated to my son Markus.

About the Author

Freelance writer and photographer Anita Cancian has made a career of celebrating the joys of outdoor activities through her writing. Her work has been published in such magazines as *Outdoor Canada, Canadian Cyclist, Explore, SkiTrax* and *Pedal.*

Cancian's love for the outdoors developed at an early age, as she spent much of her childhood camping in Alberta and British Columbia with her family. Between 1980 and 1986, she cross-country skied and cycled competitively, and she continues to enjoy rock climbing, skiing, cycling and hiking in her spare time.

Born and raised in Alberta, this Edmonton native now lives in the Vancouver area with her husband, Mike Sample.